# Opening the Old Testament

**Praise for** *Opening the Old Testament*

'This is a very successful attempt to "open" the Old Testament for the reader with no specialist knowledge. By concentrating on selected passages in detail, Katharine Dell introduces the major themes and genres of the Bible in an accessible way, and then provides the background information needed to understand the bigger picture. Drawing on much experience in teaching the Old Testament to students and in informing ordinary Bible readers through her work with the Bible Reading Fellowship, she helps everyone to see how this often mysterious book can contribute to modern thought about ethics and religious belief, as well as how it connects with the New Testament. An invaluable guide for anyone puzzled or intrigued by the Old Testament.'

*John Barton, University of Oxford*

# Opening the

# Old Testament

*Katharine Dell*

**Blackwell**
Publishing

BLACKWELL PUBLISHING
350 Main Street, Malden, MA 02148–5020, USA
9600 Garsington Road, Oxford OX4 2DQ, UK
550 Swanston Street, Carlton, Victoria 3053, Australia

First published 2008 by Blackwell Publishing Ltd

1   2008

*Library of Congress Cataloging-in-Publication Data*

Dell, Katharine J. (Katharine Julia), 1961–
    Opening the Old Testament : an introductory handbook / Katharine Dell.
        p. cm.
    Includes bibliographical references and index.
    ISBN 978-1-4051-2500-0 (hardcover : alk. paper)—ISBN 978-1-4051-2501-7 (pbk. : alk. paper)
1. Bible. O.T.—Introductions.   I. Title.

    BS1140.3.D45 2008
    221.6′1—dc22

                                                                          2007028729

A catalogue record for this title is available from the British Library.

Set in 10.5/13pt Palatino
by Graphicraft Limited, Hong Kong
Printed and bound in Singapore
by Markono Print Media Pte Ltd

The publisher's policy is to use permanent paper from mills that operate a sustainable forestry policy, and which has been manufactured from pulp processed using acid-free and elementary chlorine-free practices. Furthermore, the publisher ensures that the text paper and cover board used have met acceptable environmental accreditation standards.

For further information on
Blackwell Publishing, visit our website at
www.blackwellpublishing.com

# Contents

# Figures

# Maps

# Preface

Blackwell Publishing commissioned me to write this book and in many ways it has been a return to my own introduction to and excitement at discovering the Old Testament, as well as a reminder of what I teach to my students today. I am privileged to have attended both Oxford and Cambridge; to have studied in Oxford as an undergraduate and graduate and then begun my teaching career in Old Testament at Ripon College, Cuddesdon; to lecture, teach and research now in Cambridge in the very stimulating environment of the University in the city of my birth. This book is dedicated to those who taught and inspired me as a student at Oxford and to those to whom I now teach the Old Testament, and from whom I continue to learn, in the Faculty of Divinity in Cambridge.

Katharine Dell
St Catharine's College, Cambridge

# Chapter 1  What is the Old Testament?

> **Psalm 23**
> *A Psalm of David*
> 1  The LORD is my shepherd. I shall not want.
> 2  He makes me lie down in green pastures;
>     he leads me beside still waters;
> 3  he restores my soul.
>     He leads me in right paths
>     for his name's sake.
> 4  Even though I walk through the darkest valley,
>     I fear no evil;
>     for you are with me;
>     your rod and your staff –
>     they comfort me.
> 5  You prepare a table before me
>     in the presence of my enemies;
>     you anoint my head with oil;
>     my cup overflows.
> 6  Surely goodness and mercy shall follow me
>     all the days of my life,
>     and I shall dwell in the house of the LORD
>     my whole life long.[1]

Psalm 23 is perhaps the best-known psalm from the Old Testament, sung in metrical and hymnic versions in the worship of the Christian church.[2] Its popularity makes it as good a place to start as any when opening the Old Testament for the first time. Perhaps what has made this psalm enduringly popular and memorable is its quiet confidence. It expresses security in God's protection in the face of any adversity. God is portrayed as divine shepherd (vv. 1–4), a well-known image in the Old Testament, reminding us of a human shepherd caring for the flock.[3] The key point, however, is that it is written from the position of the individual, the 'I' ('my shepherd'). God's shepherding care is for each member of God's flock and the psalmist feels that protection in a personal way. Other psalms feature the same image but usually in reference to the whole of God's people shepherded by God.[4] It is the individualism in this psalm that is perhaps most striking.

Being in God's shepherding care the psalmist 'lacks nothing'. This phrase may well remind us of the time when the children of Israel 'lacked nothing' when God sustained them: 'their clothes did not wear out and their feet did not swell' (Nehemiah 9:21). This is an interesting echo of the **wilderness experience** that was so formative of the people of Israel. The images of lying down in green pastures and being led by still waters are restful ones suggesting solace and comfort in God's direction of one's life.[5] They are also restorative images – after rest we are renewed. So God restores one's very soul or life. As the shepherd leads the flock, so God directs one's life along the 'right paths'.[6] This is all in keeping with God's character and reputation as essential components of God's 'name'.

These restful images of letting God provide for us echo the way God provided the children of Israel with what they needed during the **exodus** and wilderness experiences. All they had to do was trust in God. God led them out of slavery (cf. Exodus 15:13), through the uncertainties of the wilderness wanderings and to the **promised land** (Deuteronomy 2:7). There are perhaps further overtones of the release of the people of Israel from **exile**, later in their history, in links with texts from the **exilic prophets** that speak of shepherding Israel home. There is a powerful expression of this sentiment in Isaiah 40:11: 'He will feed his flock like a shepherd; he will gather the lambs in his arms and carry them in his bosom, and gently lead the mother sheep.' The past is not forgotten in this note of thanks for present prosperity and hopeful expectation of a rosy future.

---

The **wilderness experience** was that of the wanderings of the children of Israel in the Sinai desert for forty years.

---

The **exodus** is the escape of the Semitic people (later known as Israelites) from Egypt under the leadership of Moses in circa 1250 BCE.

---

The **promised land** is the land of Canaan as promised first to Abraham in Genesis 12 and eagerly anticipated by the exodus group.

---

The **exile** is an event in the sixth century BCE when the Babylonians captured the kingdom of Judah and took its upper-class citizens away to enforced exile in Babylon.

---

The **exilic prophets** are those prophets who lived at the time leading up to and during the Exile (i.e. the seventh and sixth centuries BCE), notably Jeremiah, Ezekiel and Deutero-Isaiah (the author of Isaiah 40–55), whose prophecies reflect the historical turmoil and theological rethinking of that period.

However, even in this very positive and confident psalm there is a note of doubt, reflecting the fact that human life is rarely all rosy. There is an overtone of threat in verse 4 in the images of the darkest valley (probably of death, as in many translations) and later in mention of enemies.[7] But these are not dwelt on – fear is banished by God's protecting rod and staff, the two instruments needed by the shepherd. The rod is to ward off dangers to the flock, the staff to gather the sheep together. Although this is a psalm from an individual, the sense of community is never far away. Even though many of us live our lives, especially in our modern cities, far from sheep and shepherds, the imagery speaks to us in our human need – we long for rest, quiet, restoration, leadership, protection and comfort just as our ancestors did.

The main image in the psalm then switches to God as host of a banquet (vv. 5–6). We meet God in verse 5 as a host, preparing a table. Is this a table for a guest, in line with an ancient tradition of hospitality for strangers?[8] We might remember a line in another psalm (78:19) in which the question is asked, 'Can God spread a table in the wilderness?' Presumably the answer is 'yes' since God can do all things. This latter verse reminds us perhaps of the wilderness experience when God gave manna and quails for food in abundance to the wandering Israelite people. We are also told in Psalm 23 that God anoints the head of the suppliant with oil, probably part of the preparations for a feast. Possibly, if the meal was eaten outside, the function of such an action was simply to keep the sun off the head! Are there royal overtones of anointing with oil here (cf. Psalm 45:7–8), or at least evidence of this meal being one of special thanksgiving, given all the lavish preparations? We are also told that God provides in plenty – the overflowing cup makes a link between the literal banquet cup and the cup of life which is overflowing with blessings for this person. Again, care and provision from God is the theme and this thought links together the two images of this psalm – God as shepherd and God as host.

Verse 6 makes a kind of summary – the psalmist feels so blessed as to be looking forward to a future of relationship with God. The psalmist will continue to go to the house of the Lord.[9] This could indicate a yearly thank-offering, or it could be a more frequent visiting. The psalmist might be a regular member of the congregation or even a visitor – or maybe a priest, literally dwelling in the **temple** forever! The key point is that the psalmist will regularly be in the temple to praise his God. Maybe the context of this psalm was on just such an occasion in the temple

The **temple** originally refers to the Jerusalem temple as built under Solomon (circa 950 BCE), regarded as the dwelling place of God. Subsequent destructions and rebuildings occurred over time.

A **covenant** is a formal agreement between two parties, in this context the covenant between God and Israel which takes a number of forms (see chapter 4).

The **last supper** is the final meal Jesus had with his disciples at which he took bread and wine and gave them to his disciples as a representation of his body and blood. This inaugurated the **Eucharist** at which this symbolism is re-enacted in Christian churches worldwide today.

The term **eschatological** (from Greek *eschaton*, meaning 'end') refers to the end of time.

when the psalmist felt the grace of the protection God had afforded him in his life. Goodness and mercy are profound gifts, mercy or steadfast love having overtones of the **covenant** relationship enjoyed by the people of Israel with their God.

It is perhaps ironic that this hopeful psalm is very popular in Christian circles at funerals! This may be because of the message that God's protection leads a person through life and because of the strong confidence in the future expressed at the end of the psalm. In the Christian context Jesus is the shepherd who leads his flock and ultimately lays down his life for them. He is also host of the **last supper/Eucharist** and of the **eschatological** heavenly banquet, vanquishing all enemies, even death itself. Various passages in the New Testament[10] use shepherd imagery for Jesus, who is described as the 'Good Shepherd' of the sheep.

## One Psalm at a Time

So we have opened the Old Testament and looked at one psalm! This is perhaps the best way to 'open' such a book – to dip in, find something familiar and unpack it a little to expose deeper undercurrents and themes that might lead us further into other Old Testament books and ideas. We see immediately how rich the imagery is, how sustaining for our own faith and

**Egyptian bondage** refers to the period of slavery for the Israelite people just before the events of the exodus released them from it.

yet how challenging in making us look beneath the surface to see echoes of the story of Israel released from **Egyptian bondage**, wandering in the wilderness and then many years later returning from a different wilderness that was Exile and coming home to their promised land. In fact, it is only if we are familiar with the stories and themes of the Old Testament that we will pick up these deeper resonances. This is why we need to open such a psalm in a more profound way than simply picking it up and reading it, or even simply reciting the words in church. We are introduced in Psalm 23 to God and to God's people, but also to the individual psalmist as one to whom we can relate personally and this is perhaps the main appeal of many psalms.

I was inspired to begin this book with Psalm 23 by two main factors. First, by my own survey of asking people with which bits of the Old Testament they were most familiar – and this psalm out of all the Psalms seemed to come out on top. And second by Robert Davidson's comment in his *Beginner's Guide to the Old Testament* which also inspired the title of this book. He writes insightfully:

> For many people, not least those within the church, the Old Testament, apart from a few familiar, well-loved passages such as Psalm 23, is more or less a closed book, largely unread, very often misunderstood. It is a closed book because in many ways it is difficult and puzzling. Many otherwise highly intelligent people, committed to the Christian faith, will openly admit that they don't know how to handle the Old Testament.... Many people are anxious to find something which will help them to open this closed book. When they do open it and begin to learn to read it intelligently and with understanding, they often find it challenging and exciting, strangely relevant to their lives.[11]

In this book I wish to help people 'open' the Old Testament and find something of that challenge and excitement which Davidson mentions. In this first chapter I hope to introduce readers to the concept of the **canon** of the Old Testament and to the variety of different genres or types of material contained therein. I will mainly focus on five carefully chosen examples from the book of Psalms to illustrate the rich diversity of material and of the theological themes it contains.

> The **canon** is the group of authoritative texts that make up the Bible (see discussion later in this chapter). Canon means 'a rule'.

Scholars are sometimes interested in the idea of finding a 'centre' of the Old Testament and it has been sought either in a theme such as 'covenant' or in a book such as Deuteronomy. I would argue that it is indeed to be found in a book – the Psalms – which is a kind of watershed for all the different types of material produced by different social groups and for all the theological themes that we encounter elsewhere in the Old Testament.

## Clarifying Terminology

First, let us clarify terminology. I have so far referred to the Old Testament (and that is my preferred term in this book). However, it is worth remembering that these texts for Jesus were simply 'scripture' – the authoritative texts passed down to his generation after centuries of **Israelite** life. These texts are only called the 'Old' Testament or Covenant because there is a New Testament which is seen by Christians to be a fulfilment of many of the promises and hopes of the previous scriptures. Sometimes it is called the First Testament. More commonly nowadays

> **Israelite** is a generic term for the nation of Israel and also used in the plural for its inhabitants.

**Map 1**   Palestine at the time of David when the united kingdoms of Israel and Judah were at their greatest extent. Neighbouring states, e.g. Ammon, Moab, Edom and the Philistine region, are also shown.

scholars prefer to use the term Hebrew Bible, which acknowledges its roots in Judaism and its separate nature as the scripture of the Jewish faith. But the trouble with this term is that the Hebrew Bible and the Old Testament are not identically one and the same, as I shall go on to explain. Arguably also the term Hebrew Bible denudes the Old Testament of its relationship to the New in a Christian context. In Britain, scholars who belong to the Society for Old Testament Study get together regularly for conferences.[12] There has been some debate in recent years as to whether the society should change its name to something like the Society for Hebrew Bible Studies, but it has been generally felt that such a title would change the nature of what we represent, despite the increasingly diverse backgrounds and faiths of our members. Another term used for these accumulated texts, mainly in Jewish circles, is Tanak. This springs from the first letters of the three sections of the Hebrew Bible: Torah (Law), Nebi'im (Prophets) and Ketubim (Writings). But the Christian Old Testament presents the books in a different order and so arguably this term is not appropriate for this context.

Another problem with the term Old Testament is the word 'old', which suggests something outdated. Davidson puts it well:

> We talk about the 'Old Testament'. The very word *old* is unfortunate; particularly when we set it beside something we call the New Testament. It suggests that here is a book which is old hat or obsolete, something no longer needed which can have little to say to our rapidly changing world, when what is new today is in danger of being old and outdated tomorrow.[13]

It is an important part of my task in this book to show that the Old Testament is far from being obsolete and that it can speak powerfully to us today. Its antiquity is part of its enduring interest. I sometimes think that it is amazing that any of it has survived when you think that parts of it might have been written as long ago as three and a half thousand years! I also muse on the fact, from time to time, that in teaching the Old Testament I spend most of my day BCE (**Before the Common Era**) and little of it since the time of Christ!

> BCE denotes the period before Christianity, preferable to BC (Before Christ) in its neutrality.

## Books and Matchboxes

The Old Testament is a major part of our Bible and the word Bible is derived from Greek (*biblia*), and refers to a collection of books. This is a key factor, because what we have in the Old and New Testaments is a series of books, as in a library. At a point in time – the time of the closing of the canon

The **Law** (Hebrew: Torah) in this context refers to the first five books of the Old Testament in a term especially used in Jewish tradition. It also refers to the legal demands that the Israelites are meant to keep.

In this context the **Prophets** refers to the collective texts of Israelite prophets, including historical texts that contain stories about the prophets (known as the former prophets).

The **Writings** are a collection of poetic, wisdom and narrative texts that do not fit into the other two categories.

– it was decided which books would form a part of the library and which would be excluded. Davidson suggests that we see the Old Testament as a bookcase with three shelves.[14] These shelves would relate to the three categories of Tanak. The top shelf would contain the **Law** (five books), the middle shelf the **Prophets** (the former prophets, 6 books; and the latter prophets, 15 books) and the final shelf, the more miscellaneous **Writings** (the rest). This is a useful image, but again it relies on the Hebrew Bible order of books and not the Old Testament one. Also, as I shall show, the division of books is a bit more nuanced than just this division into three.

This leads me on to my own first introduction to the Old Testament canon, which used matchboxes of different colours. I find this more helpful than the

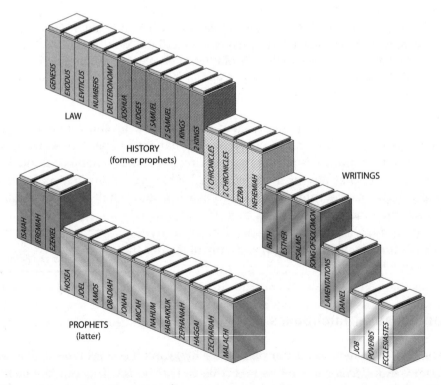

**Figure 1.1**  A long line of books, drawn as matchboxes, to represent the Old Testament.

bookshelves image. So, my first introduction to the canon of the Old Testament was a Sunday children's service experience of seeing a row of matchboxes, one for each book of the Old Testament – 39 in all. In fact, because I was the vicar's daughter, I found myself colouring different sets of matchboxes with large felt-tip pens, helping my father to prepare for his presentation. The interesting thing was that each matchbox did not have a different colour; rather, the first five matchboxes were painted blue, the second six (with one exception) were painted green, and so on. It was explained to us in church that the reason the first five books of the Old Testament, represented by the first five matchboxes, were painted blue was because they form a set of books known as the Law or **Pentateuch**, material considered some of the earliest, most formative and most important of Israel's faith. The second six, Joshua to 2 Kings, were green because they represented a 'history' of Israel known as the **Deuteronomistic history** – not to be confused with the book of Deuteronomy itself, which was one of the five blue books, but taking its inspiration from ideas in Deuteronomy and hence so named.[15] The little exception among the six green

> The **Pentateuch** is a term coined by scholarship to refer to the Law, the first five books of the Old Testament.

> The **Deuteronomistic history** is a term used in scholarship to refer to the group of historical books comprising Joshua, Judges, 1 and 2 Samuel and 1 and 2 Kings, also known in tradition as the 'former prophets'.

matchboxes was the book of Ruth, gaily coloured red, because it is counted as one of the Writings and it is unlikely that it belongs to the Deuteronomistic history. It is placed in my Protestant[16] Bible between Judges and I Samuel because the events described seem to belong to the period of the Judges, but it is most probably a separate composition, being very much a self-contained story. It is about Ruth, the Moabitess, a foreigner to Israel, who ends up being a key ancestor of an important king (see chapter 5). As I look along my line of matchboxes I see some more green, but this time a lighter green for the four books of 1 and 2 Chronicles, Ezra and Nehemiah.[17] These are also a history, hence the green, and if I were to open those books I might notice a certain element of repetition with the Deuteronomistic history. I would read again about all the kings of Israel and their reigns, although this time with a somewhat pious slant and a major concern with Jerusalem and the temple shining through. These books, I realize, belong to a later period, as they are a rewriting of the earlier history, known collectively as the Chronistic history (see chapter 2).

So are history books all we are going to get? No, because we find more red in the next group of matchboxes – Esther, Job, Psalms, Proverbs, Ecclesiastes and the Song of Solomon are their individual names, but they all share the bright red jacket. Flicking through my Bible these books don't seem to have a lot in common with each other – variety seems the order of the day. Esther is a short narrative with a woman as the heroine, rather like Ruth. On closer inspection of the matchboxes, Job, Proverbs and Ecclesiastes can be seen to be a pinker red than the others and I realize that this is a subdivision of **wisdom books**, representing a rather different world-view to the history books, one based on individual experience of human relationships and interaction with God, expressed in proverbs and in dialogues as in Job (see chapter 3). We notice that both the Psalms and the Song of Solomon have a poetic quality that makes them inspiring literature. These matchboxes then are all coloured red because they are the Writings, from all periods of Israelite life and representing a wide variety of genres of story, poetry and so on.

> **Wisdom books** is a term denoting Job, Ecclesiastes and Proverbs, books probably composed by wise men or sages. Some scholars add the Song of Solomon to the category. All are contained in the Writings section.

We then find a large chunk of yellow and this we realize is a huge section of prophets that takes up the rest of the shelf. This includes the twelve so-called 'minor' prophets (sometimes grouped together as one **Book of the Twelve**) and also the three great prophets, Isaiah, Jeremiah and Ezekiel (see chapter 4). The two books shaded a more orangey colour are Lamentations, a book traditionally attributed to the prophet Jeremiah and yet with a poetic quality that might make us want to put it into the Writings (next to the Psalms perhaps), and Daniel, a late apocalyptic work.

> The **Book of the Twelve** is a collective name for the twelve minor prophets.

This collection is known as the canon of the Old Testament,[18] which, when linked with the canon of the New Testament, forms the whole Bible.[19] But what I didn't realize when I was at my church children's service was that what I was being presented with was the Protestant canon of the Old Testament. What I know now is that there are two canons, each very different. What Protestants follow is essentially the same as the Hebrew Bible of 25 books (39 if we divide into 1 and 2 Samuel and do not group the minor prophets into a book of 'The Twelve'), also followed by some Orthodox churches. However, turning to my Hebrew Bible (so named because it is written in the original language of Hebrew[20] and is used in Jewish communities), I notice that they are not entirely one and the same, for I would have to change the order and hue of my matchboxes. After the Pentateuch and then the Deuteronomistic history (or 'former prophets') where the order is fixed,[21] the order changes, so that I have the prophets next (including the former prophets that I classified as 'history'), followed strictly by the writings which include Ruth, Lamentations, Daniel and the Chronicler's history.

## Canons and Versions

The other canon is that followed by Catholics and some Orthodox churches, based on the **Septuagint**, which is the earliest Greek translation of the Bible. So far as we know, no precedent existed at the time for any large-scale translation of a Near Eastern religious text such as the Bible,

> The **Septuagint** is the Greek translation of the Bible, begun in Alexandria, Egypt in the third century BCE, traditionally attributed to Origen, who in fact pulled together two earlier but divergent translation traditions. 'Septuagint' is from the Greek for 'seventy', reflecting another tradition (in the Letter of Aristeas to Philocrates, late second century BCE) that the translation was done at the behest of Ptolemy 2 (285–246 BCE) by 72 elders in Egypt in 72 days (rounded down to 70, for convenience). Ptolemy 2 may, however, only have commissioned the translation of the Pentateuch and the translation of other books seems to have continued piecemeal over the next two centuries. The earliest manuscripts of the Septuagint are from Qumran and are dated to the second century BCE.

so this translation was a pioneering effort by those wishing to make the Bible accessible to the large community of Greek-speaking Jews in Alexandria.[22] Now the Septuagint was the first translation of the Hebrew Bible into Greek, a translation that took place between the third and first centuries BCE,[23] so that by the time of the New Testament it was well established; indeed, it was the most widely known version at the time of Jesus and is generally the version cited in the New Testament. It is therefore an old and authoritative translation and its canon clearly includes a much larger range of material, some translated from Hebrew and Aramaic manuscripts and some composed in Greek. This is followed by the **Vulgate**, the Latin translation, which contains 46 books, including,

> The **Vulgate** is the Latin translation of the Bible from the original Hebrew by Jerome in the fourth century CE. It became the standard version used by the Western church, replacing an older Latin translation made from the Septuagint. One of the more significant Vulgate manuscripts is the Codex Amiatinus from the early eighth century CE.

as in the Septuagint, much of what Protestants know as the **Apocrypha**. I now discover that the *order* of the books in my Protestant Bible follows the Septuagint, but without the books of the Apocrypha (otherwise

The **Apocrypha** (from the Greek for 'hidden') is a group of religious writings from antiquity (15 books) included in the Septuagint and accepted by Greek-speaking Alexandrian Jews at the initial stage of the putting together of the Septuagint, but rejected by the Jewish community in Palestine and by rabbinic authorities of later times. For the first four centuries of the Christian era the Septuagint in this form was normative for the Christian community, hence the importance of these books for understanding the background to the New Testament. However, once Jews rejected the Septuagint (including Ben Sira and 1 Maccabees, which were originally written in Hebrew), the question of the canonicity of these 'extra books' became acute. When Jerome translated the Hebrew texts into Latin he rejected the books written in Greek and considered them 'apocryphal'. This alignment was accepted by Protestants at the time of the Reformation and so these books are considered uncanonical by Protestants. However, the Catholic church follows the books of the Septuagint, as do some Orthodox churches – and some Orthodox churches even add more books. The broadest canon is that of the Ethiopic church.

The **deutero-canonical** books are the books of the Apocrypha – a 'second canon' as distinguished from the first canon of books as contained in the Hebrew Bible. In Catholic circles the term is used for these books, but this is not to suggest that they are worth less than the other books in the canon.

known as the **deutero-canonical** books, rejected from the Hebrew Bible/Protestant canon). Just to add another complication to an already complex picture, there are further Jewish or Jewish-Christian writings from antiquity that are not included in any canon or in rabbinic literature, but which are associated with biblical books or biblical characters and even written in their name, and which claim divine inspiration. These books were put together as the **Pseudepigrapha**.

The **Pseudepigrapha** ('false writings') are further uncanonical books, Jewish and Christian writings from the third century BCE to the second century CE. The title refers to the assumed name under which many of the books are written. These books can also be designated 'further apocryphal writings'. They include apocalypses, testaments, midrashic stories, wisdom stories, hymns and prayers. They are an important source for an understanding of second temple Judaism and early Christianity.

So we see straight away that Jewish and Christian groups follow differ-ent 'canons' of texts.[24] This raises the issue of what is authoritative scrip-ture.[25] In some circles the Bible is a fixed entity that is 'of God' and cannot be questioned. But with a shifting canon, that claim is easy to refute. It is thought that the Law or Pentateuch – the first five books – was the first section to be collected together as an entity by the fifth century BCE (tradi-tionally by Ezra, as stated in the apocryphal book 2 Esdras 14:44–8). This may account for these first five books being primary in all the canonical orderings and explains their priority in Judaism.[26] The reasons for re-arrangements of the order are largely historical, as canonical discussions were resolved in various ways among different groups, from a period stretching from the fifth century BCE well into the second century CE.[27] While the order of the Pentateuch and former prophets was fixed early on, the most variations in order occur in the **latter prophets** and writings. The twelve minor prophets seem to have been ordered in what was thought to be a historical sequence, according to a second century CE scroll from Wadi Murabba'at. It was early Jewish practice to conclude the Hebrew

> The **latter prophets** comprise individual prophetic books such as Isaiah, Jeremiah and Ezekiel and also the twelve minor prophets or Book of the Twelve.

Bible with Chronicles following Ezra-Nehemiah (thus inverting their usual order). The reason is thought to be an ideological desire to close the canon on a positive note, the end of Chronicles stating that the fulfilment of biblical pro-phecy will involve a return of the Jews to their ancestral land. This echoes Genesis 50:24–5 in its promise of return to the ancestral land made by Joseph to his brothers. There may also be an ideological reason behind the variations in order found in the Christian versions, which save the prophets until last. One only needs to dip into the New Testament to see that much is made of the fulfilment of prophecy from the past in under-standing the life of Jesus (see chapter 5). Maybe the prophets are placed last in the Christian Bible because it leads more naturally into the New Testament, with the prophecy of Malachi ending on a note of prediction of the great day of the Lord leading us straight into Matthew's gospel and with Malachi's words concerning Elijah prefiguring the role of John the Baptist.

When mentioning the Septuagint, I strayed into the area of translations of the Bible and I would like to pause to mention some of the key texts that we have. The Old Testament/Hebrew Bible itself is written in Hebrew, with a small portion of Aramaic (Daniel 2:4–7:28 and Ezra 7:12–26). The Septuagint is in Greek. There are other early translations of the Old

Testament – the version known as the **Syriac Peshitta** was probably written in the first and second centuries CE. There are various Jewish

---

The **Syriac Peshitta** is a version of the Bible with early roots from the first half of the first millennium CE (different books being translated at different times and in different places), made from Hebrew but with reference to the Greek Septuagint. Some books were translated by Jews as evidence from links found with the Targum tradition, especially in the Pentateuch. The Targum of Proverbs actually derives from the Peshitta. By the fifth century CE the Peshitta version was the most widely used and ecclesiastically approved text of Syrian Christianity. Its oldest full version is the Codex Ambrosianus from the sixth to seventh century CE.

---

**Targums** are ancient Jewish commentary on scripture, regarded as of very high authority within Jewish circles.

**Aramaic** is the language spoken by Jesus and was in common use at his time. It is a Semitic language, closely related to Hebrew, known from the ninth century BCE onwards.

**Masoretic Text** is a consonantal Hebrew text with vowels added by the Masoretes. It is the standard text used in all Hebrew Bibles today.

The **Aleppo Codex** is a manuscript version of the Hebrew Bible from 925 CE which is the first codex ever made to contain the whole Hebrew Bible, although not the oldest surviving codex, since the Torah section was almost totally destroyed by fire in 1948.

The **Leningrad Codex** is a manuscript version of the Hebrew Bible from 1008 CE and is the oldest complete Hebrew Bible extant.

**Targums** written in **Aramaic** in the third century CE. Another major translation was made into Latin with the Vulgate in the fourth century CE. When we are translating the Old Testament, we need to refer to the other early translations, particularly when we come across problematic passages. Even when we have decided on our 'canon' of authoritative texts, we still find ourselves encountering variant translations, sometimes of quite a startling nature, and we can find huge variations between different versions of our English Bibles, such as the New English Bible (NEB), New International Version (NIV) and New Revised Standard Version (NRSV).

There is also the related issue of versions.[28] The text of the Old Testament/Hebrew Bible that we have today is known as the **Masoretic Text** and is one that has been passed down over many centuries. Some of its material may have been originally oral, but gradually cycles of written material came together and by the time the canon was closed all the material was in a fixed literary form. Until seventy years ago, the oldest actual manuscripts that we had of the Old Testament were from the eleventh/tenth centuries CE, the **Aleppo Codex** and the **Leningrad Codex**, faithfully copied by monks from earlier manuscripts. But all that changed with the discovery of the **Dead Sea Scrolls** at Qumran, among which were found versions of all the books of the Old Testament with the exception of Esther. Thus the Qumran texts, which date from the first century BCE, now form our earliest textual evidence. And the amazing thing is that the eleventh-century manuscripts do not vary from

> The **Dead Sea Scrolls** are versions of texts and other sectarian writings from the first century BCE, found in 1947 in caves at Qumran by the Dead Sea.

the Qumran versions in any significant way, indicating that the tradition copied the books of the Old Testament accurately and faithfully, providing us with a continuous tradition over many centuries. The Qumran material indicates to us that the Hebrew Bible was transmitted in scrolls – ancient sheets of leather sewn together – and that the earliest versions were purely consonantal – i.e. no vowels – as is possible in biblical Hebrew. The main difference between the Qumran material and the Masoretic Text that we have today is that the vowels have been put in. This was done in the Middle Ages between the sixth and tenth centuries CE by a rabbinic group called the **Masoretes**, who also added marks for reading and their own remarks. Hence the name, Masoretic Text. And if you look at any Hebrew Bible today you will see their work in the margins and footnotes as well as all the added consonants. The actual text of the Old Testament/ Hebrew Bible that we use today is in fact that of the Leningrad Codex.

> The **Masoretes** (notably the Tiberian Masoretes) were groups who worked during the second half of the first millennium CE, who added the vowels to the consonantal texts.

## Reading the Bible

So we have established that this is a collection of books – even though not all groups can agree on the exact boundaries of this canon or collection. It is interesting however that when we buy a Christian Bible or a Hebrew Bible we tend to perceive it as one book – perhaps because it is bound in one volume. Rather, I suggest that seeing the books that make up the larger volumes (i.e. each matchbox) as separate, might be a more successful way into 'opening' them, for the 'one volume' (often in dense print on thin paper) is somewhat daunting to approach by any standards. John Barton makes this point in his *What is the Bible?*[29] in relation to the laudable, but often failed, task that people set themselves of trying to read the whole Bible from cover to cover:

> When people set themselves to read right through the Bible they seldom think of this as if it were a matter of reading through a *pile* of books, but more as a single task (usually one that peters out around Leviticus).[30]

**Figure 1.2**    The Shrine of the Book at the Isreal Museum in Jerusalem, where some of the Dead Sea Scrolls are now housed. Photograph: Katharine Dell.

He goes on to comment on the 'getting stuck on Leviticus' syndrome:

> Genesis, and the first twenty-four chapters of Exodus, are interesting enough by any standards. They are full of great sonorous passages like the creation stories in Genesis 1 and 2, and well-told tales such as the story of Joseph (Genesis 37–50), not to mention traditional favourites such as Moses in the bulrushes (Exodus 2:1–10). But after that the going gets distinctly tougher. At Exodus 25 we enter the great central block of legislation in the Pentateuch, which concentrates almost exclusively on the exact detail of complex religious rituals . . . But for most people it is an acquired taste; and most would-be Bible readers falter, and abandon the project somewhere in the middle of Leviticus. Those who persevere are rewarded by some splendid passages in Deuteronomy, and then the whole long tale of Israel's entry into the Promised Land. But for most people by then it is too late.[31]

I would agree with Barton here that anyone who decides that they are going to read the whole Bible has a good romp through Genesis with the stories of creation, the fall and the flood. Following these, there are the rather

**Figure 1.3** One of the caves at Qumran where the Dead Sea Scrolls were found. Photograph: Katharine Dell.

**Figure 1.4**    Dead Sea Scrolls: the Great Isaiah Scroll. © The Israel Museum.

**Patriarchs** is a collective term for those early ancestors of Israel whose stories are contained in Genesis and Exodus. They were originally nomads who found their way to the land of Canaan. Their most famous ancestor is Abraham. The term specifically refers to the male leader of a family or tribe.

**Lawcodes** are sections of laws that make up a recognizable group. Different sections of laws (e.g. Exodus 21–4, the covenant code, and Leviticus 19–26, the holiness code) come from different periods in Israelite history. There are ancient Near Eastern parallels too, such as the Code of Hammurabi, king of Babylon (1792–1750 BCE), a stele containing 282 laws.

enjoyable stories of the **patriarchs**, Abraham, Isaac and Jacob, and their various antics, such as passing off their wives as their sisters – twice by Abraham and once by Isaac (Genesis 12:10–20, Genesis 20:1–18 and Genesis 26:1–11).[32] The Joseph story too is a good yarn and even into the book of Exodus with the story of liberation from slavery in Egypt to find the Promised Land we are still interested. But Leviticus seems to be the killer. If you were awake during Exodus – and there are chapters of **lawcodes** in Exodus 20–23, known as the book of the covenant – you will be asleep by Leviticus! At first glance it is nothing but a whole series of legal prescriptions, quite a few of which are about what to do when you develop a mysterious lump on your body (see Leviticus 21:16–24). In such an event you go to the priest who pontificates on whether you are deemed clean or unclean.

In fact, it has to be said that Leviticus has had a bad press and that there is much of interest in its pages. I am the Old Testament editor of some Bible Reading notes called *Guidelines*[33] and on looking through what had been covered in the last few years and what perhaps needed doing, I found that nowhere in the records was there any mention of Leviticus ever being done! So I promptly commissioned an author, Philip Jenson, to do just that and he covered it admirably. He made this comment in his introduction:

Is there any book in the Old Testament so obscure and forbidding as Leviticus? . . . So why bother? . . . The challenge is one of interpretation – to look long enough and hard enough at the text that it becomes a channel for God's grace and wisdom. Leviticus is indeed a far country but, sometimes, living only for a while in a different world can help us return to our own land and see it with fresh eyes.[34]

This comment might well be applied to the Old Testament as a whole. It does seem a 'far country' at times, with many customs, presuppositions, cultural norms and practices alien to our modern world. While we might wish to extract what is timeless from it, we cannot ignore its more unpalatable cultural aspects. I will discuss this issue in chapter 5.

## Law, Prophets and Writings

To go back to the image of matchboxes and the titles we have given to the various sets of books within the canon, we gave the title of 'Law' to the first five books, as traditionally done in Judaism and Christianity. Scholarship has generally referred to the first five books of the Old Testament as the Pentateuch. Perhaps the title 'Law' is a bit misleading. Certainly, all the major lawcodes of the Old Testament are contained in these five books – and many of the laws are in Leviticus. However, there is much more besides laws in those books – there is myth, narrative, genealogy, songs and liturgical pieces. The title 'Law' might be seen as off-putting to our 'opener' of the Old Testament, as it suggests nothing but a set of prescriptive rules and dry regulations. It also suggests that legalism is the character of the faith we are about to encounter. In scholarship, the famous nineteenth-century scholar Julius Wellhausen[35] sought to 'rediscover' the ancient faith of the Israelites that was not so dominated by 'law' as it later came to be. He realized that the Pentateuch contained many laws that were not actually from the period of the giving of the law on Mount Sinai (as it is presented in the Old Testament), but that in fact later collections of laws had found their way into that event. This was a comment largely on how material in the Old Testament might have come together, but it also pointed in the direction of the development of a religion that, while cherishing law as an important element, was not solely characterized by this one genre.

Prophecy too contains a huge variety within it. We have seen how the 'former prophets' is really a history (and I shall classify it as such), but even within the so-called latter prophets, there is huge variety in the expressions of judgement and hope, and in the different characters of individual prophecies and of the prophets who made them. This shows the problem of classifying sets of books together. Maybe, as I have suggested, we are better off taking each book as an individual item. But then we will no doubt find that even that is too limiting – for example, scholarship has found three prophets from three different periods in the one prophecy of Isaiah (Isaiah 1–39, 40–55 and 56–66). Even among those subdivisions we find very varied material. And the Writings are even more miscellaneous. Some have elements in common – such as the wisdom books – but even the term wisdom is a broad one which barely allows for an adequate definition of the three books that come in its category.[36] Among the Writings there is narrative, history, poetry – almost all the different genres of material that we find in the Old Testament are represented here and so again we are probably better off taking each book as a separate entity, but even that approach has its limitations. In fact, rather than being negative about the difficulties of categorization, it is perhaps better to be positive about diversity.

## The Worship Book of Ancient Israel

The book I want to focus on in this chapter is the Psalms. This book is among the Writings and yet it is very different from the rest of them, as it is the only book exclusively containing material used in worship in ancient Israel. If we read no other book in the Old Testament except the Psalms, we would have a good insight into the range of different genres in the Old Testament, into the different theological stances found within its pages and the emotions expressed. For this reason I regard it as a central and definitive book of the Old Testament, if not *the* central book, as mentioned earlier.[37] On closer inspection of the Psalms we might also learn about Old Testament worship and come to appreciate the wider context of Old Testament history and thought, as we did with Psalm 23. The Psalms, although seen by us as a 'book' within the larger collection of books, has always been used as a living set of poems in the context of worship. It is not intended to be read as a book, although there may be some design in its final form and subsections. Essentially, the Psalter[38] is a collection, rather like a hymn book. It contains much of the best of Hebrew poetry and can be classified in literary terms as well as in historical and theological categories.

The Psalms is of course the hymn book of the Israelites and we can learn much about the original context of their worship in its pages (see discussion below). However, in many Christian traditions it has also become some of the best-known and best-loved material in the whole of the Old Testament, if not in the whole Bible. Going back to the popularity of Psalm 23, I ask myself 'Why?' Is it because of the Christian application of it to Jesus? I remember seeing a picture in a children's Bible of Jesus surrounded by lambs with the caption 'The Lord is my shepherd' underneath it. I will never forget a paper given at the Society of Biblical Literature[39] one year on a sheep's-eye view of Psalm 23 (designed for Sunday school use). The ironic thing was that it was in the same section as my own rather erudite work on the wisdom psalms,[40] which was filled with scholarly references – it brought us straight down to earth in a really refreshing way (with pictures of fluffy sheep of course)! The image of Jesus as a shepherd mixes in my mind with a childhood picture that used to hang on my wall at home of 'the shepherd boy' (figure 1.5). I have never been quite sure whether it was meant to be David as a young shepherd boy or

**Figure 1.5** David/Jesus the shepherd boy by Margaret Tarrant. Courtesy of the estate of Margaret Tarrant.

Jesus, and that ambiguity may have been deliberate on the part of the artist – after all, wasn't Psalm 23 written by David, so isn't he in fact speaking about God, his Lord (Jesus in Christian terms), who guides him throughout his life?

## David: Shepherd Boy and King

In each chapter I wish to focus on one or more of the famous historical figures of the Old Testament, and it seems appropriate when talking of the Psalms to pause to consider David, who is traditionally their author. Davidson insightfully notes the romanticization of the figure of David that I just mentioned:

> Most of us have a fairly romantic picture of *David*. There is David the shepherd boy, probably composing some of his more familiar psalms, *e.g.* 'the Lord is my Shepherd', while he tended his flock on the hillside near his home town of Bethlehem. There is David, the young hero of Israel, slaying the Philistine champion Goliath with a pebble from his sling . . . The reality is somewhat different and more interesting.[41]

The **Philistines** are a nation who migrated to coastal areas in the southwest of Palestine from the twelfth century BCE and were the traditional enemy of the Israelites at the time of the Judges and the early monarchy. David signed on as a mercenary with the Philistine army.

The **Ark of the Covenant** is the golden casket containing the two tablets of the ten commandments. It became the vehicle and symbol of God's presence before the temple in Jerusalem was built. The Holy of Holies became its final resting place in the temple.

The **Succession Narrative** is the name given by scholars to 2 Samuel 9–24 and 1 Kings 1–2, as it seems to be a self-contained narrative about the power-politics that led to Solomon becoming king. A common theory is that it was written by a group of sages working at the king's court.

He points out David's early origins as 'little more than a guerrilla leader of a band of social misfits and desperados', with doubtful connections to the **Philistines**. David's military prowess combined with political intrigue to win him the throne among the southern tribes and eventually in the north also. He made Jerusalem his capital and the centre of religious activity, with a temple housing the **Ark of the Covenant**. He drove out the Philistines so as to take control of an ever increasing amount of territory.

The stories about David as contained in 1 Samuel 16:14 – 2 Samuel 5:12 (his rise to power), 2 Samuel 7 (his covenant with God) and 2 Samuel 9–20 and 1 Kings 1–2 (the **Succession Narrative**) give us a broad picture of this successful king, but it is not without criticism. Let us not forget that it was David who arranged for one of his own soldiers, Uriah the Hittite, to be killed because he wished to marry Uriah's wife, Bathsheba (2 Samuel 11–12). This seems a far cry from David's reputation as a composer of psalms and 'author' of the book of Psalms. In connection with that, we are told that David played the lyre to his predecessor King Saul (see chapter 2) and calmed his tormented spirit:

> And whenever the evil spirit from God came upon Saul, David took the lyre and played it with his hand, and Saul would be relieved and feel better, and the evil spirit would depart from him. (1 Samuel 16:23)

This turns out to be deeply ironic because little does Saul know that the one who calms his nerves will turn out to be his greatest rival for the throne!

We will be considering some passages about David in chapter 2 – the covenant in 2 Samuel 7 and **the Chronicler**'s picture of David. However, here we might just pause to consider the events from David's anointing as king while Saul was still on the throne, to his rule over a united kingdom of Israel and Judah

> The **Chronicler** is the presumed author of the Chronicler's history, possibly an individual, more likely a group with a particular ideology.

from Jerusalem. In 1 Samuel 16 we find the account of David being anointed as king by Samuel, at God's command. Here Samuel visits the house of Jesse, not knowing who is to be chosen. Seven sons are shown to Samuel, but they do not fit the bill. Eventually, the youngest is mentioned – David, the shepherd boy, and of course he is the one chosen by God. He is described as 'ruddy', with 'beautiful eyes' and 'handsome' (v. 12). This section is followed by the scene, already described, in which David plays the lyre for Saul and becomes his armour-bearer and much beloved by Saul.

1 Samuel 17 follows with the story of David and Goliath. Saul offers David his armour in verses 38–9, but David refuses as he isn't used to it.[42] Instead, he takes five stones to put into his sling. His defeat of Goliath is more than just the defeat of a giant man, it is the defeat of the traditional enemy of Israel, the Philistines, and also the beginning of David's power and the start of Saul's suspicion of him.[43] The rest of 1 Samuel focuses on the strange mixture of rivalry and affection that characterizes the relationship between Saul and David, and the book ends with the death of Saul.

We now jump to 2 Samuel 2, in which David is anointed king of Judah in the south, in Hebron. Judah is a separate kingdom from Israel in the north, over which one of Saul's sons, Ishbaal, has been made king by Abner, commander of Saul's army. We learn in 2 Samuel 3 of Abner's defection to David and of David's growing strength. Joab, the head of David's army, in turn kills Abner without David's knowledge and David mourns for the injustice done to Abner. We are then told in 2 Samuel 4 that Ishbaal, king of Israel, on hearing of the death of Abner, lost his courage. He too is murdered, without David's knowledge, and David is again angry with the perpetrators.[44] This however provides David with the opportunity to rule both kingdoms in a united monarchy (as described in 2 Samuel 5 with his anointing, this time by the elders of Israel), with Jerusalem as its capital and the ark brought there as the sign of God's presence and blessing (2 Samuel 6). The period of the united monarchy, continued under David's son Solomon, became the heyday of the Israelite monarchy and the time of its greatest strength and extent. After Solomon the kingdoms are once again divided.

We now turn to David's role in relation to the psalms, which is a very different portrayal of him to the military leader that we have just encountered. Although David's reputation was as a psalmist and author of the book of Psalms, when we turn to the Psalter we find only some psalms attributed to him, mainly those in the first half.[45] Other psalms are attributed to temple singers such as Asaph, notably most of Psalms 73–89. The psalms attributed to David are sometimes given a place in David's life in the **superscription**. Are we to take this at face value? Scholarship has tended to downplay David's actual role and to see the attributions as honorary and giving authority to the work rather than as in any sense historical. Some psalms can be dated later than David's reign and so would be unlikely to belong there – although most psalms are not dateable since very few historical events are mentioned in the collection as a whole. It is unlikely that David had no connection at all with the psalms and maybe we should take the superscriptions a little more seriously than some scholars have done. And yet, clearly, what we have in the book of Psalms is a collection. Rather as the whole Old Testament is made up of 'books', so the Psalter is divided into five books. This is thought to be a division made in the post-exilic temple (along the lines of the five books of the Law), possibly for singing purposes. In fact it is thought that there may have been earlier collections which were then brought together and divided along different lines later on.[46]

> **Superscription** is a psalm heading, sometimes brief (e.g. 'Of David'), sometimes longer, giving details of tunes to which it should be sung or a narrative context in the life of David.

## Scholarship on the Psalms

The psalms introduce us to the whole range of human emotions. We find joy, sorrow, lament, thanksgiving, supplication, celebration and praise. They have always been hard to classify, largely because each psalm has its own individual character. Perhaps the most successful attempt to classify the Psalms since the rise of modern biblical criticism in the late nineteenth century came from Hermann Gunkel[47] with his **form critical method**. He divided the psalms into five main types: hymns, including Zion psalms and enthronement psalms; communal laments; royal psalms; individual laments, including the psalms of confidence; and individual thanksgiving psalms.[48] This categorization was meant to be on the basis of form or type (German: *Gattung*), hence the name 'form criticism', and yet some of his categories were based more on the content and character of the psalms than on the form, arguably clearer criteria with more mileage. The idea of genre classification has proved to be a helpful one, thus seeing the psalms in literary terms. Also, there are important historical and theological dimensions that must not be forgotten. Although there is little reference to the actual history of Israel in the Psalms – hence their timeless quality – certain key events within that history are reflected in some psalms.[49] There is also an important theological dimension to the psalms: we are introduced to the major themes that are found elsewhere in the Old Testament, such as covenant, creation, exodus and wilderness imagery, kingship and so on. In my view, an approach which takes account of literary,[50] historical[51] and perhaps most of all theological considerations[52] when approaching any text, but particularly in this context, the Psalms, is an invaluable way of 'opening' our Old Testament. This is the model that I shall adopt in this book. By doing this, we start to see resonances of one text with another, of one image with a similar one, of one literary type with another, of one theological theme echoing through other texts. Thus, our experience of the Old Testament is deepened and enriched.

> The **form critical method** was that employed by Gunkel and involved isolating common forms or types of material with known content and context.

The psalms crucially give us an insight into the worshipping community of Israel and into the earliest roots of that worship. There are few historical references, but many hints of ancient liturgies.[53] Gunkel's method of form criticism highlighted the recurrent occasion on which a particular type of psalm might have been sung – a royal psalm, for example, on major occasions in the lives of successive kings.[54] This method was taken further by Sigmund Mowinckel,[55] who was interested in uncovering the original cultic context of the psalms in the early Jerusalem cult. He drew on ancient parallels from the surrounding Near Eastern world of the time[56] to suggest an annual Autumn New Year festival (at the Feast of Tabernacles) at which a wide range of psalms would have been used. The festival would have involved a celebration of God's victory at the time of creation over the waters of chaos and God's imposition of order on the world, followed by God's subsequent enthronement as king. As a part of this festival Mowinckel posited a yearly remembrance of the enthronement of the king,

God's representative, at which certain psalms would have been fitting. The festival would have taken place in the cultic celebrations at the Jerusalem temple, God's presence being symbolized by the Ark of the Covenant, which would have been carried in a procession into the temple. He thus reconstructed a festival situation from the Psalter drawing on psalms that suited that festival. This cast kingship in Israel in a new light. Up until then, the kings had been known from the historical books, with their deeds and exploits, such as David.[57] With the recognition of an important role for the king in cultic life, a new angle was brought into an understanding of the office. This showed the benefits of using the scholarly method of examining extra-biblical parallels from the ancient world[58] – notably a **Babylonian** festival context in this case[59] – to illuminate the Old Testament. But it also flagged up a potential danger: could we be so sure that Israelite models were based on those of neighbouring cultures? How far should such parallels be seen as decisive evidence for the Israelite context? The role of archaeology and cross-cultural parallels will be discussed in chapter 2 and can be seen in the illustrations in this book.

**Babylonian** refers to the nation with Babylon as its capital and to its inhabitants. This nation conquered Judah in 587–586 BCE and caused the Exile, often known as the Babylonian Exile.

Many psalms are brought to life by positing some kind of ritual lying behind them, or some kind of recurrent occasion on which they might have been used. However, scholars have found evidence for other types of festival, such as a covenant renewal festival,[60] within its pages and the quest for contexts in which psalms might have originated has tended to dominate the debate. The psalms themselves reveal singers, sacrifices and places of worship such as the holy temple at **Zion**. We are being offered a glimpse here into the worshipping life of many generations, although it is just a glimpse and not a full picture and that is why scholars have tried to fill the gaps. However, an individual as well as a communal worship context is also very strong in the Psalms, as we saw in Psalm 23, and should perhaps be more emphasized to counter this communal emphasis that scholars have tended to make. While some psalms were clearly written in response to events, on specific occasions, for formal purposes such as a coronation or for a festival, others were undoubtedly written by the individual, possibly by the sick person longing for release from their suffering or by one who simply wishes to express the joy of being alive and in relationship with God.

**Zion** is the name of the holy hill in Jerusalem on which the temple was built and hence was a symbol for God's dwelling place.

Rather than concentrating chiefly on the possible original contexts for psalms, I wish to focus on two things: (1) their genre or character in literary terms and (2) their theological content in relation to important Old Testament themes. We already saw with Psalm 23 that an apparently simple psalm of trust in God by a grateful suppliant has deeper overtones once explored further. I wish to select a few very different psalms for us to consider on these different levels. This selection of royal, wisdom and law (Torah) psalms, among others, will introduce us to the different types of material we have in the Old Testament, i.e. to the different genres which make up the Old Testament as a whole. Theological themes such as creation, covenant and individual questioning will moreover demonstrate the range of theological expression found in the Old Testament. On both levels, the question 'What is the Old Testament?' is answered in a more profound way than simply counting matchboxes (useful as that method may be as a starting point)!

## A Selection of Psalms

### Psalm 2

1 Why do the nations conspire,
 and the peoples plot in vain?
2 The kings of the earth set themselves,
 and the rulers take counsel together,
 against the LORD and his anointed, saying,
3 'Let us burst their bonds asunder,
 and cast their cords from us.'
4 He who sits in the heavens laughs;
 the Lord has them in derision.
5 Then he will speak to them in his wrath,
 and terrify them in his fury, saying,
6 'I have set my king on Zion, my holy hill.'
7 I will tell of the decree of the LORD;
He said to me, 'You are my son;
 today I have begotten you.
8 Ask of me, and I will make the nations your heritage,
 and the ends of the earth your possession.
9 You shall break them with a rod of iron,
 and dash them in pieces like a potter's vessel.'
10 Now therefore, O kings, be wise;
 be warned, O rulers of the earth.
11 Serve the LORD with fear,
 with trembling kiss his feet,
 or he will be angry, and you will perish in the way;
 for his wrath is quickly kindled.
Happy are all who take refuge in him.

Psalm 2 concerns itself with the king and so is widely regarded as a royal psalm. It is well known in Christian circles, with the language of kingship being applied to Christ. It can be interpreted on a number of different levels, as we shall see. On the surface it seems to be concerned with other nations versus Israel and the message is that God is on the side of the Israelite king who will vanquish other nations. This sounds somewhat nationalistic and rather typical of what many people think of the Old Testament – that it is about a small, insignificant nation which thought rather more highly of itself than it should have done and that it is rather violent in its warlike language (see the discussion in chapter 5). However, we need to see beyond that accusation because it becomes clear that what this psalm is really concerned with is serving God and God's vanquishing of the wicked. So in fact the offer is to all kings and rulers to serve God in righteousness, and through them the rest of the population. The psalm then has a more universal than nationalistic flavour after all.

The psalm begins with the question why the nations plot – it is all in vain in the face of the power of God. They love to engage in power-politics, but lack that deeper trust in God that is needed.[61] In verse 2 we have mention of 'the LORD and his anointed' against whom the nations prepare for battle. They wish to cast off the bonds of subjection, i.e. rebel against authority. In verse 6 it becomes clear that it is the king who is God's anointed (Hebrew: messiah), set by God on the holy hill of Zion, where the temple and palace were to be found, to rule Israel.[62] This mention of anointing which may well have happened at a coronation ceremony has led scholars to believe that this psalm concerns royal **enthronement** (as do also Psalms 72, 101 and 110). It is God, however, who does the consecrating with oil and the crowning.[63] The moment of enthronement may be the 'today' in verse 7 where the king becomes God's adopted son and 'begotten' of the godhead from that moment. At this point of coronation also the king received a 'decree' from God, possibly the substance of the **Davidic covenant**. This may have festival overtones – possibly an annual remembrance of the enthronement of the king as Mowinckel suggested; or alternatively a psalm used on special royal coronation occasions only. Once the Davidic king has been adopted by God, the other nations are under his power just as they are under God's. The king will break them and dash them in pieces like a vessel. Of course, the historical reality was a far cry from this rather idealistic picture of domination over the nations painted here. Israel was a small, **vassal state**

**Enthronement** refers to the process of becoming a king in relation to the coronation ceremony. It was believed that God too was enthroned as king.

The **Davidic covenant** is summarized in 2 Samuel 7. Interestingly, father and son language is used there too.

A **vassal state** is one beholden to another, more powerful state. The vassalage usually involves paying a tribute of money to the host nation.

of other major nations such as Assyria, Babylonia and Persia for most of her history. It is best seen as an expression of God's power over the world rather than as a realistic hope of world domination by Israel.

In verses 4–5 we are given two pictures of God: one of God laughing scornfully at the plotting nations and the other of God's anger. These views of God could be seen as problematic, but they are part of the use of human language to describe God's emotions and they are expressions of God's power (cf. Psalms 37:13; 59:8). In verse 10 the rulers are enjoined to be wise, a quality particularly needed in leaders (see the discussion of King Solomon's wisdom in chapter 3). In verse 11 the **fear of God** is mentioned and the nations are called to kiss God's feet in submission. God is powerful and in that sense frightening, commanding respect and rightful trust. There is a note

> The phrase the **fear of God** (or 'the LORD') is familiar from the book of Proverbs, particularly from Proverbs 1–9 (e.g. Proverbs 1:7) and elsewhere, and denotes a proper state of reverence and obedience before the godhead, hence a praiseworthy wisdom quality.

of conflict in this psalm in the mention of the consequences of God's anger, but it is resolved at the end by suggesting that seeking refuge in God is the path to true happiness.

In verse 7 the king appears to be speaking, which might suggest different speaking roles in a ceremony. Verses 4–6 are in the third person and the scene shifts from earth to heaven. The change of speaker may have been done for poetic or dramatic effect. Maybe the psalm reflects something of the power-games that go on before a new king comes to the throne – at a moment of national weakness other nations like to plot. On another level, however, we could see the psalm as being about the conflict between order and chaos. World politics may appear to be in chaos and yet the message is that God's divine power can bring order to the world and overcome human attempts at mastery. In a post-9/11 world this has a meaningful message for us today. God is sovereign in the world and in history and is in charge of the historical process, even at times of chaos and terrifying disorder. God reigns over all through the mediation of the king who is the anointed son here.

It is clear why this psalm quickly became a favourite in Christian circles, because Jesus was seen, even during his lifetime, as a king – notably King of the Jews (John 18:33) at the time of the resurrection and as God's 'anointed son'. He was crucified by the 'nations' of the world who were ruled by an earthly ruler, the Caesar. And yet he was king of God's everlasting kingdom that was not of this world, and hence Jesus' kingship was not like any human kingship. More than that, he was God's only begotten son. He did not even behave in a kingly manner – his aim was not to gain power or glory but he was sent to give himself up to sinful humanity. Interestingly, in one of the gospel accounts of his baptism, 'You are my son,

**Messianically** relates to the period when the messiah (Hebrew: 'anointed one') is expected to come, notably in the future. It is particularly linked with the restoration of the Davidic royal line.

today I have begotten you', a direct quotation from Psalm 8:7, is cited (Matthew 3:17).[64] In his death and resurrection Jesus conquered death itself and hence was victorious over human death and destruction.[65] In Jewish circles, before and after Christ, the psalm was interpreted **messianically** as describing the coming David or Davidic line (Daniel 9:25). After the Jewish Exile, the monarchy had ended and so having a king again became a more and more distant dream. The idealistic language of this psalm suited such hopes and reinforced ideas about the ideal end-time when God's kingdom will be established. This is true in Christian circles where the universal dominion of God's kingdom is still a future reality – so Psalm 2 is cited in the book of Revelation (1:5; 2:27; 4:2; 6:17; 12:5; 19:5), which is about the coming of Christ's kingdom at the end of time.

## Kingship in Israel

This psalm then is rich in its message on a variety of levels and gives us a real insight into the way kingship was viewed in ancient Israel as God-given. It offers us a glimpse of the kinds of ceremonial that may have taken place in the ancient temple, notably a royal coronation either occasionally or possibly annually. It shows how Israel saw herself as part of a global community, with God having concern for all nations and ultimate power over them. It demonstrates the triumph of serving God in trust and ruling in wisdom. It also points to an ideal of a just and Godlike world.

The genre of 'royal psalm' into which this psalm falls was one of Gunkel's classifications.[66] It shows us the importance of kingship in Israel and may lead us to reflect on the history of that kingship. Of course, Israel didn't always have a king – there were **judges** and prophets and some who combined these roles. Samuel, for example, combined the roles of judge and prophet and was leader in Israel at the time when the kingship was initiated. This leads to a lack of clarity about who is in

**Judges** denotes those in the role of judge over Israel, the accounts of whom are contained in the book of Judges in the Old Testament. There were 12 judges who ruled Israel in the times before the monarchy: Othniel, Ehud, Shamgar, Deborah, Gideon, Tola, Jair, Jephthat, Ibzan, Elon, Abdon and Samson. The reason that many of these names are not familiar to us is that the amount of material on each varies enormously and the best documented are those such as Deborah, Gideon and Samson.

charge in Samuel's dealings with King Saul. Although Samuel anoints Saul king in 1 Samuel 10, Saul is very dependent upon Samuel's guidance. When the idea of having a king arises in Israel, it is said to be the people who want one, rather than God (1 Samuel 8). However, God concedes and appoints King Saul (1 Samuel 8:22). Samuel and Saul have an uneasy relationship, with the boundaries of power being unclear. Saul fails to live up to God's expectations on a number of occasions (for example, when he makes an early sacrifice and hence disobeys God's command – 1 Samuel 13). Gradually, it becomes clear that the kingship is not going to survive under him and this is where David enters the frame. We have already noted how David's lute playing soothed Saul in his frenzied frame of mind. David ultimately gained the kingship and the promises of an everlasting kingship were made most famously to him and his line in the covenant contained in 2 Samuel 7. The kingship suffered many ups and downs. The time under David and his successor Solomon was a golden era with the extent of the nation Israel at its greatest. After Solomon the kingdom was divided between north and south and this continued until the fall first of the northern kingdom, Israel, in 722 BCE and then of the southern kingdom of Judah in 587 BCE, when many inhabitants were taken into Exile. The Exiles did eventually return, but Judah became a vassal state in the Persian Empire and never again had a king in power. However, hopes attached to the Davidic line and to the temple in Zion persisted and were pushed into an idealistic future.

Most of our information about the kings of Israel comes from the historical narratives as contained in the Deuteronomistic history and Chronicler's history. The Chronicler makes much of David as the founder of the temple in Jerusalem and this, of course, became the focus of power for the Jews in the post-exilic period, on return from Exile. However, Psalm 2 has shown us that there is another important source for information on kingship in Israel – in the psalms. This source is less historical and specific; rather, it is a festal view of kingship as an institution and as it might have been celebrated in the worship of ancient Israel.

If Mowinckel is right that there was an annual ritual in the cult of the enthronement of the king, this would suggest that pride of place was given to that institution in Israel's life (by comparison with the ambivalence over kingship found in the Deuteronomistic history).[67] What do we know about the festivals that might have been celebrated in ancient Israel? Mowinckel suggested that the re-enactment of enthronement rituals might well have accompanied a celebration in the autumn of the New Year, the harvest, the seasons and the creation. Weiser had an alternative idea of an annual covenant festival at the same occasion and there have been other variants upon these suggestions. There were three major festivals in the year in ancient times: the Feast of Tabernacles in the autumn (mentioned in Exodus 23:14–17; 34:22–3; Deuteronomy 16:16 as an occasion at which all male Israelites had to appear at the sanctuary); the Feast of Unleavened Bread in the spring at the time of the barley harvest (which came to be associated with Passover); and the Feast of Weeks at the time of the wheat harvest in May/June. It is interesting that these were all originally agricultural festivals, probably taken over from ancient Canaanite festivals that already existed in the land. It seems that in Exile, the Jews took over the Babylonian calendar. Modern Jewish festivals (as shown in figure 1.6) reflect the ancient festivals and a calendrial view of the year.

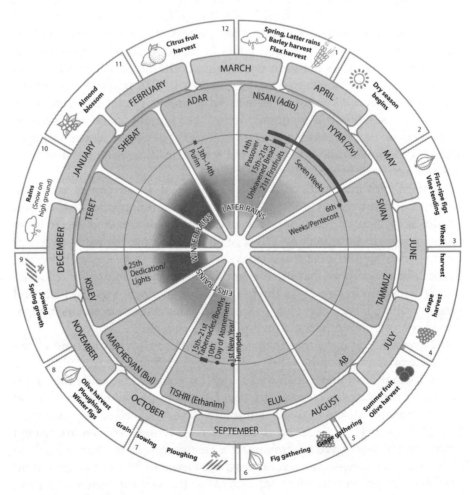

**Figure 1.6**    The Jewish worship year.

The next psalm to which I wish to turn is Psalm 19.

**Psalm 19**

*To the leader. A Psalm of David*

1 The heavens are telling the glory of God;
    and the firmament proclaims his handiwork.
2 Day to day pours forth speech,
    and night to night declares knowledge.
3 There is no speech, nor are there words;
    their voice is not heard;
4 yet their voice goes out through all the earth,
    and their words to the end of the world.
  In the heavens he has set a tent for the sun,
5 which comes out like a bridegroom from his wedding canopy,
    and like a strong man runs its course with joy.
6 Its rising is from the end of the heavens,
    and its circuit to the end of them;
    and nothing is hid from its heat.
7 The law of the LORD is perfect,
    reviving the soul;
    the decrees of the LORD are sure,
    making wise the simple;
8 the precepts of the LORD are right,
    rejoicing the heart;
    the commandment of the LORD is clear,
    enlightening the eyes;
9 the fear of the LORD is pure,
    enduring forever;
    the ordinances of the LORD are true
    and righteous altogether.
10 More to be desired are they than gold,
    even much fine gold;
    sweeter also than honey,
    and drippings of the honeycomb.
11 Moreover by them is your servant warned;
    in keeping them there is great reward.
12 But who can detect their errors?
    Clear me from hidden faults.

> 13    Keep back your servant also from the insolent,
>           do not let them have dominion over me.
>           Then I shall be blameless,
>           and innocent of great transgression.
> 14    Let the words of my mouth and the meditation of my heart
>           be acceptable to you.
>           O LORD, my rock and my redeemer.

Psalm 19 is a psalm of mixed genre incorporating elements of wonder at God's creation and enjoining the importance of keeping the law. There is also an element of teaching in the psalm and a note of prayerfulness at the end. This means that the psalm touches on some rather different areas of Israelite life and thought to those we have already encountered. We have seen how the first five books of the Old Testament are collectively known as the Law and this in itself indicates the importance and primacy of that concept in Israelite life into Jewish life today. But we have also seen how a legal emphasis may not have actually characterized Israel's earliest faith, if scholars such as Wellhausen are to be believed. This psalm demonstrates the important place that the law had in the life of every individual Israelite and opens the door for us into consideration of this genre. However, the element of teaching and exhortation accompanying it in this particular psalm is interesting. It perhaps provides a bridge with the wisdom tradition – those educationalists and wise men who were responsible for disseminating knowledge largely gained from tradition and experience. It also shows that the different genres of Old Testament life are easily combined and often falsely separated one from another. The wisdom books, however, as we saw, do form a distinctive part of the writings section of our canon. The third important element of this psalm is the emphasis on creation. We have encountered two psalms that indicate links to Israel's historical life – to the wilderness in Psalm 23 and to the kingly scene and covenant with the Davidic house in Psalm 2. Here we are reminded of another important doctrine of the Old Testament – creation – most famously expounded at the beginning of Genesis (see chapter 4), but with the psalms being another strong source of reference (e.g. Psalms 8, 104, 148). Finally, the note of prayerfulness is interesting and suggests that at some point in its history this psalm was used as a personal prayer, despite its possible original use in a worship situation. This would have been the case with many psalms, so that as situations changed, so did their use and function. When the time came that there was temporarily no temple in

Jerusalem, or indeed in a growing Jewish **diaspora**, these psalms were still cherished and passed on in the tradition and today they are mainly used as private or communal prayers.

> The **diaspora** refers to the phenomenon of Jews living outside the homeland of Israel, nowadays a far greater number than live in Israel.

C. S. Lewis wrote of Psalm 19, 'I take this to be the greatest poem in the Psalter and one of the greatest lyrics in the world.'[68] He is praising the psalm's imagery and its changes of style, which he sees as 'effortless' in the mind of the psalmist. It begins with a hymn to God as creator,[69] mentioning especially the sun (vv. 1–7). It then turns to a poem about the delights of keeping the law (vv. 8–11) and then a personal response from the psalmist is appended (vv. 12–14). What is interesting about the opening four verses, which form a kind of hymn, is that God's creation is itself praising God. Creation is thus personified as if it is speaking[70] – proclaiming God's glory and handiwork to the world and yet without the strictures of real languages (the number of which mean that people often cannot understand each other).[71] The realization then is that there is no real speech in the terms we would describe it; rather, the 'voice' of the heavens[72] and the firmament[73] reaches out throughout the earth, as we all recognize the wonder of the created world.

The psalm then moves on to the specific example of the sun[74] and here we find overtones of pre-scientific beliefs shared in the ancient world of the sun dwelling in a tent. People asked the question, 'What happens to the sun at night?' Not knowing that the world is round, they supposed that the sun rested in a tent above the sea overnight, a tent set up by God. It resembled the canopy under which bride and bridegroom get married in a Jewish wedding, and indeed it is to the image of a bridegroom that the next verse turns – as the bridegroom emerges from the canopy, so the sun. The next image is of a strong man – there is real energy in the sun and in the speed with which it goes on its cycle across the sky. Their cyclical view of the world is revealed – it goes from one end of the heavens to the other and its heat permeates everything. Just as the heat of the sun permeates everything, so does the law of the Lord.[75] Here we have the somewhat abrupt break between verses 6 and 7 of the psalm which may indicate some cutting and pasting by the author, as one might do on one's computer today. Maybe some or all of verses 1–6 represented an older hymn, taken over and put into a fresh context by the author of the rest of the psalm. Scholars have suggested that the first half of this psalm might have had a place at the autumn New Year Festival alongside psalms that mention creation such as 8, 104 and 148.

There is a very eloquent praising of the value of the law in this psalm from verse 7 – it is perfect and revives the soul. One can have confidence in it and it makes even the simple wise.[76] Both heart and eyes are fired up by it. There is a very personal aspect of its benefits in that it renews a person's inmost being. It all springs from God[77] and the fear of God. It is more precious than gold (cf. Psalm 119:72, 127) and sweeter than honey (cf. Psalm 119:103).[78] In many ways the description of the law and its benefits could be seen on another level as a description of the benefits of belief in God.

From verse 11 a note of caution is heard for those who might transgress, even without realizing it. There are hidden dangers lurking and insolent people around. The psalmist here asks God for protection from them. The great reward mentioned for keeping the law is more than monetary, recalling the benefits listed earlier. One wonders what the 'great transgression' (which may simply parallel the great reward) might be – **idolatry** perhaps, which was greatly frowned on throughout the Old Testament period, or even **the fall**. The last verse of the psalm has the character of a formula of dedication, perhaps originally of a sacrifice, but in this context of the speaker himself. The prayer is for acceptability to God in whom the psalmist trusts. He calls God his rock and redeemer.[79]

---

**Idolatry** is the worship of idols that represent gods in any religion. It was especially frowned on in Israelite religion, in which any image of God is prohibited. Cf. the Ten Commandments.

---

The **fall** refers to the events that are recorded in the second and third chapters of Genesis, when Adam and Eve fall from grace and are expelled from the garden of Eden. This is symbolic of the 'fallenness' of humankind in general.

---

The emphasis on speech and communication in this psalm recalls the wisdom tradition with its emphasis on the importance of speaking appropriately (e.g. Proverbs 15:1, 'A soft answer turns away wrath, but a harsh word stirs up anger'). Wisdom in verse 7 is itself mentioned alongside law (cf. Proverbs 7:1–3) and the fear of the Lord (cf. Proverbs 8:13), which is the beginning of all wisdom and the attitude that the pious person should adopt. Law and wisdom are thus linked as God's divine teaching. The 'great reward' in wisdom terms might be monetary, since riches and honour were highly desirable (cf. Proverbs 8:13; 22:4).[80] One of the most interesting features of this psalm is the way it moves from the universe to the individual. The heavens proclaim God's glory to the world, and yet each individual has their body and soul renewed by the law and wise living. We might muse on the fact that just as life would not exist on this planet without the sun, so is God's law, in the broadest sense, integral to human life.

The superscription to this psalm states that it is 'Of David', but there is nothing in the psalm to link it to him and it seems unlikely to have been written by him. It is more likely an example of one attributed to him, in honorific or traditional terms, rather than actually composed by him. We see in the mix of genres the possibility of earlier sections and later sections and this is to introduce us to the idea of composite psalms, not just of varied genre but possibly too of different times of writing. We know also that psalms were 'updated', as was much literature in the Old Testament (see discussion in chapter 2). In this psalm, it is possible that the prayerful final verse is a **doxology** and, as mentioned, the first half of the psalm may be the earliest section. Dating questions continue to fascinate scholars when they discuss the psalms, but the truth of the matter

**Doxology** is from the Greek *doxa*, meaning 'glory' and is used to describe pious endings to psalms, often thought to be added later to an existent psalm.

is that it is very difficult to date any with certainty. Decisions largely rest on what we know of other parts of the Old Testament – so, for example, if we thought from elsewhere that law-keeping was a preoccupation of the post-exilic age when there was no king, then we might say that a section of the psalm mentioning law was 'later'. This kind of conclusion can be rather subjective, however.

Unlike the other two psalms we have considered so far, this psalm is not particularly popular in Christian circles, and there is little that can be linked to Christ, except perhaps the final reference to a redeemer. It has proved more popular in Jewish circles because of the emphasis on the law in that religion and its integral nature to life. We saw in C. S. Lewis's remark an indication of his appreciation of the poetry and imagery of the psalm. Another area of scholarly interest in relation to the psalms is that of their character as poetry. Lewis particularly liked the idea that the law was 'sweeter than honey', an image which he thought no one could improve upon.

The next psalm I wish to consider is Psalm 105, the longest of the group I have chosen.

**Psalm 105**

1  O give thanks to the LORD, call on his name,
    make known his deeds among the peoples.
2  Sing to him, sing praises to him;
    tell of all his wonderful works.
3  Glory in his holy name;
    let the hearts of those who seek the LORD rejoice.
4  Seek the LORD and his strength;
    seek his presence continually.
5  Remember the wonderful works he has done,
    his miracles, and the judgements he has uttered.

6   O offspring of his servant Abraham,
      children of Jacob, his chosen ones.

7   He is the LORD our God;
      his judgements are in all the earth.

8   He is mindful of his covenant forever,
      of the word that he commanded, for a thousand generations,

9   The covenant that he made with Abraham,
      his sworn promise to Isaac,

10  which he confirmed to Jacob as a statute,
      to Israel as an everlasting covenant,

11  saying, "To you I will give the land of Canaan
      as your portion for an inheritance."

12  When they were few in number,
      of little account, and strangers in it,

13  wandering from nation to nation,
      from one kingdom to another people,

14  he allowed no one to oppress them;
      he rebuked kings on their account,

15  saying, "Do not touch my anointed ones;
      do my prophets no harm."

16  When he summoned famine against the land,
      and broke every staff of bread,

17  he had sent a man ahead of them,
      Joseph, who was sold as a slave.

18  His feet were hurt with fetters,
      his neck was put in a collar of iron;

19  until what he had said came to pass,
      the word of the LORD kept testing him.

20  The king sent and released him;
      the ruler of the peoples set him free.

21  He made him lord of his house,
      and ruler of all his possessions.

22  To instruct his officials at his pleasure,
      and to teach his elders wisdom.

23  Then Israel came to Egypt;
      Jacob lived as an alien in the land of Ham.

24  And the LORD made his people very fruitful,
      and made them stronger than their foes,

25  whose hearts he then turned to hate his people,
      to deal craftily with his servants.

26  He sent his servant Moses,
      and Aaron whom he had chosen.

27 They performed his signs among them,
    and miracles in the land of Ham.
28 He sent darkness, and made the land dark;
    they rebelled against his words.
29 He turned their waters into blood,
    and caused their fish to die.
30 Their land swarmed with frogs,
    even in the chambers of their kings.
31 He spoke, and there came swarms of flies,
    and gnats throughout their country.
32 He gave them hail for rain,
    and lightning that flashed through their land.
33 He struck their vines and fig trees,
    and shattered the trees of their country.
34 He spoke, and the locusts came,
    and young locusts without number;
35 They devoured all the vegetation in their land,
    and ate up the fruit of their ground.
36 He struck down all the firstborn in their land,
    the first issue of all their strength.
37 Then he brought Israel out with silver and gold,
    and there was no one among their tribes who stumbled.
38 Egypt was glad when they departed,
    for dread of them had fallen upon it.
39 He spread a cloud for a covering,
    and fire to give light by night.
40 They asked, and he brought quails,
    and gave them food from heaven in abundance.
41 He opened the rock, and water gushed out;
    it flowed through the desert like a river.
42 For he remembered his holy promise,
    and Abraham, his servant.
43 So he brought his people out with joy,
    his chosen ones with singing.
44 He gave them the lands of the nations,
    and they took possession of the wealth of the peoples,
45 that they might keep his statutes
    and observe his laws.
    Praise the LORD!

**Salvation history** denotes the history of the people of Israel from their early origins. They believed God to be a God of history who acted on behalf of his people, performing salvific acts.

**Settlement** refers to the period when the land of Canaan was starting to be settled with Israelites, both the families of the patriarchs and those returning from Egypt after the exodus.

This is perhaps the least well-known of the psalms I have selected, but its chief interest lies in the fact that it gives us a potted version of the **salvation history** and so introduces us to how the people at worship viewed the historical events that had led to their creation, blessing and continuance. The salvation history recounted here is the earliest period of the promises repeated to Abraham, Isaac and Jacob down to the time of the **settlement**. Joseph is mentioned, as is the time in Egypt and the plagues, followed by the wilderness period.[81] Another aspect of this psalm is its character as a hymn of praise or thanksgiving[82] – it gives the most positive presentation of the salvation history in the Psalter, with no mention of any going astray by the people (unlike Psalm 106 which follows it). Underlying the psalm is a strong note of praise to God for having guided events in the formative days of the people of Israel, for fulfilling the promises that were made and for guiding events in the wider world. We also have hints of the context of worship in the Jerusalem temple with its recitation and possible re-enactment of saving events accompanied by singing. We might get an insight from this psalm into how ancient traditions were passed down over the centuries, since one intriguing aspect of this psalm is that the first 15 verses are quoted in one of the historical books of the Old Testament, 1 Chronicles 16:8–22.[83] In this latter passage the quotation is put into the context of cultic celebrations at the time of David following the placing of the Ark of the Covenant in Jerusalem. This citation suggests that the psalm was known to the Chronicler who wrote this book, probably in the post-exilic period, any time from the fifth century BCE, and so it is likely to pre-date this author. It could even belong to earliest times, representing the recital of history in the cult in either pre-Davidic times or Davidic times (when the Ark came to rest in Jerusalem, as the Chronicler portrays it).[84]

The first six verses of this psalm are a call to the people to sing the praise of God and tell of God's deeds and miracles. This may suggest a call to worship and to a ceremony in which the covenant was specifically remembered.[85] The past events fuel the relationship with God in the present, leading the people to 'seek his presence continually' (v. 4). It is made clear that it is to the chosen people of God as represented by Abraham[86] and Jacob that the promises have been made (v. 6), but in verse 7 it is clear that God's sphere of action is the whole world. In verses 7–10 we are reminded that God made a covenant with Israel – to Abraham (Genesis 17:8; 22:16) and then repeated to Isaac (Genesis 26:3ff.) and Jacob (Genesis 28:13ff.; 35:12) – and that it was chiefly about land and offspring. In verses 12–15 the improbability of such a small and insignificant group becoming the recipients of God's great promises is highlighted. They were semi-nomadic and had no land of their own. God gave them protection against the odds and so the emphasis falls on divine guidance of events.[87] In verses 16–23 we have a potted history of the story of Joseph, perhaps most famous for his 'technicolor dreamcoat' (see Genesis 37–45).[88] Here there is no mention of that part of the story of Joseph, only of the time when he was in Egypt. He was enslaved until his prophetic dreams and the interpretation of the dreams of his fellow prisoners were believed and he was elevated to high office under Pharaoh and was able to instruct others in wisdom.[89] The message here is again that God was guiding events and 'testing' his faithful servants (v. 19).[90]

The next phase of the salvation history is a recalling of the period in Egypt when Israel was under oppression. Verses 24–5 are a kind of theological summary of the time spent there. It is even emphasized that God made the Egyptians hate the Israelites – it was all part of God's divine plan. Here Moses and Aaron enter the frame and there is an account of the plagues in the verses that follow. Interestingly, the order of the plagues as in the Exodus account (Exodus 7–17) is different here and indeed plagues 5 and 6 are omitted altogether. This might suggest that the account in Exodus had not reached its final form when this psalm was written. Therefore it could be a testimony to the earlier date of this psalm before the tradition had become fixed (see the discussion of Pentateuchal sources in chapter 2). So the ninth plague of darkness begins the account;[91] then plagues 1 and 2 of rivers of blood and frogs, followed by flies (plague 4) and gnats (plague 3), hail (plague 7) and locusts (plague 8). The climax is the slaying of the first born (plague 10) – no wonder Egypt was glad when they departed (v. 38) (see the discussion of the exodus in chapter 5)! We are told that Israel left Egypt laden with valuables (cf. Exodus 3:21; 11:2). Again, God is guiding the people so that no one stumbles along the way.[92] The power of God overcomes any and every obstacle. A cloud is mentioned in verse 19 – possibly a cloud (or angel) of guidance (Exodus 13:21) or perhaps more likely of protection, either from the Egyptians (Exodus 13:21) or from the sun during the day.[93] The fire is to give light at night and also perhaps lead the people in the right direction. We then have reference to the manna (bread) and quails (meat) given to the people of Israel by God in the wilderness. There is also mention of the miraculous opening of a rock (at Rephidim, cf. Exodus 17:1–6) to provide life-giving water to the people as they traversed a desert land. The end of the psalm recalls the beginning – the note of praise continues with a remembrance of the joy and singing at the time of the deliverance (cf. the Song of Moses sung in Exodus 15), linking up with the joy and praise expressed at any time that this psalm was sung. God is seen to have kept the covenant promise of land, a promise that is valid forever. We might find the idea of taking over the land of others problematic today, but the Old Testament does not perceive it as such. Land is always transferring from one group to another through the natural processes of law, but the difference here is that someone else's land is seen as God-given to the Israelites. While it is in a sense an extension of the idea that God wins wars on behalf of his own people – he can raise up conquerors and establish his land – there are difficult issues of prior ownership and land-sharing that remain pertinent today, especially in Israel/Palestine. This shows the extraordinary contemporaneity of so many issues raised by seemingly innocent verses in the Old Testament! The psalm ends with a reminder of Psalm 19 – obedience to the law being the inspiration that follows from such a remembrance of God's saving deeds (cf. Exodus 19:5ff.; 20:1).[94]

This psalm is closely linked to the historical events that led to the formation of Israel as a nation and a people. It tells of the inauguration of the special relationship between God and his chosen people. The note of universalism in verse 7 almost seems a token gesture to a wider world. On nationalistic grounds, then, one might have thought that this recitation held little appeal for a Christian audience, except to affirm their Old Testament roots. However, this is not the case. I remember attending a United Reformed service in which a 'creed', recited by the congregation, recalled the early days of the exodus and wilderness wanderings of the people of Israel, as in this psalm. The New Testament definitely saw itself as a continuance of the covenant relationship and indeed as a new fulfilment of old promises (Luke 1:72, 73). The church was regarded as the seed of Abraham, fellowship in Christ replacing the promise of land (Galatians 3:16–29), and the recipient of a new covenant (1 Corinthians 11:25).

Although the psalms are not in general the best place to look for Old Testament history, we have already seen that hints of that history keep appearing and this gives us an insight into how the Israelites at worship presented their own history. I want finally to consider another psalm that gives a hint of history, but is in fact more of a communal lament. The part of history that it reflects is very different from Psalm 105 – it speaks of the Babylonian exile. After the period of the kings, Jerusalem finally fell to the Babylonians in 587 BCE. At that point the upper classes were deported to Babylon. This was a common practice in the area – the victors basically exiled the important people in order to weaken and subjugate the country. The Israelites found themselves in Babylon for fifty years and it was only in 537 BCE, when the Persians took over Babylon, that they were allowed to return. Psalm 137 reflects that situation and it is to that psalm that we shall now turn; the last in our selection.

---

**Psalm 137**

1  By the rivers of Babylon –
    there we sat down and there we wept
    when we remembered Zion.
2  On the willows there
    we hung up our harps.
3  For there our captors
    asked for us songs,
  and our tormentors asked for mirth,
    saying,
  "Sing us one of the songs of Zion!"
4  How could we sing the LORD's song
    in a foreign land?
5  If I forget you, O Jerusalem,
    let my right hand wither!
6  Let my tongue cling to the roof of my mouth,
    if I do not remember you,
  if I do not set Jerusalem
    above my highest joy.
7  Remember, O LORD, against the Edomites
    the day of Jerusalem's fall,
  how they said, "Tear it down! Tear it down!
    Down to its foundations!"
8  O daughter Babylon, you devastator!
    Happy shall they be who pay you back
    what you have done to us!
9  Happy shall they be who take your little ones
    and dash them against the rock.

---

This psalm is clearly set in the period of Exile from the homeland and specifically in Babylon. The Exile was a key moment for the Israelites, a moment at which their history seemed abruptly to have come to an end, and along with it all the institutions on which they had relied. It was a time when theological assumptions had to be revisited and revised. Ironically, it was also a very formative period in Israelite thought and theological under-standing, and also in her production of literature – isn't it often said that human beings only feel inspired to write during the bad times? This psalm is primarily a lament, but it contains elements of a song of Zion and of a diatribe against enemies. Thus it is a psalm of mixed type, like Psalm 19. Verses 1–3 transport us to Babylon with the exiles grieving over their destroyed city of Jerusalem, with its holy mount of Zion. They were unable to sing because their captors asked them to play happy songs – presumably, all they wanted to sing were sad ones. Their captors are clearly mocking them about their Zion hymns (e.g. Psalms 76, 84, 87, 122). There was a tradition that Zion would never be overcome – that it was in some way impregnable.[95] Presumably the captors were rejoicing in the fact that to all intents and purposes it was now overcome – by them, the Babylonians. The psalmist then asks how any song about the Lord could be sung in a foreign land – the implied answer is that it couldn't. It wouldn't be right to sing about Zion there, given that Zion is God's earthly dwelling place. And yet the psalmist is highly concerned not to forget Jerusalem and in that context utters a self-curse. He hopes that his right hand will wither or his tongue stick to the roof of his mouth if he ever would forget his 'highest joy'.[96] The psalm changes gear in verse 7 and becomes a diatribe against enemies. The **Edomites** were neighbours of Israel and particular enemies just after the Exile.[97] Given that verses 1–3 are in the manner of past recollection, scholars have suggested that the psalm might actually belong in the home-land just after the return, when the temple was still in ruins and people were building their own houses instead of the temple (cf. Haggai 1:9). The psalmist here remembers the Edomites' part in Jerusalem's fall – the temple was in ruins. Then, for Babylon, the chief enemy who caused the devastation, the law of retribution is alive and well. In a war, crimes and horrors are committed on both sides[98] and verse 9 of this psalm indicates that. Israel would be happy to take the little children of the Babylonians and dash them against the rock as an act of retribution. Perhaps the impli-cation is that this crime has been done by them. This is one of the most difficult verses in the Psalter (and is often bracketed in Christian Psalters) and yet the actual context is that of retribution, hate and despair on behalf of the beleaguered psalmist. We could of course read the verse symbolically, but maybe that would be refusing to face up to the difficulty of the verse (see the discussion of 'difficult passages' in chapter 5). A cultic setting seems unlikely for this psalm. It represents a time in Exile

The **Edomites** were descended from Esau, the brother of Jacob who, through Jacob's trick-ery, lost his birthright (Genesis 27). Edom is to the southeast of Israel, in modern-day Jordan.

**Figure 1.7** David playing the harp. Vellum Manuscript by a scribe called Benjamin. Image taken from North French Miscellany. Originally published/produced in northern France circa 1280. © akg-images/British Library.

and just after, when the exiled Israelites couldn't hold their ceremonies and hence perhaps couldn't sing their songs. Would there have been days of lamentation on which prayers would be offered for the restoration of Jerusalem (cf. Zechariah 7:1–5; 8:19)? In Jewish tradition this is sung on the 9th Ab[99] at a service commemorating the destruction of Jerusalem. This psalm has not formed an important part of Christian tradition, although Babylon becomes, in the book of Revelation, an archetype of evil and a new Babylon is envisaged (cf. Revelation 17–18).

There is an overtone of the diatribes of the exilic prophets in the last two verses of this psalm. Bad-mouthing one's enemies is well documented, as is reprisal for misdeeds. There is little prophecy in the Psalter – arguably the genre that is most missing from its pages (and an argument against my 'centre' theory). And yet hints of prophecy's existence and its sentiments find echoes too, as here in Psalm 137. However, the overwhelming impression of this psalm is one of lament; in that, it joins a large majority of psalms in the Psalter.

We might relate the Psalter to another of the 'Writings' of the Old Testament, the book of Lamentations. Lamentations is highly poetic, like the psalms, and is a kind of bewailing, along similar lines to Psalm 137, of the destruction of Jerusalem in 587 BCE. It is traditionally attributed to the prophet Jeremiah who lived around the same time. The difference is that this work is set during the actual siege of Jerusalem and it concerns the horrors of that event. There is a strong note of lament in this short book, showing the link between lament psalms and prophecy. The prophet Jeremiah lived through the events of the Exile and stayed in Jerusalem, so one can see where the attribution came from. We also have poems of lament within the book of Jeremiah that form his 'confessions' (Jeremiah 11:18–12:6; 15:10–21; 17:5–10, 14–18; 18:18–23; 20:7–18), telling of the personal anguish that the prophetic task of preaching judgement caused him.

## The Diversity of the Old Testament

In Christian circles, the Psalter goes on being used and is given pride of place in many liturgies. Of all the Old Testament, therefore, it is the part that people often know. Its many laments and thanksgivings clearly resonate in the lives and hearts of modern men and women. Although we have focused on some of the 'time-bound' and more 'historical' aspects of some psalms, that is not their general character. In fact, it is their very timelessness that has made them so endurable.

We have seen in this brief survey of five psalms something of the range of theological expression in the Psalter: from trust in God, shepherd and host, to praise to God as the redeemer of Israel; from the heyday of kingship in Israel, to God as king; from horror at the realities of exile and destruction, to calm confidence in God's law, in God's creative activity and in his wise word. We have also been introduced to the range of genres found in the Psalms which reflect the genres of the Old Testament canon. So within the canon we will find the patriarchal history (Genesis), the exodus and wilderness wanderings (Exodus), the law (Leviticus and Numbers) and the Promised Land (Deuteronomy, Joshua). We will find ancient history about kings such as David and his descendants (the Deuteronomistic history) and laments over the 'bad times' (Psalms and Lamentations). We will find wisdom, praise to God as creator and much more. The Psalms is just a starting point, and we will go on in subsequent chapters to explore other parts of the canon of the Old Testament.

So in response to our opening question 'What is the Old Testament?' we can see that the answer is far from simple. It is not a straightforward body of authoritative texts – history has conspired to give us a complex set of canons, translations and versions. We have noted its diversity as a collection of books and from a study of just one of its key genres, the psalms, we have been given a glimpse into the richness of material that we will encounter as we take our study further.

## Notes

1   I use the NRSV translation throughout.
2   One recent use of the psalm is as the theme music for the BBC television series *The Vicar of Dibley*, music by Howard Goodall.
3   First found in Genesis 49:24 in a list of names with which to describe God, 'Mighty One of Jacob, by the name of *the Shepherd*, the Rock of Israel'. See also Psalm 80:1 in which God is described as 'Shepherd of Israel'.
4   Such as Psalm 77:20 in which God leads his people 'like a flock'. See also Psalm 95:7, in which 'We are the people of his [God's] pasture, and the sheep of his hand', and Psalm 100:3, which echoes 95:7.
5   We are perhaps reminded of Isaiah 11:6–7 in which 'the wolf shall live with the lamb, the leopard shall lie down with the kid', a vision of harmony between different animals and between animals and human beings. In Jeremiah 33:12 there is a similar image of flocks lying down to rest in a wasteland (amid the destruction of Judah at the Exile). God decrees in a hopeful oracle that 'there shall again be pasture for shepherds resting their flocks'. Ezekiel goes a step further to describe God as the true shepherd and to give us an extended diatribe (in chapter 34) on false shepherds versus the true one.

6   This idea of direction by God along life's path is known to us from the wisdom literature, e.g. Proverbs 4:11, in which the parent states to the child that 'I have led you in the paths of uprightness', an image easily applied to God as in Psalm 16:11: 'You show me the path of life.'

7   'Enemies' are a perennial problem for psalmists it seems, as in Psalm 71:10–11 where enemies lie in watch hoping to take the psalmist's very life.

8   As indicated in Genesis 18:1–8. For a discussion of this and other examples, see K. J. Dell, 'Hospitality in the Old Testament', *Guidelines*, Vol. 20/3, eds. J. Duff and K. J. Dell, Oxford: Bible Reading Fellowship, 2004, pp. 100–6.

9   Cf. similar sentiments in Psalms 27:4–6; 36:7–9; 52:8–9; 61:4.

10  Notably John 10:11–12; 1 Peter 2:25 and 5:4.

11  Robert Davidson, *A Beginner's Guide to the Old Testament*, Edinburgh: St Andrew Press, 1995, pp. vi–vii. This is, in my view, one of the best beginner's introductions on the market.

12  www.sots.ac.uk.

13  Davidson, p. vii.

14  Davidson, p. 33f.

15  Of course these historical books are collectively known as the former prophets and so placed under the prophecy category on the Tanak scheme. Straight away we are being introduced to the problems of genre classification!

16  I use the term Protestant here to distinguish it from Catholic. The Protestant tradition has accepted as canonical the same books that are in the Jewish Hebrew Bible, but presented them in a different order. In Anglican circles, this is also true, except that the apocryphal books, that are canonical in Catholic circles but rejected in Protestant ones, are included in the lectionary (but not to be preached on for foundational Christian doctrine). This sounds like a typical Anglican *via media*!

17  Included as Writings (Ketubim) in the Tanak scheme.

18  The term Old Testament was not however coined until the late second/early third centuries CE by Tertullian and Origen. Some scholars therefore prefer to use other terminology, e.g. Jewish scriptures or Jewish Bible. However, in the interests of clarity and simplicity I use the familiar term, Old Testament.

19  In recent scholarship a particular interest has emerged in the period of canonization as a decisive time for not only the collecting together of certain canonical texts, but also as the time at which those texts were decisively finalized and no longer allowed the kind of fluidity that may well have characterized some of them earlier on. Brevard Childs pioneered the method of 'canonical criticism' which sees the period of canonization as decisive in historical, literary and theological terms and not simply in relation to the Old Testament alone but to the New Testament also. He argues that interpretations that are supported in many examples across the canon are more authoritative and decisive than lone ideas in isolated places. This is part of a wider interest in the shaping of texts during and after the biblical period. However, with the various different canons that we discuss in this chapter, one wonders whether one can be so decisive about the authority of this particular 'stage' in the evolution of both individual texts and their collection together.

20  With the exception of a section of Aramaic in Daniel 2:4 – 7:28 and in Ezra 7:12–26.

21  The order of the Pentateuch and former prophets has never changed. The Pentateuch was the first section to be made canonical (probably as early as the fifth century CE) and the prophets in the third century CE. It is the question of which books should make up the Writings that most exercised those responsible for the canonization of the whole, and indeed the 'Apocrypha' is mainly writings that were excluded for various reasons, largely because they were originally composed in Greek (with the exception of Ben Sira and 1 Maccabees). Interestingly, Ben Sira (from the second century CE) writes in his prologue, 'Many great teachings have been given to us through the Law, and the Prophets and the others that followed them', showing his awareness of groupings of authoritative books. And 2 Esdras 14:44–8 suggests that Ezra knew a canon of 24 books, other books being kept back from public reading. Even if this is an exaggeration, Ezra would certainly have known the Pentateuch. His successor, Nehemiah, is said to have 'founded a library and collected the books about the kings and prophets, and the writings of David, and letters of kings about votive offerings' (2 Maccabees 2:13).

22  The tradition of translating the Bible into the vernacular and hence into every single language in the world therefore has ancient roots.

23  The Septuagint took a long time to come together in a definitive form because there were two translation traditions that developed, one in Alexandria and one in Palestine. Palestinian Jews sought to correct and revise certain translations to bring them more into line with the Hebrew text – Aquila's second century CE version is the most famous of these. Others, such as Philo, thought the Alexandrian Septuagint inspired and of equal status with the Hebrew text. Early Christians seem to have adopted the latter position; however, Jewish Greek speakers preferred Aquila's version. These divergences inspired Origen to revise the Septuagint so as to come closer to Hebrew and Jewish versions. This became known as the Hexapla. Interestingly also, the earliest forms of the Septuagint date from a time prior to the finalization of the Hebrew text itself and so provide an important witness to early textual forms of the Hebrew Bible. Hence the Septuagint was and continues to be invaluable to translators attempting to uncover the original meaning of a text.

24  For a detailed discussion of the different texts and versions, see G. Khan, 'The Hebrew Bible', *The Oxford Illustrated History of the Bible*, Oxford: Oxford University Press, 2001, pp. 60–96.

25  Feminist scholarship has raised this in connection with the question of what are authoritative texts for women. See chapter 5.

26  Interestingly, the Samaritans have only ever accepted the Pentateuch as their 'canon' of scripture.

27  Decisions over the classification of the 'Writings' took the longest, with the Synod of Jamnia (or Jabneh) in 90 CE famously debating the canonicity of Ecclesiastes and the Song of Songs.

28  For the oldest manuscripts of the Septuagint, Vulgate and Peshitta, see the explanations related to those discussions, above.

29  John Barton has written many introductory books on the Bible as a whole and on the Old Testament in particular and is eminently readable. A particularly useful volume for the novice to the Old Testament is his *The Original Story: God, Israel and*

*the World* (written with Julia Bowden), London: DLT, 2004; Cambridge: Eerdmans, 2005.

30   John Barton, *What is the Bible?* London: SPCK, 1991, p. 21.

31   Barton, pp. 143–4.

32   This repetition is evidence of 'good yarns' being repeated of different characters. It is highly unlikely that Abraham tried to pull off this stunt more than once, especially the second time after Sarah had just conceived Isaac, and it is also highly unlikely that King Abimelech was tricked in the same way twice by father and son. It is much more likely that we have doublets in the tradition here that can be explained best on literary grounds.

33   Published by the Bible Reading Fellowship: www.brf.org.uk.

34   P. Jenson, 'Leviticus' in *Guidelines to the Bible*, Vol. 21, Part 2, Oxford: Bible Reading Fellowship, 2005. Quotation on p. 37.

35   Julius Wellhausen, *Prolegomena zur Geschichte Israels*, Berlin: W. de Gruyter, 1905 (English translation: *Prolegomena to the History of Ancient Israel*, New York: Harper Torchbooks, 1957). This is a foundational book in Old Testament studies. Wellhausen also stated in a more definitive way than his predecessors the four-source theory that came to dominate Pentateuchal study. See the discussion in chapter 2.

36   Although some categorization is useful: see Katharine Dell, *Get Wisdom, Get Insight: An Introduction to Israel's Wisdom Literature*, London: DLT, 2000.

37   The debate about finding a 'centre' has been overplayed in discussions of Old Testament theology, and indeed in discussions of biblical theology as a whole, and there probably is no need to prioritize one book or set of ideas over another.

38   The Psalter is another way of referring to the book of Psalms used particularly in Christian circles in a liturgical context.

39   The main American conference in biblical studies (www.sbl-site.org). The conference was SBL, Boston 1999, Book of Psalms section, and the paper was by Carol J. Dempsey, 'Psalm 23: A Literary, Social-Scientific and Creative Interpretation'.

40   Published as '"I will solve my riddle to the music of the lyre" (Psalm xlix:4 [5]): A Cultic Setting for Wisdom Psalms?', *Vetus Testamentum* 54/4 (2004), pp. 445–58.

41   Davidson, pp. 12–13.

42   The armour could be symbolic of handing over the kingship (ironic, at this point, as Saul does so unwittingly) and yet the rejection of it could symbolize the fact that David's type of kingship will be very different to that of Saul. There is a disjunction between 1 Samuel 16 and 1 Samuel 17: in 1 Samuel 16 Saul knows David and has made him armour-bearer, but in 1 Samuel 17 he does not appear to know who he is and offers him armour for the first time. This looks like a source-critical problem and it is clear that whoever stitched sources together did so rather clumsily here.

43   Interestingly, it is a women's song in which they chant 'Saul has killed his thousands, and David his ten thousands' that leads to Saul's anger and subsequent suspicion of David.

44   It has been suggested in the scholarship that this absolving of David for all responsibility for these deaths is a literary ploy (rather than a historical fact) in order to cast him in a better light than reality might suggest.

45  Notably in books 1 and 2 of the Psalter. See J. Day, *The Psalms* (OT Guides), Sheffield: JSOT Press, 1990, as an excellent introduction to scholarly work on the Psalms.

46  For example, a group of psalms (42–83) known as the Elohistic Psalter which feature Elohim much more frequently than Yahweh as the name for God; see Day, pp. 113–14.

47  H. Gunkel, *The Psalms: A Form-Critical Introduction*, Philadelphia: Fortress Press, 1967 (German 1926).

48  He also noted other smaller categories such as communal thanksgivings, wisdom psalms, pilgrimage psalms and entrance liturgies.

49  For example, Psalm 89 tells of the covenant with David as known from 2 Samuel 7, although the ending of the psalms shows that covenant to have been broken. We have a glimpse here into the period of the exile when Israel felt that the covenant had well and truly been broken. This psalm has clearly been updated historically as events unfurled.

50  Literary approaches to the Old Testament traditionally refer to the isolation of sources and interest in how the material came together historically, including the work of authors, editors, canonizers and so on. This includes an interest in different genres and their function. However, the term has broadened out to include any literary approach, whether it be looking at the function of narrative, or the style and language of an author, the structure of a text and so on. I take the sense in the broadest way, to include both types of category.

51  Historical approaches essentially seek to draw out the historical worth of a piece of material, but there is a broader sense of historical which includes sociological, cultural and socio-economic factors. While some would deny the strictly historical value of much in the Old Testament (in relation to its being provable, say, by archaeology), nevertheless many would argue for its historical 'ring' or even its historico-ideological nature in a possible back-projection of 'history' as perceived by a later generation.

52  Theological considerations link up with literary and historical categories and include anything in the area of theological ideas or concepts at any stage in the historical process or in the development of the texts.

53  For example, references to the temple, to cultic processions, sacrifices, dancing, singing and musical instruments.

54  Royal psalms include the king's coronation (Psalms 2, 110), marriage (Psalm 45) and battles (Psalms 18, 20, 144).

55  S. Mowinckel, *The Psalms in Israel's Worship*, Oxford: Blackwell, 1962; originally published in a six-volume study of the Psalms in 1921 and 1924.

56  To cross-refer to the cultures surrounding Israel and their practices is an important scholarly method. After all, no country exists in a cultural vacuum.

57  In the Deuteronomistic history, as mentioned above.

58  See W. W. Hallo and K. L. Younger (eds), *The Context of Scripture*, Leiden: Brill, 1997–2002, for a three-volume collection of texts from the surrounding cultures of the ancient world.

59  The Babylonian Akitu festival involved a recitation of the Babylonian creation epic, *Enuma elish*, which recounts the god Marduk's victory over Tiamat, the dragon of chaos, and the consequent creation of the world and enthronement of Marduk as king. Although hints of ancient mythology lurk in the Old Testament,

Genesis 1 as we have it contains no monsters of chaos that need to be overcome, just the watery depths of the firmament, and so one wonders how close the parallels really are here.

60   For example, A. Weiser, *The Psalms* (Old Testament Library), London: SCM Press, 1962, argued that many psalms had their context at a ceremony of covenant renewal held at the Autumn New Year festival. There is some evidence for covenant renewal being associated with the Feast of Tabernacles in Jewish tradition, notably Psalms 50 and 81 (cf. Deuteronomy 31:9ff.), but it is generally felt that Weiser overplayed this particular emphasis.

61   This message very much echoes that of the prophet Isaiah, a major part of whose message was the call to trust in God rather than play power-politics, e.g. Isaiah 30:15. The nations were a religious as well as a political threat.

62   God also dwelt on Mount Zion, which paralleled his heavenly throne (cf. Psalm 11:4; 103:19). Zion could refer to the whole city of David (e.g. 2 Samuel 5:7) or just to the temple hill (e.g. Psalms 65:1; 132:13; Micah 4:2) or to the whole city of Jerusalem (e.g. Isaiah 10:24; Jeremiah 3:14; Amos 6:1).

63   Cf. the anointing of the king in 1 Samuel 24:6; 10; 26:9, 11, 23.

64   Also at the transfiguration (Matthew 17:5) and resurrection (Acts 13:33).

65   Cf. Acts 4:24–8; 13:33; Hebrews 1:5; 5:5; Romans 1:4.

66   His genre of 'royal psalm' was criticized for being one of content rather than form, which contradicted his method of 'form' criticism.

67   Scholars have found pro- and anti-monarchic sources in the Deuteronomistic history.

68   C. S. Lewis, *Reflections on the Psalms*, London: Geoffrey Bles, 1958, p. 63.

69   The name for God used here in verse 1 is El, the generic name for God (usually found in the plural, Elohim) that precedes the revelation of the name Yahweh at the burning bush (Exodus 3). El is also used for the head of the Canaanite pantheon and so there is a suggestion of wider ancient Near Eastern origins and connections of the name. Otherwise 'the LORD' in our translations indicates the divine name, Yahweh.

70   Scholars are appreciating afresh the concept of nature's 'voice' in biblical texts, an area which has been hitherto under-appreciated but is speaking again to our more environmentally aware world. See especially the *Earth Bible* project, ed. N. Habel and S. Hurst, Sheffield: Sheffield Academic Press, 2000–2.

71   We might be reminded here of the story of the Tower of Babel in Genesis 11, which is an origin story about how different languages emerged.

72   'The heavens' could refer to the dwelling place of God or to the divine beings there as 'heaven' personified – either is possible.

73   The firmament was thought of as a metal plate or mirror. Cf. Job 37:18; Deuteronomy 28:23.

74   The sun was deified in ancient Mesopotamia, where Shamash, the sun god, was represented at times as bridegroom and as strong man. Thus the images here could have been influenced by such parallels. No aspect of nature is ever deified in the Old Testament and this is an important distinction between ancient Near Eastern religions and the religion of the Old Testament.

75   The law is not an absolute entity at this point, but a written expression of Yahweh's will and already of considerable importance.

76  Quite a feat if the Proverbs are to be believed! In Proverbs 1:32, for example, the simple are gullible and wayward.

77  God in this verse is Yahweh rather than El.

78  There are similarities between Psalm 19 and the longest psalm in the Psalter, Psalm 119.

79  The term 'redeemer' (Hebrew: go'el) is familiar to us from the book of Job (notably Job 19:25) and the book of Ruth, where Boaz is Ruth's redeemer. 'Rock' recalls the constancy of God as in Psalm 23.

80  This emphasis on reward is echoed in the New Testament, e.g. Mark 9:41; Luke 6:23, 33f.; Romans 7:5f.; 2 Corinthians 5:10.

81  The Sinai events are omitted and this has suggested to some older scholars (e.g. Wellhausen) an earlier stage in the formation of the tradition in which the Sinai traditions had not yet been incorporated into the story. If this is right it would be a fascinating insight into how traditions gradually develop, link up and become embellished.

82  This was one of Gunkel's dominant genre categories in the Psalter.

83  Along with Psalms 96 and 106:47.

84  M. Noth, *The Laws in the Pentateuch*, London: SCM Press, 1984 (German 1966) suggested a twelve-tribe 'amphictyony' at the point when the twelve tribes came together in early Israel, realized that they were worshipping the same God and combined their stories and experiences (see discussion in chapter 2). If this was the setting for this psalm it would place it very early in the pre-exilic period. Alternatively, some scholars have suggested a later, post-exilic date for the psalm, thus showing the uncertainties of psalm dating. See L. C. Allen, *Psalms 101–150*, Word Biblical Commentary, Waco, TX: Word Books, 1983.

85  Cf. Weiser's covenant festival theory mentioned above.

86  Interestingly, Abraham is rarely mentioned in the Psalter.

87  In verse 15 'anointed ones' probably refers to anyone called by God (although it later came to refer specifically to kings). 'Prophets' were not really around (not in any formal institutional sense, anyway) in patriarchal times, so prophets in a general sense are probably meant here. Of the patriarchs, only Abraham is ever called a prophet (Genesis 20:7).

88  The account of Joseph in this psalm is probably independent of the Genesis account and shows different traditions at work. I use the phrase 'technicolor dreamcoat' in reference to the Lloyd Webber/Rice musical *Joseph and His Amazing Technicolor Dreamcoat*, which has popularized this famous story for our time.

89  Joseph is the ideal 'wise man' who rises to power from lowly beginnings. He may have been an inspiration to more lowly administrators.

90  One thinks perhaps of Abraham as a parallel, whose faith was tested to the limit with the near-sacrifice of his son, Isaac (Genesis 22).

91  A possible indication of God's power over the sun god, for the benefit of worshippers of the sun-god in the wider ancient Near Eastern world.

92  Cf. the wisdom image of life as a path in Proverbs 1–9 (e.g. Proverbs 2:20).

93  There are possible connections with the cloud of theophany (i.e. of God's presence), as in Exodus 33:7–11 at the entrance to the Tent of Meeting.

94  Weiser suggested it was possible that there was a recital of the Decalogue (the Ten Commandments) in the liturgy of the festival cult.

95  This tradition is apparent in Isaiah 1–39 when there is a miraculous deliverance of Zion from the Assyrian army. See, for example, Isaiah 37:30–4 for a reflection of these ideas.

96  A solemn vow of commitment is found in Zion psalms (e.g. Psalms 84, 122) and this echoes that commitment.

97  See Obadiah 11–14; Ezekiel 25:12ff.; 35:5ff.; Lamentations 4:21.

98  Cf. 2 Kings 8:12; Isaiah 13:16; Hosea 10:14; 13:16; Nahum 3:10.

99  This is a Jewish month of the year. See the chart of the Jewish worship year (Figure 1.6).

## Chapter 2 | How to 'Open' the Old Testament

### The Bible in Order

In chapter 1 we dived into the Old Testament by looking at one of its important genres, a psalm. This was one way to open the Old Testament. We also got a sense of the different books and genres that make up the Old Testament by looking at the canon. When we moved on to other psalms, the sheer diversity of types of material and theological concerns contained in them became apparent. We also became aware of a history echoed in some psalms.

I put the point that reading through the Bible cover to cover was probably not the best way fully to appreciate its content. One problem is that events and material presented in the Old Testament are not in the historical order in which we believe they actually happened. Rather, clusters of material, say on the law, were attracted to the key law-giving event, which was to Moses on Mount Sinai. Hence we find Leviticus and Numbers and Deuteronomy adjoining that account which actually represent largely later material. It is as if certain key events were magnets attracting fuller and often later material to them.

A rather different version of the Jerusalem Bible[1] came out in the 1970s by Joseph Rhymer called *The Bible in Order*.[2] This was designed to reflect scholarly consensus about the historical order of events and the development of ideas in the Old Testament and hence to put material in its proper chronological place. Interestingly, it opens with the patriarchs, Abraham, Isaac and Jacob, then Joseph, and then moves on to the exodus and wilderness traditions, reflecting exactly the same order of events as we saw in Psalm 105. The notable difference with this Bible is that it does not begin with the creation stories. This is because scholarly consensus places the actual writing of those stories (even if they have older oral roots) in a slightly later period than this very early time.

| Early period | | |
|---|---|---|
| 2000 BCE | c. 1925 Abram leaves Ur | The Patriarchs |
| 1900 BCE | 1900–1720 Isaac | |
| 1800 BCE | 1800–1700 Jacob<br>1750–1640 Joseph | |
| 1700 BCE | | Israel in Egypt<br>c. 1700–1280 |
| 1400 BCE | c. 1350–1230 Moses | |
| 1300 BCE | 1300–1190 Joshua<br>c. 1280 Exodus from Egpyt<br>c. 1280–1240 The Ten Commandments<br>c. 1240 Conquest of Canaan<br>1224–1184 Deborah<br>1224–1137 Gideon | Judges 1220–1050 |
| 1200 BCE | 1115–1075 Eli | |
| 1100 BCE | 1075–1035 Samuel<br>1070 Samson<br>1070 Jephthah<br>1050 Philistines destroy Shiloh<br>1050–1011 King Saul<br>1011–970 King David | 1050–930 United Kingdom of Israel and Judah |
| 1000 BCE | 970–930 Solomon<br>966–959 Building of the temple of Jerusalem | 930 The kingdom divides |

The story of Israel probably began in the mists of time, in around 2000–1800 BCE when Egypt was the dominant power in the area. It is clear that the story of Joseph links up with Egyptian dominance. The exodus too happened during the time of Egyptian domination, but probably a bit later than the patriarchs, in around 1280 BCE.[3]

Once settled in the land, there began the period of the Judges from around 1300 BCE in which the main 'enemy' was the Philistines, sea peoples who lived in the coastal areas of present-day Israel (see map 2). It is not until around 1000 BCE that the kingship was properly founded under Saul and then definitively under David. This is thought to be a period when many

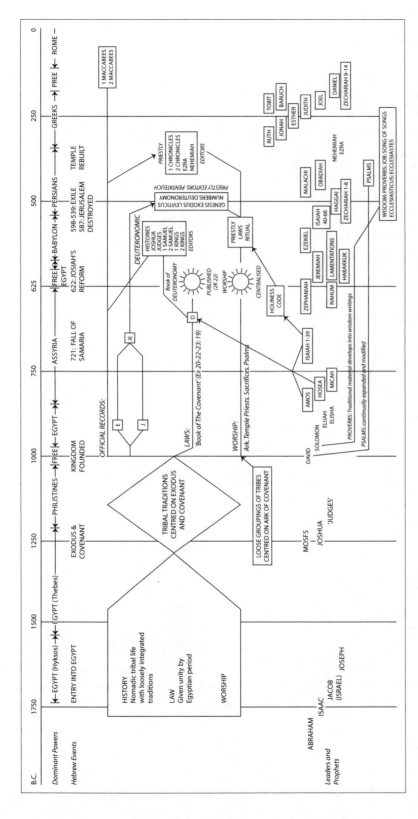

**Figure 2.1** A chronology of Old Testament events and literature. Redrawn from J. Rhymer, *The Bible in Order*, London, Darton, Longman and Todd, 1975.

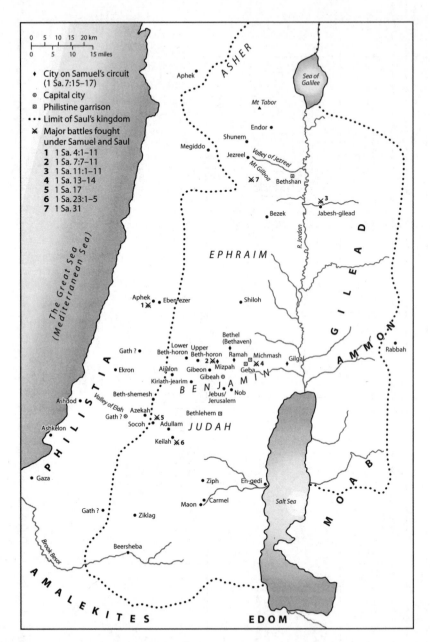

**Map 2** Philistine regions and northern shrines.

oral traditions took written form in a settled city and court environment. This process probably continued and was extended in the reign of Solomon, who was renowned for his wisdom and had international contacts that no doubt enabled the wider dis-
semination of material. It is to this period that Rhymer attributes the earliest stories of Genesis (known as J), the earliest proverbial collections (Proverbs 10–31), early laws in the Book of the Covenant (Exodus 20:22–23:19) and psalms from the early monarchic period, including Psalm 2, which we looked at in chapter 1.

> J is the common designation of the Yahwistic source, thought by scholarship to be the earliest literary source that features in the Pentateuch. German scholarship first posited this source and labelled it the work of the 'Jehovist', hence the initial letter 'J'.

This kind of presentation gives us perhaps a better picture of the historical order of events and might suggest to us that we should read Genesis 12 to the end of Exodus, followed by Joshua, Judges and 1 and 2 Samuel, finish-
ing off in 1 and 2 Kings, Genesis 1–11, Proverbs 10–31 and a selection of psalms. That sounds a rather daunting reading list in itself! I suggest that a mere listing of the books we might read still doesn't really 'open' the Old Testament for us. We need to look beneath the surface at the stories themselves and get a sense of the power of Hebrew narrative. The Israelites from earliest times told stories – probably initially around the campfires of their nomadic existence and then, as they gradually became a more settled people in towns and cities, about their heroes and leaders. These stories were lively and entertaining and were designed to be remembered orally. We need to look at the stories themselves in order to re-enter their world. Until the partially settled, but not centralized, period of the Judges there would have been little written material and the material from that period has the character of tribal cycles of stories.[4] It is not until the time of the monarchy that writing down stories, proverbs, lawcodes and psalms really got under way – hence Rhymer's reluctance to place them earlier in his Bible.

Scholarship today would probably write a rather different 'Bible in order' because some of the conclusions on which Rhymer based his book have been challenged in recent times. One particular area of debate is how late the actual writing process was. Perhaps Rhymer attributes too much material to the early monarchy. Since the final form of many of the books of the Old Testament was not reached until towards the Exile or even after, perhaps it is safer to focus on that final writing-down period. W. Brueggemann argues in his *Theology of the Old Testament*[5] that every text has to be considered in relation to its exilic interpretation, whether that be reflected in the text itself or simply the way the exilic community might have interpreted earlier texts. He argues this because he sees the Exile as such a formative period in Israelite thought, especially in the development of theological ideas. More radically, could there even have been a deliberate ideological 'back projection' of events and ideas from a later age?[6] Are these texts so much the production of a later age that they are more adequately to be described as the 'creation' of such an age? This is to adopt a position highly sceptical of being able to say anything about Israelite 'history' in strictly historical terms, preferring to regard the literary texts as a 'late' attempt to create a past that did not really exist. I would argue that seeing all the material as a late presentation, whether simply on a literary level or in historical terms also, can distort as much as seeing it all as early.

One crucial aspect of opening the Old Testament is to look at the development of ideas which accompanied 'historical' events.[7] For example, how did the Israelites' understanding of God develop? Early encounters with God by the patriarchs and **matriarchs** of Israel were largely localized and family affairs. By the time of the exodus, the Israelites were a beleaguered group saved by **Yahweh** – the new name for their God, revealed to Moses (in Exodus 3). By the time of the settlement and monarchy Yahweh was a national God, supporting kings, prophets, wise men and priests (i.e. a nation and a land). The Psalms give us an insight into the nature of the relationship between Israel and her God – the moments of thanksgiving and the moments of lament. Understandings of God and of God's purposes for Israel clearly developed over time.

---

**Matriarchs** is a collective term for the wives of the patriarchs, their most famous representative being Sarah, wife of Abraham.

---

**Yahweh** is the divine name revealed to Moses at the burning bush in Exodus 3. It is thought to be derived from the verb 'to be', with the probable meaning 'I am who I am'. In some Jewish circles uttering this name is avoided for reverential reasons.

---

## Abraham and Sarah

So it looks from this discussion that if we are to open the Old Testament at the right place (if indeed there is ever a right place), we need to begin where it all started, with Abraham. He is going to be our 'famous figure' in this chapter, along with his wife Sarah. Abraham is perhaps best known as the 'father' of three major world faiths today (Judaism, Christianity and Islam) and hence as ancestor of many nations. God promised him both land and progeny. His and Sarah's story is contained in Genesis 12–25. Their 'history' is potted into a few short incidents – life-changing moments perhaps – which have key significance and which are unpacked theologically for us by the writers of the stories. We might just draw out a few of the key points and first and foremost enter into the world of the story.

At the end of Genesis 11 a genealogy links the family of Abraham with the descendants of Shem after the flood. Abraham is at this point called

Abram and his wife is called Sarai, of whose barrenness we are immediately told (Genesis 11:30). His father is Terah, who takes Abram, Sarai and his fatherless grandson Lot away from Ur of the Chaldeans to go to the land of **Canaan**. Ur of the Chaldeans is actually ancient Sumer, the **Sumerian culture**, which was eventually incorporated as part of Babylonia (also known as Chaldea), so it may well be that this culture provides the family's background.[8] We are not told why they left, nor why they didn't in fact make it all the way to Canaan at this point, but ended up in Haran, where Terah died. It is in this context that God calls Abraham at the beginning of Genesis 12:

> **Canaan** is the 'promised land', already inhabited by Canaanites with their own gods, culture and city-states, later to become the land of Israel.

> The **Sumerian culture** is the oldest in the world, pre-dating even the Egyptians. The Sumerians inhabited southern Mesopotamia in the fourth millennium BCE. Their culture was taken over by the Babylonians. They were the first to invent the alphabetic system of writing, among other inventions.

Now the Lord said to Abram, 'Go from your country and your kindred and your father's house to the land that I will show you. I will make of you a great nation, and I will bless you, and make your name great, so that you will be a blessing. I will bless those who bless you, and the one who curses you I will curse; and in you all the families of the earth shall be blessed. (Genesis 12:1–3)

Here we have the promise that God will make a great nation of Abraham's descendants and that God will bless him. We are not told why God chooses Abraham in this way – but it is the first covenant with a specific person and ultimately with a specific nation. Abraham then completes the journey to Canaan and arrives in **Shechem**, where he builds an altar to God, and then in **Bethel**, where he does the same. Although this is someone else's country, Abraham is promised the land by God and so he feels able to pitch his tent there. Abraham and his family are essentially nomadic tribesmen at this point.

> **Shechem** is an early northern city and shrine. This moment of Abraham's arrival marks the beginning of the altar there in the Ephraimite hill country in the region of Samaria at a strategic junction between north and south.

> **Bethel** is another early northern city and shrine established by Abraham on the border of the tribal areas of Ephraim and Benjamin.

The first real 'story' about Abraham and Sarah is a rather strange one. They go down to Egypt because of a famine and Abraham tries to pass off his wife Sarah as his sister so that she might be taken into Pharaoh's harem. This leads to Abraham being given plentiful gifts by Pharaoh, of animals and slaves (in which wealth was measured in nomadic circles; cf. Job 1), a kind of dowry. We are not told how Sarah feels about this and whether she is 'in' on the plot. God seems to be, since plagues are inflicted upon Pharaoh because of his housing of Abraham's wife. Pharaoh finds out and packs them off. This is a kind of mini-exodus – plagues

**Figure 2.2** 'Ram in a Thicket.' Symbolic figure of a goat about to nibble at a tree, made of lapis lazuli and gold. Sumerian, from Ur, Babylonia, c. 2500 BCE. One of an almost identical pair found in a grave at Ur. It was named the 'Ram in a thicket' by the excavator Leonard Woolley, alluding to Genesis 22:13 where a ram is sacrificed by Abraham in place of his son, Isaac. The ram is more accurately described as a goat, since goats often adopt this kind of pose in a tree when looking for food. © The British Museum, London UK/Bridgeman Art Library.

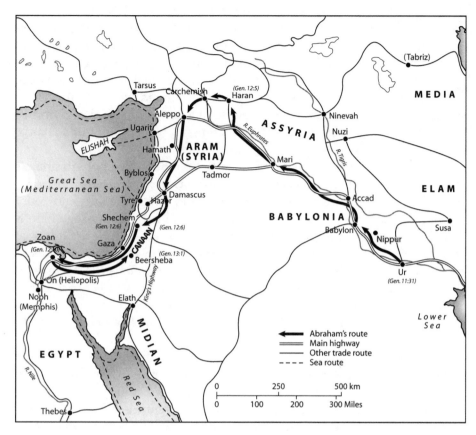

**Map 3**  Abraham's journey from Ur to the Promised Land.

in Egypt and Abraham escaping. Could it be that the writer of this story (possibly a later writer) was deliberately modelling it on its more famous counterpart? At any rate, the story gives us the explanation of how Abraham became wealthy and it also demonstrates that God is on his side.

In Genesis 13 we move on to a conflict between Abraham and his nephew Lot. It seems that the land around Bethel is not big enough for them and so they quarrel. Abraham suggests that they take different parts of the land rather than quarrelling and he magnanimously gives Lot the choice of 'right or left'. Lot decides that the plain of Jordan looks plentiful and so journeys east, little knowing that this is where the **Sodomites** live, who will not prove easy neighbours (Genesis 14 tells the story of Lot's capture, which stirs Abraham into fighting to save him). We then have a

> The **Sodomites** are an infamous group associated with sexual perversity and outrageous inhospitality. Sodom is often paired with Gomorrah and they are jointly representative of evil.

**Hebron** is another city and shrine established by Abraham. It is on the Judean mountain ridge south of Jerusalem.

reiteration at the end of Genesis 13 of the promise to Abraham of the whole land and of offspring, prompting Abraham to pitch his tent in another area, at **Hebron**, where he builds another altar. We have thus had listed three of the main shrines in Israel: Shechem, Bethel and Hebron,[9] all reputedly founded by Abraham. These stories, as well as telling us about the famous ancestor, are also giving us 'origin stories' for the various shrines, telling us where their authoritative status comes from.

So far we have heard God's promise to Abraham, but not Abraham's response. However, in Genesis 15 he questions the promise of offspring, since he has no child. God takes him outside to look at heaven and count the stars – that's how many his descendants will be! The message here is that God can do anything and Abraham has to trust God. We are told that he believed the Lord, despite the odds, and that he was thus considered righteous by God (Genesis 15:6). Abraham then questions the promise of land and is asked to sacrifice to God. He is warned that it is not going to be easy in the land for his offspring – there will be 400 years of oppression, but a final reward. Through the sacrifice, God makes a covenant with Abraham: the promise of land.

We then enter a round of stories essentially about offspring. Sarah employs the first 'surrogate mother' in Hagar her slave, whom she encourages to sleep with Abraham and bear a child for him. Of course, she conceives straight away, underlining Sarah's barrenness. We are told that, having conceived, Hagar started to look down on Sarah – fertility was power in such circles of women! Sarah is upset, but Abraham reminds her that she is the one with real power. So Hagar runs away into the desert. Interestingly, God is with her in the wilderness and promises that her son Ishmael will also be 'father' of many.[10] He will also be a 'wild ass of a man' who will invite enmity.

The first half of Genesis 17 provides an interlude from the offspring theme in which the covenant is reiterated (possibly a later source), this time accompanied with directives about **circumcision**. Genesis 17 also describes how Abraham and Sarah are given their new names. In the second half of the chapter we are back with the offspring theme and the promise is made that Sarah, despite her old age (and they are all very old at this time),[11] will conceive and bear Abraham a son. Although Ishmael will found a great nation, he will not be the recipient of the covenant. That will be reserved for Sarah's son, Isaac.

At this point in the cycle of stories Abraham receives a visitation from God, although he doesn't

**Circumcision** is the outward sign of God's covenant with Israel. It is the rite of removal of a boy's foreskin from his penis, performed in early infancy.

know it at first. Three men appear requesting hospitality. Abraham obliges, rushing into the tent to instruct Sarah in her wifely role to make cakes to accompany the calf that he has killed along with curds and milk. The men have come, it seems, to tell Abraham that he will have a son.[12] Sarah overhears and laughs to herself – she is beyond childbearing age.[13] It is then revealed that this is a divine visitation. God questions why Sarah laughed – surely nothing is too wonderful for God? Sarah out of fear of God denies that she laughed. But God puts her straight! Here Abraham and Sarah seem to be able to converse with God openly and in the second half of the chapter Abraham actually argues with God as to whether Sodom should be punished. If righteous people are in the city, is God right to destroy it?[14]

After an interlude on Sodom and Gomorrah and stories chiefly about Lot, Genesis 20 returns us to Abraham and Sarah, who move to Gerar and Abraham tries his 'passing off his wife as his sister' stunt again.[15] This is somewhat incredible in the light of the promise just received from God that Sarah is going to conceive – why would Abraham want to risk that? Luckily, King Abimelech of Gerar, who is about to bed Sarah, receives a dream from God threatening death. Abimelech pleads innocence with God and then turns on Abraham, who pleads some truth in the sister relationship in claiming that Sarah is his half-sister. Abimelech is generous towards Abraham in the end, giving him animals and slaves and money as well as restoring his wife to him and inviting him to stay in his land (where they make a covenant together at Beersheba at the end of chapter 21). For Abimelech and his family, there is the reward of renewed fertility – it is interesting that this theme continues in relation to a foreigner's family also.

Finally, in Genesis 21, we have the climax – the birth of Isaac, named 'laughter'. There is still jealousy between Sarah and Hagar and Sarah asks that Hagar be sent away with her son. In the wilderness Hagar again calls upon God as she has run out of water and God provides for her and her son and again renews his promise and protection to Ishmael.

Perhaps the most distressing story of the Abraham cycle is the last, in Genesis 22, the command from God to sacrifice Isaac. Perhaps we can get a better sense of the nature of that demand having read through the whole cycle and having seen how much of it has been about the promise of offspring and the difficulties faced by Abraham and Sarah in producing a son and heir. One wonders what Sarah would have thought of this command from God! We don't hear her opinion on the matter.[16] That Abraham is prepared to go to the brink of killing his son as a sacrifice to God is a demonstration of his fidelity to God, first and foremost. And, of course, a ram caught in a thicket provides the perfect alternative for the sacrifice and so Isaac is saved. This is seen as a test of faith – and yet we might ask how reasonable

The **Hittites** were a nearby nation to Israel, dating from the second millennium BCE and comprising much of what is now modern Turkey.

that request really was.[17] When Sarah dies in Hebron (Genesis 23) Abraham seeks a burial place among the **Hittites** who own the land and he pays for a suitable field with a cave in it. Abraham lives on a little longer to marry his son Isaac to Rebekah (a native of his own land, who, we are told in Genesis 24:67, was a comfort after Isaac's mother's death) and indeed to marry again with considerable progeny as the result. It is also revealed that Abraham had a few concubines who also had children (Genesis 25:6). In Genesis 25:7 we are told of his death and burial alongside his wife Sarah in the field purchased from the Hittites.

## History and Story

We are reading here a connected account made up of a series of stories. Some are self-contained stories, fairly domestic at times; others have the character of more theological pronouncements.[18] Many of the stories are intended to teach us a lesson or a truth rather than being strictly historical. Some tell us of the origin of a shrine in a particular place. Some of these stories may well have originated as oral tradition among the tribes, told around the campfire in nomadic circles. They may well have been embellished and grown in the telling. Sometimes they may have been told simply because they were a ripping good yarn! This was ancient entertainment as well as an important reminder of significant events in the story of one's origins.

However, we need to make an important distinction between history and story. We are looking here ostensibly at the beginning of a history, but told through the medium of story. It is the only source of information we have about Abraham as far as the literature goes. One might point out that it is amazing that we have any information at all, given how long ago he may have lived! This storytelling is typical of much of the Old Testament. Rather than write these stories off as 'unhistorical', we might pause to remember that we all tell stories about our past. In fact our accounts of our own pasts are largely a series of narratives that were sufficiently significant to have become part of our 'life story'. We may well shape and alter the stories over time, or even forget some of the detail, but they are essentially our guides to our own historical existence and our witness to others of our developed identity over time. We should not be too quick then to renounce narrative as a historical medium.

Provan, Long and Longman, in their attempt to counter the minimalist position and reaffirm the 'historicity' of much of the Old Testament (but not simply by trying to prove history through archaeology), make this point well when they liken narrative art to portraiture. They write,

> Our argument is that a biblical narrative, as verbal presentation, . . . does not duplicate but, rather, depicts the past. Like a portrait, a biblical narrative is in one sense a fabrication, because it consists of words on paper and not the actual past. Nevertheless, these words on paper, like paint on canvas, can accurately represent the historical past.[19]

We might be able to back up the account in a more strictly historical way through archaeology, but Provan, Long and Longman argue that the uncertainty regarding that method has led to the kind of minimalist position that postmodern scepticism has spawned (it is unlikely anyway that archaeology could prove Abraham's actual existence).[20] We may decide that the question of historicity is secondary to the account's nature as theologically significant story. At the end of the day, what we have in the Old Testament is what the tradition has passed down and perhaps the key is that these stories were seen as theologically important as they revealed God's action on behalf of God's people. It is the testimony of this people that has been passed down to us, and to a certain extent we need to trust it. As Provan, Long and Longman put it, 'history *is* the telling and retelling of unverifiable stories. Knowing any history aside from the story in which we are personally involved requires trust in an unverified and unverifiable testimony.'[21]

Scholars have devised different approaches to try to penetrate beyond the surface of this material which we will briefly explore. One approach is to look beyond the question 'How historical is this account?' to try to reconstruct the world of the text, looking at not only archaeological findings but also at the wider cultural context of the ancient Near Eastern world. The focus in this case is on social history rather than strict history. Let us look at these arguments step by step.

## Archaeology and Social History

Perhaps we should first ask the traditional question, 'Does archaeology shed any light on the existence of the patriarchs – Abraham, Isaac and Jacob?' No records from other countries near Israel mention Abraham – later on in the history, such records become a useful point of comparison, but not this far back. Archaeological evidence has been sought for an invasion of

**Semites** refers to Semitic peoples, of which the Jews are one. It describes groups of ancient Near Eastern people whose cultures and languages were closely related.

**Nuzi** is the name of the ancient city where texts were discovered by archaeologists that gave a fascinating insight into the customs of the people who lived there circa 1450 BCE.

The **Hurrians** were a small nation in northern Syria, third to second millennium BCE, who produced the Nuzi texts.

nomadic **Semites** into Palestine between 2100 and 1550 BCE which might be correlated with the movement of the Hebrew patriarchs into the area. This quest has had limited success since the period is so early, but would place the patriarchs in the middle Bronze Age.[22] Other scholars have placed the patriarchs in the late Bronze Age on the basis of alleged comparable social customs in the **Nuzi** texts of the **Hurrians** from the 1400s BCE. For example, it was claimed that the occasions on which the patriarchs pass off their wives as their sisters (in Genesis 12, 20 and 26)[23] are to be interpreted in the light of a Nuzi custom of adopting a woman as one's sister and that the childless Abraham's adoption of a slave, Eliezer, as his heir in Genesis 15 makes sense in the light of the Nuzi practice of childless couples adopting slaves. However, in each case, either the Nuzi or the biblical evidence has to be forced in order to make the equations fit properly and so such parallels are generally not felt to be completely convincing. Kitchen lays out the evidence for these various possibilities, noting that the patriarchs at least have to be prior to the exodus and so earlier than the thirteenth century BCE at the latest.[24] Other scholars, such as J. van Seters,[25] have dated the patriarchal narratives to the first millennium BCE and argued that the stories reflect the conditions of this later age. Such a range of views about dating, and from scholars who are by no means radical in their views, shows how fluid the archaeological evidence is. Perhaps we need to ask whether trying to 'prove' the Bible from archaeology is really possible. Perhaps all it can offer is a 'balance of probabilities', as Bright puts it.[26]

There has been some questioning in recent times of the assumption of older scholars (based on the biblical story) that there was an invasion of Semites into the land of Canaan. The text presents Abraham as coming from Ur via Haran and gradually making settlements in different parts of the land of Canaan. On this supposed pattern it is essentially a nomadic people who gradually become settled and bring with them their distinctive faith. What if this is just a 'story' and in fact the Israelites (as they came to be known) were in fact indigenous pastoralists in the highlands in the late Bronze Age (i.e. enclosed nomads, living in proximity to Canaanite cities so that some of the Canaanite culture rubbed off on them, but they had their own stories and traditions)? What if 'Israel' was not just a 'separate group' of (originally) nomads, but rather a mixture of Israelites and dis-affected Canaanites? One idea is that some Canaanites might have rejected city life and made their homes with the pastoralists who gradually became more and more sedentary. The highland group might have developed agriculturally and socially to such an extent that the centre of power started to shift.

These are all theories based mainly on social factors about the movements of peoples and on economic factors. Like the archaeological evidence, these theories are largely speculative. One recurring point is how distinctive and separate the Israelite group were, or how far they represent a mixed community with Canaanites and possibly others. It is clear that a number of tribes came together to form 'Israel' and one question is whether this process happened at this early stage. Was an indigenous, earlier settled group joined by others – for example, outsiders from Egypt with the memory of the exodus experience, who received a sympathetic hearing from the people who had experienced Egyptian rule in Canaan? Did other groups join them from **Syria**, such as dispossessed farmers, bringing with them customs such as circumcision and the rejection of pork?[27] On this model, by 1050–1000 BCE they would have existed in a tribal confederacy united by economic

> **Syria** is a neighbouring nation of Canaan/Israel, in ancient times the region bordering the eastern Mediterranean from Palestine and Phoenicia up to the Euphrates in the northeast and the Taurus mountains in the northwest. It incorporated ancient Ugarit.

concerns and gradually taken control of the lowlands and established a monarchy. The diversity of the different groups led to the emergence of different 'camps' as reflected in the stories of Judges. Thus some would perhaps have been Canaanites who became Israelites and some would have come from outside.

The question whether this was a separate group or a mixed nomadic/indigenous one is of considerable significance when considering how distinctive the religion of the earliest Israelites was. Halpern, for example, argues that there was no pure Yahwistic past – other gods were recognized in conjunction with the elevation of the High God or national Deity, Yahweh, such as **Asherah**, his possible consort, and other subsidiary members of Yahweh's assembly. They were worshipped as a normal part of Yahweh worship until the time of kings Hezekiah and Josiah in the seventh century BCE. However, the memory of a pure Yahwistic past was

> **Asherah** is the Queen of Heaven, one of the chief goddesses of the Canaanite pantheon and mother of many minor gods. She is chiefly known to us through Ugaritic literature. Some have associated her with the Israelite god Yahweh, as the missing female consort of the god. She was widely worshipped in ancient Israel, although worship of her was loudly condemned by the prophets. The word asherah is used in another sense in the Old Testament to denote a pagan cultic object in the temple.

created by the prophets and reformers of a later time who brought the past into a neat synthesis.

## Scholarly Views on Early Israelite History and Religion

This takes us into the broader area of the nature of early Israelite religion. We noticed in the Abraham cycle that a number of different names for God occur: Yahweh ('the LORD' in English translations, a name that hasn't actually been revealed yet); El Elyon ('God most High') (used by Melchizedek, priest of Salem in Genesis 14:18–20);[28] El Roi (a name given to God by Hagar in Genesis 16:13, meaning 'God of seeing' or 'God who sees'); Elohim ('God' in English translations, the more usual generic name for God).[29] Does this show that the patriarchs worshipped different gods? Or did the group come to recognize that in fact they were worshipping one and the same God? And how do we handle this idea of 'back projection' of later theological ideas onto the earlier material? It can't have been that systematic, otherwise we wouldn't find the evidence of other names for God or other discrepancies that suggest the welding together of earlier traditions.[30] This brings us around in a circle, as many scholarly discussions tend to do!

A more traditional 'historical' approach to these questions is perhaps represented by the work of Martin Noth in his *History of Israel* (1958).[31] Noth does not begin his history of the Israelite nation where the Old Testament begins it – with Abraham in Genesis 12. Rather, he begins with the period sometime after 1200 BCE when, he believes, the settlement of the Israelites in Canaan started and when the name 'Israel' was first used by a confederation of tribes in Canaan. To this confederation of tribes were brought the stories of individual tribes, stories which were very old, such as those about Abraham. These stories from individual tribes were then woven together into a history of the Israelites, thus giving them a corporate identity. They do not represent chronological history. Thus Noth questions the basic framework of the biblical story of Israel before the settlement period. More radically, he even questions the historical existence of the patriarchs, in that 'story' doesn't necessarily equate with 'actual historical existence'.

We saw when we looked at Psalm 105 how the story of early Israel seemed to be neatly catalogued in a historical order, almost like a recitation. We find such summaries elsewhere in the Old Testament, for example in Deuteronomy 26:5–9:

A wandering Aramean was my ancestor; he went down into Egypt and lived there as an alien, few in number, and there he became a great nation, mighty, and populous. When the Egyptians treated us harshly, and afflicted us, by imposing hard labour on us, we cried to the LORD, the God of our ancestors; the LORD heard our voice and saw our affliction, our toil, and our oppression. The LORD brought us out of Egypt with a mighty hand and an outstretched arm, with a terrifying display of power, and with signs and wonders; and he brought us into this place and gave us this land, a land flowing with milk and honey.

This is how the Old Testament remembers and presents its own history. We need to decide how much authority to give this presentation over the reconstructions that scholars would have us believe. Noth questions this biblical framework, i.e. that the patriarchs Abraham, Isaac and Jacob lived in Canaan, that their descendants went down to Egypt and that, having escaped at the exodus, they wandered in the wilderness and occupied the land of Canaan. He believes this framework to be essentially unhistorical. He does not deny that some Hebrews escaped from Egypt, or that some other Hebrews spent time in the wilderness south of Judah. But he believes that this is an artificial framework which crystallized in the process of the formation of the tribal confederation in Canaan. Thus it was when the twelve tribes of Israel came together that stories drawn from separate traditions became normative for all. History – and much of it was reliable historical information – was reshaped in a meaningful way for them in a clearly ordered series of events in which the hand of God was seen to be at work. From earliest times, interest was not focused upon the patriarchs as personalities but in the divine promises made to them – the theological element was stressed. Thus what we have in the patriarchal narratives is cultic history rather than history in the modern sense.

Whether or not we accept Noth's reconstruction of Israel's history – and it has been very influential in scholarly circles – it does try to penetrate beyond the surface meaning of the biblical account and recognize a process of the collecting of stories and traditions which had early origins but have been reshaped by the literary or theological concerns of later generations. Some more conservative scholars see this kind of reconstruction as a threat to the authority of the Bible.[32] However, in the view of many (including myself), realization of the kind of process at work in the collecting and shaping of material serves ultimately to enhance the Bible's authority as a testimony to history as well as to faith. One needs to remember that the tribes would have come together for a whole host of reasons – political, cultural, military and religious – and these texts reflect all those concerns, whether they be the primary concerns of the actual historical period in which they are set or those of a later age. The Bible is a sociological document, reflecting faith and other factors, interpreting historical events in many different ways and at different stages in Israelite life. It is important not to be doctrinaire about our reconstructions, which may well change in the light of new evidence – either internal or external. This is important in developing an understanding of how the ancient Hebrews conceived of history. They did not have any sense of critical evaluation of evidence. It is not plausible that the Bible was written at one sitting – its authors used older sources and oral traditions when writing their history, but their primary motivation for recording such events was surely religious. They wished to explain events for faith.

This emphasis was famously formulated by another German scholar working at the same time as Noth. Gerhard von Rad[33] regarded Deuteronomy 26:5ff. as a statement of Israel's faith – as a theological interpretation of the historical events – and argued that such a summary may well have been recited in a cultic situation, such as we might recite the creed in church today. He argues that Israel's faith is grounded in a 'theology of history'. It is important to recognize, he argues, that there was a historical basis for that history on which the theology was built and yet he maintains that the older stories contained in the patriarchal narratives are not strictly historical in the sense that we would use the term. What was important for Israel's faith is that Israel regarded the events in which it saw the hand of Yahweh at work as based on historical fact and reshaped by God's continuing action in the world (e.g. the **Red Sea**).[34] I think this is a good way of understanding how the stories of the ancient Israelites have come down to us. Stories may contain nuggets of historical fact, they may contain information about the origins of peoples and places, but fundamentally they are told because they demonstrate the action of God in the lives of individuals, they demonstrate the nature of God's great promises and they show human beings and God in a relationship of trust that will have immense consequences for the future of not just one people, but ultimately the rest of the human race and for the whole of the created world.

The **Red Sea** refers to the great event of the parting and crossing of the Red Sea at the time of the exodus. The term is sometimes used synonymously with the exodus to denote the miraculous events of that time.

Although I am citing here the scholarship of an earlier age than our own, it seems to me that there were lasting insights in this period, much of which has been lost today. With the pronouncement of the 'death of biblical history' by K. Whitelam,[35] an agenda-driven negativity seems to have entered the debate that runs counter to the positive claims of a previous age. While older certainties may need to be questioned, there is a sense in which to deny not simply the validity of external 'evidence' from archaeology or the surrounding cultures but also the entirety of the 'historical' testimony of the literary texts is to reduce to nothing what actually is an amazing *something*. That *something* is that we have so much information about a small, arguably insignificant (on the wider international scale) and beleaguered people who were the inheritors of the promise of God. That promise of God went on to apply not simply to one people but to whole nations and to the world. Surely such a testimony, while not necessarily seen as strictly historical in every sense of that word, should be taken seriously in an evolving theological context.

## Complementary Approaches

As we delve deeper into the Old Testament we start to learn something of the complexity of the questions that scholars ask and the number of theories can seem overpowering. Perhaps we will never really know how these stories have come down to us and how they were shaped. Perhaps we will never be able to reconstruct exact history. But that won't stop scholars trying to uncover these conundrums! I have tried to show that a historical approach, including archaeological and sociological factors, needs to be complemented by a literary approach that takes account of the texts that we have in front of us and their character and by a recognition of the importance of theology in the shaping of both the history itself and the writing process. This triumvirate of historical, literary and theological is a crucial one in our opening of this ancient document.

The story of Abraham is essential for an understanding of the roots of a people and the promise of land, but it is also the first stage in a complex and deepening relationship with God that applies to the whole world and not just to a tribe or even a nation. It is through the stories that have come down to us and through the development over time of ideas about relationship with God, the world and of human beings with each other that, I would argue, the keys to opening the Old Testament really lie.

## A Continuing History

After Abraham, the Old Testament relates that the relationship between God and the people developed under Isaac, Jacob and Joseph, the other main patriarchs of Israel (Genesis 25–36). Narrative highlights are Jacob's trickery in robbing Esau of first his birthright and then of his father's blessing (Genesis 25, 27); Jacob's dream of a ladder ascending to heaven in which he is promised land and progeny just as Abraham was (Genesis 28); Jacob's courtship of Rachel and eventual marriage to both her and her sister Leah (Genesis 29); offspring difficulties culminating in the birth of Joseph by Rachel (Genesis 30); Jacob's wrestling with a man at Peniel who turns out to be God, with the resultant founding of the nation Israel with the changing of Jacob's 'name' (Genesis 32:22–32); reconciliation with Esau (Genesis 33); Joseph's dreams and betrayal by his brothers (including his special robe) (Genesis 37); and Joseph's time in Egypt in which he interprets dreams and becomes a powerful administrator, later tricking his brothers and ultimately reconciling with them (Genesis 38–46).

The defining tribal story for the whole group was probably the exodus from Egypt as related in Exodus 4–14.[36] It may only have happened to one or two tribes, as Noth argued, but the story of liberation from slavery became a theological example of what God was prepared to do for his chosen people. The wilderness wanderings (Exodus 15–18) were a time of testing – with highlights such as the foundation of the law in the giving of the Ten Commandments (Exodus 19–20), but also with times of strife and questioning (such as the golden calf in Exodus 32). We will go on to consider the exodus and law-giving in chapter 3.

The history of the birth of the Israelite nation as I have presented it so far is contained in the Pentateuch – the first five books of the Old Testament – notably in Genesis and Exodus. In some ways these are the most famous parts of the history because they are the defining moments

| Monarchic period | Kingdom of Israel (930–722) | Kingdom of Judah (930–587) |
|---|---|---|
| 1000 BCE | 930–910 King Jeroboam<br>910 King Nadab<br>908 King Baasha | 931–913 King Rehoboam<br>925 Pharoah Shishak (Sehshonq) invades Palestine<br>913–911 King Abijah<br>911–870 King Asa |
| 900 BCE | c. 879 Samaria, capital of Israel | |
| | 886 King Elah<br>885 King Zimri<br>885–880 King Tibri<br>880–874 King Omri<br>874–853 King Ahab<br>c. 870–850 Elijah | 870–848 King Jehoshaphat<br>848–841 King Jehoram<br>841 King Ahaziah<br>841–835 King Athaliah<br>835–796 Joash<br>c. 810–750 Joel |
| | 853–852 King Ahaziah<br>852–841 King Joram<br>c. 850–790 Elisha<br>841–813 King Jehu | |

| | | |
|---|---|---|
| 800 BCE | 798–781 King Jehoash<br>781–753 King Jeroboam II<br>760 Amos<br>760 Jonah<br>755–732 Hosea<br>753–752 King Zechariah<br>752 King Shallum<br>752–742 King Menahem<br>742–740 King Pekahiah<br>740–722 King Pekah<br>731–722 King Hoshea<br>722 Fall of Samaria<br>722–705 King Sargon II | 796–767 King Amaziah<br>767–740 King Uzziah (Azariah)<br>742–687 Micah<br>742–700 Isaiah<br>740–732 King Jotham<br>732–716 King Ahaz<br>716–687 King Hezekiah<br>c. 704 Assyria besieges<br>Jerusalem |
| 700 BCE | 705–681 King Sennacherib<br>681–669 King Esarhaddo<br>669–627 King<br>Assurbanipal<br>612 Fall of Nineveh<br>609 End of Assyria<br>605–562 King<br>Nebuchadnezzar II<br>605 Battle of Carchemish | 640 Zephaniah<br>640–609 King Josiah<br>621–580 King Jeremiah<br>609–597 King Jehoiakim<br>609 King Jehoahaz<br>605 Habakkuk<br>604–535 Daniel<br>597 King Jehoiachin<br>597–588 King Zedekiah<br>687–642 King Manasseh<br>664–612 Nahum<br>642–640 King Amon |
| 600 BCE | 556–539 King Nabonidus<br>550–539 King Belshazzar | 597–538 Exile<br>597 First deportation<br>593–570 Ezekiel<br>587 Obadiah<br>587 Fall of Jerusalem –<br>second deportation<br>582–581 Third deportation |

'when it all began'. We have seen the nature of the history as 'story'. But in fact there is a continuing history throughout the Old Testament as contained in the so-called 'historical books' (or perhaps more accurately 'cycles of books') known as the 'Deuteronomistic history' and 'Chronicler's history'. In order to get a broader view of Old Testament history and the kinds of issues that scholars address, we will consider parts of 1 Samuel and 1 Chronicles in the context of these histories. The question of the nature of these texts as 'history' will again emerge, but in a slightly different context.

## Deuteronomy and the Deuteronomistic History

Often, one hears an individual story from the Old Testament – as in the Old Testament reading in a church service – and one has no real context for the chronology of events surrounding it. Examples might be an individual battle or any individual story of a famous personage. This is where some understanding of the historical timeline as represented by these books comes in handy. We need a framework in which isolated incidents can be interpreted.

One might be confused at the title 'Deuteronomistic history' for the books from Joshua down to 2 Kings. Isn't Deuteronomy in the Pentateuch, one of the first five books of the Old Testament? We are in danger of mixing matchboxes here! In fact the reason that the history is known as 'Deuteronomistic' is because its literary and theological character is such that it seems to have close connections with the book of Deuteronomy. Chronologically the history, although much of it happened in early Israel, is likely to have been written down after the book of Deuteronomy itself. We start to encounter again the important distinction between the time that the history happened and the way stories about that history circulated first in oral tradition and then formed cycles of tradition that eventually ended up in written form. When we speak of the 'Deuteronomistic history' we are essentially talking about the writers of that history who pulled together disparate traditions and combined them into a continuous 'history' of the nation. Probably, independent cycles of traditional material were brought together by a writer (or a group of writers) who gives himself away in important linking passages in Deuteronomistic style which stitch the whole together.

So let us consider briefly the nature of the book of Deuteronomy itself. It is one of the five books of the Pentateuch and it is chiefly a law book presented as by Moses on the plains of Moab, a continuation of the covenant-giving on Mount Sinai. It is thus closely related in subject matter to Exodus and Numbers and completes the history of Moses begun in Exodus 2. Although it is technically a law book, in fact it is not narrowly legalistic. Rather, it represents a whole outlook on life. It calls for centralization of the cult on Jerusalem and purification of worship, and obedience to its laws (which include humanitarian laws on the treatment of slaves and widows). It calls Israel to love their God; it has a well-defined scheme of reward and punishment, a strong sense of past history and future hope, and it is concerned to counter **apostasy** in all its forms.

> **Apostasy** is any kind of falling away from God, notably the worship of other gods or of idols.

A widely accepted scholarly finding, made by De Wette in 1806,[37] is that the 'book of the law' found in the temple in the reign of Josiah, as related in 2 Kings 22:8–10, is none other than the book of Deuteronomy, or at least an early version of it (possibly Deuteronomy 12–20). The measures taken in Josiah's purification of Yahweh worship in 622 BCE (as related in 2 Kings 23) show striking affinities to the demands of Deuteronomy – notably those of a centralized sanctuary and purification of the law. We know that such centralization of the sanctuary in Jerusalem did not take place before Josiah's reign. These conclusions affect our assessment of the date of both Deuteronomy and the Deuteronomistic history. The account in 2 Kings 22 has the finding of what was supposedly an ancient law book in the temple by the priests of King Josiah. King Josiah then consults the prophetess Huldah, who tells him that failure to comply with the law had led to Yahweh's punishment in the past. Josiah's response is to rend his garments in an act of devotion and comply with its demands, notably that of centralization of the worship in Jerusalem:

> When the king heard the words of the book of the law, he tore his clothes. Then the king commanded the priest Hilkiah, Ahikam son of Shaphan, Achbor son of Micaiah, Shaphan the secretary and the king's servant Asaiah, saying, "Go, inquire of the LORD for me, for the people, and for all Judah, concerning the words of this book that has been found; for great is the wrath of the LORD that is kindled against us, because our ancestors did not obey the words of this book, to do according to all that is written concerning us." (2 Kings 22:11–13)

Thus it appears that the book of Deuteronomy is older than the reign of Josiah in the 620s BCE, although some scholars have suggested (somewhat cynically) that it was written to justify the reforms that Josiah wanted to make, so that the ink is barely dry as the document is read out to the people! If, however, we accept that some of its formulations might be earlier than the 620s, we might regard the book as having come together during the previous century. The dating of the book of Deuteronomy has implications for the dating of other books and sources relative to it and thus is an important scholarly conclusion.

This leads us to the Deuteronomistic history, with which Deuteronomy has a great deal in common in terms of style and theology. Martin Noth[38] coined the term 'Deuteronomistic history' for these books when he noticed, in the 1950s, that much of the same style, vocabulary and outlook found in the book of Deuteronomy is to be found in the history. He found in the books of Joshua, Judges, 1 and 2 Samuel and 1 and 2 Kings evidence of a continuous chronological scheme, similar style and thematic concerns, and evidence of summary speeches which were clearly composed with hindsight and put retrospectively into the mouths of great speakers. These speeches summarized the deeds of Yahweh in the past and outlined the apostasy of the people, using the opportunity to exhort the nation to be true to Yahweh. A prime example is found in Joshua 24 in which Joshua describes to the gathered tribes of Israel how God led the Israelite ancestors to the homeland and acted in their history. He recalls the exodus and the settlement. This then becomes the ground for the demand to Israel to 'revere the LORD, and serve him in sincerity and in faithfulness; put away the gods that your fathers served beyond the River and in Egypt, and serve the LORD' (Joshua 24:14). This then evokes a response in the people: 'Far be it from us that we should forsake the LORD to serve other gods' (Joshua 24:16) and a pact is made in the presence of God and the people. Noth saw these speeches as having been composed in Deuteronomic circles since they fitted in so exactly with Deuteronomic ideology, linking existing material together in a grand scheme of salvation history.

The theory that these two works – Deuteronomy and the Deuteronomistic history – are linked has been very widely accepted by scholars. The Deuteronomistic history is likely to have been inspired by the Deuteronomic reforms at the time of Josiah and may well have been gathered together during his reign. Nowadays, it is often seen as a two-stage document – a good deal of older traditional material such as sagas about the Judges and stories of Kings was brought together into the history, possibly in the time of national renewal under Josiah. However, as the events that led to the Exile started to unfold in the fifty years between Josiah's reign and the Exile to Babylon, the history was continued. It does in fact end with the Exile itself and then the hopeful release of King Jehoiachin from his Babylonian prison (2 Kings 25).

Noth's idea was that an author living at the time of the Exile brought together older materials to create a complete history of Israel. He did so by means of **redactional** links and editorial expansions of existing material. So he was an author who composed a new literary and theological entity out of older traditions. Noth says 'he' and sees the 'author' as an individual – most scholars nowadays see the Deuteronomists as a group or movement within Israel, strongly devoted to Yahwism and to Josiah's reform ideology. Noth thought the origins of the Deuteronomic movement dated to the time of

---

**Redactional** refers to the work of redactors – those who changed parts of texts or added material at a later stage than that of the main author or authors.

Josiah, but he ascribed the written form of the history to the Exile. He saw the negative attitude towards kingship as the product of an age disillusioned with the monarchy. The overall thrust of the history was an explanation of the failure that had led to the Exile and the overall tone was pessimistic. Subsequent scholars, while agreeing with Noth's basic analysis, revised the view of one Deuteronomistic history writer at the Exile. A number of scholars[39] thought that the main writing would have been done at the time of Josiah and that there was much in the history that was positive – the denunciation of idols, for example, was seen as part of the call to reform, not as bitter reflection on a hopeless situation, as Noth saw it. There would then have been an exilic update by a second hand, taking the events up to the Exile with which the history ends. As to who these people were, many theories have been suggested. They were clearly educated, possibly a group with close associations to court and temple.

**Figure 2.3** The Israelite Tribute to Shalmaneser III of Assyria. Detail from the Black Obelisk, Nimrud, Assyria c. 825 BCE. This is the only representation of an Israelite king in existence. © akg-images/Erich Lessing.

Our decisions about chronology affect what we see as the different stages in the development of theological ideas. I follow the mainstream suggestion here of a date for Deuteronomy in the seventh century BCE, and for the Deuteronomistic history in the seventh/sixth century as containing fresh viewpoints, but also older material. The distinction between the time that events took place and the time of writing becomes clear here. A further issue is whether these historians were writing history, or at least history as they saw it and as far as their sources would allow, or whether they were creating history from their present standpoint. The question is raised about the faithfulness of the 'historians' to their sources and their motivation in writing. One might think that one was on firmer historical ground in these books than with the patriarchal narratives, but in fact they contain similarly oral, tribal history alongside accounts of the reigns of kings that cannot be seen as unbiased and were often written with a political motivation in mind. Only at the end of the history do events become more contemporary with the writers, as they reach the events of their own time. So the historical ground is still shifting under our feet! Perhaps one difference however is that as the 'history' progresses and we move from tribal story to more detailed chronologies of events in the reigns of kings, its nature changes. Our evidence from the great cultures of the ancient Near East also becomes fuller and firmer and can be used to 'back up' the Bible at certain points. The Black Obelisk, for example, is the only depiction of an Israelite king on an Assyrian relief, or anywhere else for that matter.

## 1 Samuel and King Saul

Let us turn to one of the key books of the Deuteronomistic history – 1 Samuel – in order to get a flavour of the text and the issues addressed to it by scholars. In fact with 1 Samuel we have the beginning of a new set of coloured matchboxes, for together with 2 Samuel and 1 and 2 Kings it is categorized as the **former prophets**, the first of the 'historical books'. With the title 'historical books' we might wish to reassert their claim to 'history'.

The book of I Samuel has a historical flavour – we are given details of events which are each assigned a historical context in terms of place, names of main characters and details of what people said in certain contexts. Thus the first chapter of 1 Samuel introduces us to 'a certain man of Ramathaim, a Zuphite from the hill country of Ephraim, whose name was Elkanah son of Jeroham son of Elihu son of Tohu son of Zuph, an Ephraimite. He had two wives; the name of the one

**Former prophets** refers to the group of historical books that scholars call the Deuteronomistic history. These books contain numerous stories about early prophets such as Samuel, Elijah and Elisha – the 'former prophets' (to distinguish them from the 'latter prophets').

was Hannah, and the name of the other Peninnah. Peninnah had children, but Hannah had no children' (1 Samuel 1:1–2). Why give these details of place and name if there were not some historical basis for the story? Why go on to discuss battles against the Philistines, relationships between competing sons, competing kings and king and prophet if there is no historical basis for the events?[40]

When we start to look closely at 1 Samuel, however, we see that the primary character of the material is still story. What we have in 1 Samuel is a whole series of stories mainly centring on different characters and some other traditions in the form of songs or lists. These stories contain truth that goes beyond the importance of the details of place and name – they tell of human reactions, of relationships, of interaction with God and God's messengers. While some key characters are clearly focal to the stories, the details are in most cases irrelevant – a cynic might say that circumstantial details are mainly there to give a historical ring to stories that actually do not belong in a specific historical context. These stories then constitute our 'sources', if you like, for reconstructing historical truth. The history is thus not presented as a dry list of facts and dates. (Some of the dry style, such as we just read at the beginning of 1 Samuel, is often attributed to later editors who wanted to ground these stories in a longer sequence of familial and clan relationships.) Rather, the ancient material that was preserved came down to us in the form of stories which, we need to recognize, may contain more or less historical information.

So what stories do we actually have in 1 Samuel? To outline the book's contents very briefly, it begins with the story of the birth of the prophet Samuel in 1:1–28. It is followed in 2:1–10 by the Song of Hannah – not a story, but rather a song that may have had a separate existence as a psalm before it reached its present context. This is followed by a story which serves to contrast Eli's bad sons with Samuel, who then takes centre-stage in the next chapter when he is called to the service of Yahweh in 3:1–21. Then in chapters 4–6 we have an interruption of these stories about Samuel and a new theme of the Ark of the Covenant. We are told the story of how the Ark went into Exile and was then recovered by the victorious hand of Yahweh. It certainly looks as if we have a separate set of Ark traditions here which have been merged with the Samuel stories at a later stage. In chapter 7 we re-encounter Samuel as he judges Israel and in chapter 8 a new theme starts to emerge, that of the people's demand for a king. In chapter 8 we find a list or summary of the rights of the king, which looks to many scholars like a summary after the event, a kind of measuring stick for kings in the light of a number of rather negative experiences. In chapter 9 we begin our introduction to Saul, the first and ill-fated king of Israel. The next chapters all contain stories about Saul – his calling and anointing and then his condemnation and rejection. In chapter 16 we encounter David, whom Samuel anoints. From 1 Samuel 16:14 to 2 Samuel 5:10 we find the account of David's rise to power and Saul's decline and eventual death at the end of 1 Samuel.

There are powerful narratives contained in this book – perhaps one of the most engaging is that of Saul's failed attempt at kingship. Scholars have found immense literary artistry in this section (1 Samuel 9–31), suggesting that even though older sources may lie underneath, there has been a creative hand shaping the material in the form in which it has come down to us. In the account of Saul, the stories about him at times seem trivial (in 1 Samuel 9 he goes to find lost asses and ends up being anointed king!). However, they build to a climax when Saul – who to begin with was a king so blessed, popular and full of hope for the future – turns into a bitter and disappointed man seeking revenge on David, whom he loved but who will eventually usurp him. We see a man in a complex relationship with God, in some sense inexorably destined to fail as king and unable to control his own anger and desires. The story of Saul has been likened to Greek or Shakespearean tragedy in its exploration of 'fate' and 'flaw'. This comparison in itself demonstrates the richness of the Hebrew narrative.[41]

Saul is unexpectedly chosen by God to be the first king over Israel. Samuel anoints him to the role in 1 Samuel 10. There is a mixed attitude to having a king, as the role is seen in some ways to usurp God's authority (1 Samuel 10:19). When the proclamation is made, Saul is nowhere to be found, as he is hiding among baggage, a sign perhaps of his own reluctance to take on the position (1 Samuel 10:22). Initial deliverance from the Ammonites seems to be a good sign and Saul is keen to renew his kingly vows (1 Samuel 11). Things start to go wrong in 1 Samuel 13 when Saul misjudges the timing of his sacrifice. He had been told by Samuel to wait until the prophet arrives before making his sacrifice. He waits for seven days and Samuel is nowhere to be seen. Worried that his supporters will start to flee (they are on the verge of battle at this point), Saul decides to perform the sacrifice anyway and for that he is severely scolded not only by Samuel, but by God. In fact he is told that this action has cost him the kingship for his descendants – a rather harsh punishment in the light of the quite trivial nature of the crime, one might think.

There is another rather curious story concerning Saul in 1 Samuel 14: he rashly makes an oath before battle commences that anyone who eats before the battle is won will be cursed. It then turns out that his own son, Jonathan, who had not heard Saul's words, had eaten some honey, to which he owns up. Saul decides that Jonathan will have to die, but the people intercede on Jonathan's behalf and Saul spares him. There is an increasing feeling here that Saul is not entirely in control – he seems to rely on Samuel a good deal to tell him what to do (and indeed when Saul does take the initiative he often does things wrongly) and he also bows under pressure from the people. His character has clear weaknesses and despite his best efforts one gets the feeling that he is a pawn in a larger game. In 1 Samuel 15 he goes against God's command again in sparing the King of Agag – he appears to be innocent of his transgression and yet Samuel (and God) come down hard on him once more. At this point in the Saul cycle one starts to feel rather sorry for him – he has been trying his best in an untested role and he keeps being punished severely, to the point of losing the king-ship itself, for seemingly small mistakes. Later on, when Saul starts to be vindictive towards David, his rival for the kingship, some of our sympathy for him wanes. But it is interesting that the Deuteronomic historians have managed, perhaps partly in the clever use of their sources,[42] to convey the ambivalence in Saul's character – is he fated to fail, or are there elements of fatal flaw in his own character that lead him inexorably to a humbling fall?

## Oral Tradition and Narrative Art

We see in the Saul cycle the power of Hebrew narrative. There is real artistry in the writing and we are drawn into the stories in a powerful way. It is probable that the characters concerned existed as historical personages – there would be little motivation to make that up – and yet it is possible (and this is true of the patriarchal narratives as well) that stories attached themselves to famous people even if they did not originate with them, since the stories cluster around characters rather than events. This is unlikely in relation to Saul, where the narratives have a ring of authenticity in their very triviality of subject matter, but the prophet Samuel may be a different case. It is likely that the birth narrative of Samuel, for example, could have been formulated after the event, as with other birth narratives of famous personages (e.g. Moses in Exodus 2). Stories may also have arisen at different sanctuaries and cult-centres, thus explaining the very different Ark narrative transposed into the Samuel and Saul stories, for example (1 Samuel 4–6). This again raises quite sharply the question of what is and is not historical truth. Not only stories, but attitudes (for example, the ambivalence to kingship in this section) are woven into the narratives in order to shape the perspective of the reader.

Most of the stories may well once have existed in an oral form, so we need to deal with the fact that one person's way of relating a story may have differed greatly from another's and either grew or was distorted in the telling. Having said that, some accounts have an eyewitness feel to them, and others mention local place names that are probably authentic. Oral tradition is a malleable process, but it is also one that acts as a check on itself, for once people knew the stories, the changes one could make were limited. At some point these stories gained a more fixed literary character and a new literary context. Again, the literary shaping of material may well have influenced the presentation of the story, but if people knew the story told one way, then there were limits on the number of changes that could be made. And yet when setting any story down in writing there will inevitably be changes in style, and the use of literary techniques such as character development and irony.[43]

Stories do not come from nowhere and are often told and preserved for a reason. However, the original purpose of telling a story may then be overlaid with another purpose as that story becomes part of a whole series of stories. For example, the stories about Saul in 1 Samuel may originally have been told separately to those about Samuel and those about David, but in the book as we now have it they are all welded together and are shaped and changed in their new context. This shaping process may well have continued on and on, with embellishments and additions made to the stories as and when it was felt appropriate to add information or to update the stories in some way. Later generations wished to add their 'two pennyworth' to the stories and show their own generation how the stories were theologically relevant to their situation, rather in the way that a sermon not only expounds a text but also applies it to our own situation. This process might have gone on indefinitely had it not been for the fixing of the canon of the Old Testament, after which time redactions and additions ceased.

A good example of the points I have been making is found in 1 Samuel 28. In this chapter it is reported that Samuel had died and that Saul had driven mediums and wizards out of the land. However, in desperation, seeing himself confronted with a huge Philistine army and with no word from God, Saul decides to summon a medium to give him access to Samuel, whose advice he desperately relies on, even in death. Saul disguises himself and goes to the woman[44] at night. Samuel duly appears:

> The woman said to Saul, 'I see a divine being coming up out of the ground.' He said to her, 'What is his appearance?' She said, 'An old man is coming up; he is wrapped in a robe.' So Saul knew that it was Samuel, and he bowed with his face to the ground, and did obeisance. Then Samuel said to Saul, 'Why have you disturbed me by bringing me up?' Saul answered, 'I am in great distress, for the Philistines are warring against me, and God has turned away from me and answers me no more, either by prophets or by dreams; so I have summoned you to tell me what I shall do.' Samuel said, 'Why then do you ask me, since the LORD has turned from you and

become your enemy? The LORD has done to you just as he spoke by me; for the LORD has torn the kingdom out of your hand, and given it to your neighbour David.' (1 Samuel 28:13–17)

The narrative point of the story is clear – it is finally to show Saul that he has lost the throne by the will of Yahweh and that David is the chosen one.

It is a remarkable story because it is the only account in the Old Testament of a person coming up from the dead – the general view of death was that you went to a place of shadows – **Sheol** – where there was no contact with human beings or with God. This is unheard of therefore in Old Testament theology. **Necromancy** was regarded as the opposite of prophecy and hence condemned. Saul is participating in a forbidden art. Having just driven out mediums and wizards he is directly countering his own beliefs and policies.

> **Sheol** is the land of the dead, a place of shadows and of no further communion with God.

> **Necromancy** is the practice of black arts, notably the raising of spirits from the dead, ostensibly to speak to the living.

The narrator thus demonstrates Saul's confused state of mind and psychological despair – maybe we are to regard this story as more of a character study of Saul.

However, the same story also serves an ongoing theological motif that has been running through the story of Samuel and Saul: that of Saul's dependence upon Samuel and Samuel's role as God's spokesman, a role kept by the prophet rather than given at this stage to the king. One of the problems in regarding this story as strictly history is the miraculous element, i.e. Samuel appearing from sheol. Maybe the story simply grew in the telling – but if so it is hard to think what the story might have consisted of without the miraculous element. Perhaps we are just afraid of the miraculous in any story nowadays and should simply regard this story as historical as any other. Or maybe we should simply see it as an expression of Israelite faith – the element of the miraculous has thus come in as part of the story of God's dealings with humankind. All the way through these stories God is in control through his messengers, his prophets, his chosen rulers. This is to be seen as just another expression of that belief, a story recorded chiefly for its theological import but also as an expression of faith in God's action in history.

## History and Faith

It is clear that what we think of as history and what the ancient Israelites thought of as history are two different things. They clearly did not preserve history in the same way that we would. They did not do their utmost to preserve stories in an untarnished form. Rather, they changed them with each unfolding situation. For them, their history was a living thing and so it needed to change with their developing faith. The stories and traditions about the past are offered in such a way as to express what the Israelites believed that past experience to mean. There is no assessing of information for historical value or choosing of the most reliable account of an event or estimate of a person. Rather, the ancient writer is more likely to set down both accounts side by side or in an interwoven form, leading to the rather disorganized and haphazard form in which we find the stories presented. So we find a text in which there are numerous duplications and con-tradictions. For example, Samuel dominates the first three chapters, then disappears in 4–6, and returns in 7. In chapter 8 kingship is offensive to Yahweh, while in 9–10 the first king is anointed at Yahweh's command. Saul becomes king by lottery in 10:17–22 but apparently by popular proclamation in chapter 11. He seems to be rejected by Yahweh, not once but twice (in chapters 13 and 15), and he acquires the services of David not once but twice (in chapters 16 and 17). There are two accounts of David's betrothal to a daughter of Saul (chapter 18), two of his defection to the Philistine King of Gath (chapters 26 and 27) and two of his refusal to take Saul's life (chapters 24 and 26).

So the Old Testament does not contain an exact history of ancient Israel, and we know that would be an impossibility anyway, since any history is dis-torted in the telling. Rather, what we have is the historical testimony of ancient Israel expressed through the medium largely of story and written up by authors and redactors with the necessary literary skills to give expression to that history, the ultimate purpose of which was to express the faith of the ancient Israelites that God had been involved in the events of their history.

When looking at Abraham, we asked about evidence from archaeology and we might want to ask this again in relation to 1 Samuel. Once more, the nature of our text as story makes this difficult – while places and names can perhaps be verified, it is unlikely that we will be able to prove that events related in stories took place and that characters said what they are purported to have said. Older scholars such as John Bright in his *History of Israel*[45] were very positive about the role of archaeology in helping to date and prove the Bible. However, others such as Martin Noth[46] argued that biblical scholars have been carried away by the significance of small finds that are not necessarily reflective of the larger picture. He suggests that they should instead be looking back to the Bible itself as the best witness of events, even if events are hidden under literary layers and in theolo-gical reflection. Noth argues that it is possible to use archaeology only to assign a context for the Bible in the ancient Near East (e.g. there is much preoccupation in I Samuel 11 and 12 with asses. This clearly reflects the situation of the time in which asses were valued property and a way of measuring wealth and status). It is difficult to be more specific about events and times. Noth believes it is important to begin from the tradition of the Old Testament but using archaeology as a back-up.

## The Role of Archaeological Evidence

Perhaps we need to evaluate the archaeological contribution for ourselves. There are generally agreed to be three types of archaeological evidence, one of which is direct evidence – the kind of find that directly backs up the existence of a place or provides an account of a battle recorded in the Bible. Such evidence is scarce, but very exciting when it is found. Needless to say there is no such evidence in relation to 1 Samuel. The second kind of evidence is circumstantial, and this we do have in 1 Samuel. Thus we can look at customs of the time and at utensils and inscriptions on pottery and the like to measure probability with regard to the accuracy of the biblical account. Third, we can look at analogies from the ancient Near East, in particular at the literature and annals of other nations, and draw parallels that illuminate our own texts.

So what can archaeology tell us about 1 Samuel? We sadly do not have any documents which mention by name any of the characters in 1 Samuel, so our finds are limited.[47] Apart from confirming a generally plausible cultural milieu – for example, confirming that asses were to be found in the area at the time – archaeology can confirm the dating by reference to the annals and chronicles of other nations. Israel was a less developed nation-state than its ancient Near Eastern neighbours. The Israelites did not date years in the way that we do, by number; rather, they dated them by the reigns of their kings. Other more sophisticated nations used numerical systems and on the basis of these we know that the events recorded in 1 Samuel are likely to have happened in the period 1050–970 BCE.

This dating was thought for many years to have been supported by archaeological evidence from the site of the ancient city of **Shiloh**, where the stories of Samuel and Eli are set. A major destruction at Shiloh was dated to 1050 BCE and this date neatly fitted in with the natural supposition that the Philistines would attack and destroy Shiloh after capturing the Ark (1 Samuel 4). But a recent re-examination of the evidence and further excavation at the site have shown this to be uncertain. The destruction is more probably to be assigned to the period when the northern kingdom fell into Assyrian hands in the late eighth century BCE.

**Shiloh** is a holy site, a chief one during much of the pre-monarchic period, and the site of the Ark (1 Samuel 1–3). Along with Bethel, it is particularly hallowed in Priestly tradition. After the reign of Saul, the chief sanctuary moved permanently to Jerusalem.

When Jeremiah (in Jeremiah 7:12; 26:6, 9) speaks of the ruins of the Shiloh sanctuary as a warning of what can and will happen to the Jerusalem temple, he is likely therefore to have known the place as it was after that disaster. This revised understanding of the archaeological evidence is a good example of the need for caution in using archaeology to prove biblical chronology.

## Historical and Literary Concerns

What about the general historical background? Can we reconstruct this from what we know from surrounding nations and from the biblical text itself? The general background to this period is one of weakness in Egypt and in the northeastern and **Mesopotamian** areas; it was therefore a time during which Israel was free of external pressures. However, there were internal difficulties and much of the narrative of 1 Samuel is concerned with this. In particular it was the Philistine threat which affected Israel. Was it to be the Philistines, based on their cities in the coastal plain, who would establish a unified rule over the whole area? They pressed hard into the hill country, establishing garrisons and controlling Israelite movement and military power. At Saul's death, they controlled the important city of Beth-shan at the eastern end of the plain of Jezreel (Esdraelon). It was only with David that the Philistine threat could be fully met (see 2 Samuel 5). But already in the stories of Eli, Saul, Jonathan and David we can see the danger and the movements to meet it.

Mesopotamia is a generic term for the land between the two rivers of the Tigris and Euphrates, incorporating Assyria and Babylonia (modern-day Iraq).

This general historical outline is clear enough. However, it is in the detail of events that we face the problems we have discussed: literary embellishment and theological shaping. Ancient peoples clearly preserved much sound tradition about their own past, but such popular tradition, handed down over centuries, imparts its own twist to the material. It selects, it interprets, it transfers tales told about one area to another or from one person to another, and stories gather around particular personalities. Even where the time lapse between events and written records is shorter, we must recognize that selection and interpretation play an important part in producing what is only one way of describing what happened. This means that in the end we find greater interest in discussing how the story is interpreted than merely in trying to discover what happened. This process in itself reveals the beliefs held by the ancient Israelites in what God did and continued to do for them in their history.

It is likely that what we have in 1 Samuel is a final selection and interpretation, probably formulated by the Deuteronomists. As we have seen, they had their own historical and theological context to address and so shaped the material at their disposal accordingly. They probably used earlier oral and written sources, some probably in quite a fixed form already, as well as adding their own comments and interpretation. Sadly, we do not have the evidence of what such earlier narratives might have looked like before they were woven into the final text. However, we are lucky that another of the oddities of these ancient authors was to incorporate existing material – even risking repetitions and contradictions, which do not seem to have bothered them unduly – rather than excising and editing too much, as we would be tempted to do today. This may lead to a text that does not flow smoothly and to difficulties in the reconstruction of events, but it also probably means that we have a good witness to earlier narrative cycles contained within the later version itself.

We can uncover different evaluations of characters within the one text that seem to contradict and yet probably represent different sets of traditions. For example, the story of David and Saul, as it is told in 1 Samuel 16–31, is clearly written with an eye to the establishment of David as the great king whose name was to live as a pattern of kingship in Israel. But not all the stories about David are very creditable; his behaviour was certainly sometimes of very doubtful morality. Even as the stories are told, we may sympathize with Saul's difficulties. And although Saul is depicted as failing as a king, we find stories which show him as a hero, as a noble warrior, as a man of generous impulse. We must, therefore, in reading the stories, be continually aware of the interpretation being given. It is in establishing the precise development of changing perspectives that we may encounter more difficulty. For example, did a pro-Davidic stance precede or succeed a less favourable picture? What is the more primitive picture of Saul – was he always regarded as a failure or is the ambivalence found in the source reflective of what people generally felt about him?

## The Chronicler's History

We can find evidence of this selection and interpretation process in a comparison of 1 and 2 Samuel with the Chronicler's history which I mentioned earlier as a second history contained in our Old Testament. This has a different character again from the early tribal stories and from the Deuteronomistic presentation. It illustrates particularly well the point about a 'theology of history' being written, in that we can see the process of the rewriting of an earlier history for a later age, through comparison with the Deuteronomistic history. It is written by another group or individual called 'the Chronicler' and it includes 1 and 2 Chronicles and arguably the books of Ezra and Nehemiah.[48] It is a later work thought to be from the fourth century BCE, one which interestingly covers the same period of history but from a later theological standpoint. This comparison is fascinating as it gives us some insight into how ancient writers thought. It is clear that the Chronicler knew the material of 1 and 2 Samuel, although we cannot be sure whether the writer knew the books as we knew them or whether he (and it probably was a he) was working with a somewhat different edition. We notice that in 1 Chronicles a great deal of what is in 1 Samuel disappears. For example, the monarchy of Saul is very briefly dismissed by comparison with the 23 chapters concerning Saul in 1 Samuel. There is a short passage giving the family to which Saul belonged (1 Chronicles 9:35–44); only one chapter (1 Chronicles 10) tells of Saul's death at Mount Gilboa – the story told in 1 Samuel 31. But to this story, the later author has added his comment: 'Thus Saul paid with his life for his unfaithfulness' (1 Chronicles 10:13–14). The author has selected part of the story of Saul and has made it the vehicle of a particular judgement, drawing out ideas which may be detected in a less developed form in the 1 Samuel narratives. The focus is upon unfaithfulness on Saul's part in seeking guidance from other than God.

## The Chronicler's David

One of the most interesting points of difference in the Chronicler's portrayal is that of David. In the Deuteronomistic history there is a much fuller account of his life, including some of his more shameful acts such as the purloining of Bathsheba from her husband and details of his early life. We touched upon some of these stories in our discussion of David in chapter 1. In the Chronicler's account the main concern is to portray the unblemished and established King David as temple-builder, because for the Chronicler the temple is at the centre of post-exilic life. So as Wellhausen[49] put it, in the hands of the Chronicler, David's 'clearly cut figure has become a feeble holy picture, seen through a cloud of incense.' The shepherd boy, then politician and womanizer, has been replaced by a pious king who sets up all the ordinances for the temple, its life, its priests, its fitments and fittings.

David's story begins in 1 Chronicles 11 after chapters of genealogies and the very short account of Saul's reign. This is nearly as heavy-going as Leviticus! It seems in the post-exilic period that the writers were obsessed with lists of genealogies, warriors, priests and so on. David is anointed king at Hebron in 1 Chronicles 11 and then captures Jerusalem. Then there follows lists of David's warriors, a show of his military strength perhaps. In chapter 12 it is made clear that David was joined by many warriors not his own, including the armies of Saul, and that members of all twelve tribes of Israel supported his accession. 1 Chronicles 13 is a highlight with the Ark of the Covenant being brought from Kiriath-jearim to Jerusalem, not at first to the temple (which was not yet built) but to the private house of Obed-edom the Gittite. David is then established at Jerusalem and building materials are even supplied to him from other kings to help him build the temple. The Philistines are still a perennial problem in 1 Chronicles 14, but they are quickly subdued. The Ark of the Covenant is a far more interesting topic! Chapter 15 returns us to it. As soon as he has a roof over his own head, David prepares a place for the Ark under a tent. Only the **Levites** are allowed to carry the Ark and that will be one of their continuing roles in the new temple, alongside singing and playing musical instruments. And so we read that 'all Israel brought up the Ark of the covenant of the LORD with shouting, to the sound of the horn, trumpets and cymbals, and made loud music on harps and lyres'

> The **Levites** are a particular caste of priests of the tribe of Levi with a largely secondary role in the post-exilic temple as musicians, temple officials, conductors of sacrifices and preachers.

(1 Chronicles 15:28). The Ark is placed in the tent (1 Chronicles 16) and then David sings a psalm of thanksgiving. It is interesting that a psalm (Psalm 96 in all but the first and last lines) is here put into his mouth within a narrative text, not just in the Psalter itself.

As we read on in the Chronicler's story of David concern with building a proper temple for the Ark arises (this contrasts with just a couple of verses on the Ark in 2 Samuel 6:17–19). In chapter 17 David feels guilty that he is living in a proper house while the Ark isn't, but he is told by God that not he but his successor as king, his son Solomon, will be the one to build the Lord's house. This is as part, however, of the prophetic promise, through Nathan the prophet, to the Davidic house, that their rule will continue, for which David is more than grateful. He establishes his kingdom against the Philistines and indeed extends its boundaries (1 Chronicles 18) and 'the Lord gave victory to David wherever he went' (1 Chronicles 18:13b). He also defeats the Ammonites and the Arameans (chapter 19). His chief commander Joab defeats the inhabitants of Rabbah (chapter 20) and descendants of giants were defeated at Gath. The only foot wrong that David puts is in chapter 21 with his request for a census of fighting men. We are told in 1 Chronicles 21:1 that this was incited by Satan (and interestingly by God in the parallel passage in 2 Samuel 24 – is God being exonerated here by the Chronicler?). This displeases God and leads to the infliction of a pestilence upon the people. David has to sacrifice to God to make reparation and he does so on the threshing floor of a character called Ornan the Jebusite which he buys from its owner (a passage that may well remind us of Abraham's purchase of the cave for the burial of his wife Sarah in Genesis 23:9–13). This then becomes the place where the temple is to be built (chapter 22). Most of the rest of the section is on the preparations to build the temple. David primes his son Solomon on his key role (chapter 22), he sorts out the Levites and their functions (chapter 23) and those of other priests (chapter 24). He organizes the music (chapter 25), gatekeepers, treasurers and judges (chapter 26). He also manages affairs of state, such as military divisions, tribal leaders and other civic officials (chapter 27). He even has the plans of the temple in place for his son Solomon and all the precious temple fittings (chapter 28). He makes repeated calls on the people to bless their God and make offerings for the temple in a joyous spirit (chapter 29). He truly is a pious figure, concerned to do what is right in the eyes of God and the people.

## The Chronicler's Handling of Sources

One of the key differences between this history and its forerunner is that we have lost that sense of 'storytelling'. This is a much drier history, with many lists and much theological 'shaping', although the joy of worship, making music and praising God is a positive aspect of the account. As Grace Emmerson writes:

> 1 Chronicles stands high in the list of least-read books of the Old Testament. It tells, in part, much the same story as Samuel and Kings but with little of their human interest. Gone are the tales of tension and intrigue, of dysfunctional families and sibling rivalry. There is more of liturgy and ceremonial. Add to this that its first nine chapters are undiluted genealogies, and there is little wonder that it fails to attract today's readers.[50]

Yet she goes on to argue for patient reading, and I think we have seen in considering the Chronicler's portrayal of both Saul and David that the account is not without interest.

If we look at an example of what the Chronicler omitted from the Deuteronomistic history we will see how different the portrayals are. A good example is 1 Chronicles 20 in relation to the portrayal of David. Verse

1 corresponds to 2 Samuel 11:1 and verses 2–3 to 2 Samuel 12:30–1. The Chronicler has missed out nearly two chapters of 2 Samuel. Those just happen to be the story of David's adultery with Bathsheba, his plot to get rid of her husband, Uriah the Hittite (only mentioned in a list in 1 Chronicles 11:41, a man crushed and defeated in 2 Samuel 11:2–27), and Nathan's denunciation of the king through the parable of the lamb.

The Chronicler then juxtaposes his verse 3 from 2 Samuel 12:31 with his verse 4 from 2 Samuel 21:18, thus bypassing stories concerning David's family that are less than favourable, such as his daughter Tamar's rape by her half-brother Ammon and a challenge to his authority by his son Absalom and from Sheba ben Bichri. It may not just be that the Chronicler is ignoring David's failures – David is portrayed in a poor light in chapter 21 – but rather that the Chronicler's interests are very different, and family intrigue is not high on his list of priorities. It may be of course that readers were expected to be familiar with the stories about David in 1 and 2 Samuel, so that all the Chronicler had to do was allude to them. His main concern is with a theological presentation of the high point of Israelite kingship under David and promised to his successors, in which the Ark was in its rightful place, the temple was in mind (if not yet built) and the twelve tribes were united in their joyful worship of God. This opens up another question of 'authorial shaping' in deciding what is presented. How far are these texts the products of individual authors and how far are they a group presentation reflecting the wider concerns of a different age?

## The Two 'Histories'

The two histories taken together and accompanied by the patriarchal history cover pretty much the whole Old Testament period. This 'history' runs in parallel with that of the ancient Near East and those empires rise and fall while – incredibly – Israel keeps going. Although it goes from early beginnings to the high point of becoming a monarchical state and then to being disbanded at the exile, followed by vassalage to other states, the nation that is Israel survives repeated calamity. And although its outlook on history and its accompanying theological perspective change and develop over time, there is a constant looking back to its roots and understanding of its history in terms of God's deliverance of God's people.

Old paradigms such as the exodus keep being reused in new situations. The Exile becomes another paradigm of liberation from oppression. The Israelites shape and reshape their history through their preservation of the old stories and their constant theological updating, which helps to keep their

| Exile and after | | |
|---|---|---|
| 600 BCE | 556–539 King Nabonidus<br>550–539 King Belshazzar<br>539 Fall of Babylon<br>539–530 King Cyrus the Great<br>530–522 King Cambyses<br>522–486 King Darius | 597–538 Exile<br>597 First deportation<br>593–570 Ezekiel<br>587 Obadiah<br>587 Fall of Jerusalem – second deportation<br>582–581 Third deportation<br>538 First return of exiles to Judah<br>537–516 Rebuilding of Jerusalem<br>526 Zerubbabel<br>525 Second return of exiles to Judah<br>520 Haggai |
| 500 BCE | 486–465 King Xerxes I<br>464–423 King Artaxerxes I<br>404–359 King Artaxerxes II | 460 Malachi<br>458 Ezra returns to Jerusalem<br>445–433 Nehemiah rebuilds Jerusalem |
| 400 BCE | 336–331 Darius III | |
| 300 BCE | 285–246 King Ptolemy II Philadelphus<br>283 Septuagint translation<br>223–187 King Antiochus III, the Great | |
| 200 BCE | 175–163 King Antiochus IV Epiphanes | c. 167 Antiochus desecrates temple<br>166–161 King Judas Maccabeus<br>164 Temple rededicated<br>160–143 King John Hyrcanus<br>143–135 King Simon Maccabeus<br>135–104 King John Hyrcanus<br>104–103 King Aristobulus<br>103–76 King Alexander Jannaeus<br>c. 100 Rise of the Essenes |
| 100 BCE | 46–44 Julius Caesar<br>27 BCE–14 CE Augustus (Octavian) | 76–67 Salome Alexandra and King Hyrcanus II<br>67–40 King Aristobulus II and King Kyrcanus II<br>63 Pompey captures Jerusalem<br>47–43 King Antipater II<br>37–4 King Herod the Great<br>8/7 John the Baptist |
| | | c. 4 Birth of Jesus<br>4 BCE–39 CE King Herod Antipas (Galilee)<br>4 BCE–6 CE King Archelaus (Judea)<br>4 BCE–34 CE King Herod Philip (Iturea) |

faith and traditions alive. So, for example, David's charge to Solomon to build the temple in 1 Chronicles 28:20 – 'Be strong and of good courage, and act. Do not be afraid or dismayed; for the Lord God, my God, is with you. He will not fail you or forsake you, until all the work for the service of the house of the Lord is finished' – has strong echoes of the words of Moses as he looked out over the promised land knowing that he himself would never go into it, and so handing over to his successor, Joshua: 'Be strong and bold. . . . It is the Lord who goes before you. He will be with you; he will not fail you or forsake you. Do not fear or be dismayed' (Deuteronomy 31:7–8; cf. Joshua 1:5–9).

Looking essentially at the history of Israel, as presented through 'story', has helped to give us a framework for understanding other developments and hopefully a way into opening the Old Testament. It has also given us a basic understanding of the rough outline of events so that we can place odd fragments of text more easily within the wider picture. We have aired questions about the historicity of that history and wider scholarly questions regarding social history, the role of archaeology and questions of writers and sources. Focusing on the history, however, necessarily gives us a slightly one-sided view of the richness of Israel's testimony. We need to turn to the two other aspects that I have stressed alongside the historical: literary and theological approaches. We need then to look at other parts of the Old Testament's rich literature with its many different genres (chapter 3) and then at some of the great theological themes that sprang from and then transcended that history (chapter 4).

## Notes

1   *The Jerusalem Bible*, London: Darton, Longman and Todd, first published 1966.
2   J. Rhymer, *The Bible in Order*, London: Darton, Longman and Todd, 1975.
3   While the dating of the earliest settlement in Canaan is subject to some debate, the general idea is that the oppression of the Hebrews in Egypt who were led out by Moses can be dated to the reign of the Egyptian Pharaoh Rameses II (1290–1224 BCE). It is only by cross-reference to other nations that we can attempt to work out this biblical chronology.
4   Some 'Judges' are much better documented than others, which suggests that 'sources' varied.
5   W. Brueggemann, *Theology of the Old Testament: Testimony, Dispute, Advocacy*, Minneapolis, MN: Augsburg Fortress, 1997.
6   The view of the so-called 'minimalists' is that a lot of the 'history' was a back-projection of a later age, much of it imagined. See P. Davies, *In Search of Ancient Israel*, JSOTS 148, Sheffield: JSOT Press, 1994; N. P. Lemche, *Ancient Israel: A New History of Israelite Society*, Sheffield: JSOT Press, 1988; T. L. Thompson, *Early History of the Israelite People*, Studies in the History of the Ancient Near East 4, Leiden: Brill, 1992.

7   Even if one challenges a historical approach that takes the narratives as products of their own age, or a marginally later one, the point remains that theological development is found in the texts. This is one of the problems of the flattening out of the historical continuum that is the result of very late dating proposals.

8   This connection with Sumerian culture is stressed in D. Rosenberg, *Abraham*, New York: Basic Books, 2006.

9   Shechem, Bethel and Hebron were key shrines throughout the monarchic period. Later in the period these shrines were often polluted by pagan worship, leading ultimately to their closure under King Josiah when he undertook centralization of worship in Jerusalem in circa 622 BCE.

10  Ishmael is traditionally the ancestor of the Arab race.

11  The description of the patriarchs, and even more so of some of the generations before the flood, as very long-lived is a problem in relation to their historical veracity as people. This is most easily interpreted as storyteller's licence, designed to show how long and blessed their lives were. Or perhaps years were counted differently in those times. It is likely that Sarah is on the verge of menopause here (Genesis 18:11 tells us 'it had ceased to be with Sarah after the manner of women', which is a euphemism for the female monthly cycle), although she must have been considerably younger than the 90 years old that the text suggests.

12  This was revealed to Abraham in the previous chapter, so maybe we have evidence of a doublet or different 'writers' here.

13  An excellent treatment of this story of Sarah and indeed of the story of Hagar from a feminist perspective (although written by a man!) is Trevor Dennis, *Sarah Laughed: Women's Voices in the Old Testament*, Nashville: Abingdon Press, 1994, chs 2 and 3.

14  See a fascinating discussion of Abraham's arguing with God and its significance in relation to a wider Old Testament theme of challenging God, in R. Davidson, *The Courage to Doubt: Exploring an Old Testament Theme*, London: SCM Press, 1983, ch. 3.

15  Likely to be a doublet in the oral tradition that has found its way into literary form.

16  Feminist scholarship has helpfully considered the 'silences' in texts when the woman's perspective is simply excluded.

17  See again Davidson, *The Courage to Doubt*, ch. 3, and also an interesting discussion in J. L. Crenshaw, *A Whirlpool of Torment*, Overtures to Biblical Theology 12, Philadelphia: Fortress Press, 1984.

18  The variation in type of account may provide evidence of different oral or written sources. Older scholars found different criteria by which to decide different source strata, but the attempt is slightly out of vogue today in that much uncertainty abounds as to what criteria to use. It was thought, for example, that more sophisticated theological pronouncements were generally 'later' than family sagas, but with the theological shaping of much of the material (see below) that distinction is far from clear-cut.

19  I. Provan, V. P. Long and T. Longman III, *A Biblical History of Israel*, Louisville, KY: Westminster John Knox Press, 2003, pp. 85–6.

20  Some attempts have been made to date these stories on the basis of the date of the domestication of the camel, thought to have happened after 1100 BCE. However,

K. Kitchen in *On the Reliability of the Old Testament*, Grand Rapids, MI: Eerdmans, 2003, contests such a presupposition. Although references to camels are few in the patriarchal narratives – and camels were the last and least of Abraham's possessions according to Genesis 12:16 – external sources such as a camel skull from Egypt from circa 2000–1450 BCE and a figurine of a kneeling camel from Byblos dated nineteenth/eighteenth century BCE (among other evidence) prove, for Kitchen, that 'the true situation' is that 'the camel was for long a *marginal* beast in most of the historic ancient Near East (including Egypt), but it was *not* wholly unknown or anachronistic before or during 2000–1100' (p. 330). However, even if we accept this evidence, it does not prove that Abraham existed, it simply confirms an aspect of the 'world' that he inhabited and to which the text bears witness.

21    Provan, Long and Longman, p. 74.

22    Kitchen, pp. 353–5. Kitchen concludes that the external data (such as it is, and what there is he helpfully lists) is overwhelmingly in favour of a date in the first half of the second millennium BCE and that this coincides with internal data from the narratives themselves, such as information about the ages and lifespans of the patriarchs. He notes the process of transmission of the narrative and how this may have changed the selection of what has come down to us, but is more optimistic than most scholars about the historical nature of this witness. He writes, 'Originally the patriarchs probably told more episodes about themselves than we now possess in Genesis; but a basic nucleus was retained, while seemingly less germane episodes were discarded. By the thirteenth century the basic catena of material was essentially what we have now. It would then stand as a foundation or "charter" document to remind the Israelite tribal group of their origins, as the people of the God of their forefathers who was now to take them further on in life, to the exodus (and all that followed, of course)' (pp. 367–8).

23    The repetition of this story twice in relation to Abraham and once to Isaac suggests that it was a popular story that was told of more than one person and on more than one occasion. Its historicity might be questioned on such grounds. Alternatively, we may have doublets in the text as a result of source amalgamation.

24    Of course, this presupposition rest on a traditional dating of the exodus, which is also open to question, and so the sand starts to shift under our feet!

25    J. Van Seters, *Abraham in History and Tradition*, New Haven, CT: Yale University Press, 1975.

26    J. Bright, *History of Israel*, 4th edn, London: SCM Press, 2000.

27    See, for example, B. Halpern, ' "Brisker pipes than Poetry": The Development of Israelite Monotheism', *Judaic Perspectives on Ancient Israel*, ed. J. Neusner, B. A. Levine and E. S. Frerichs, Philadelphia: Fortress Press, 1987, pp. 77–115.

28    The question is raised as to whether this is Melchizedek's own god or another name for the same God. Salem is often used as an abbreviation for Jerusalem and may be an early name for the place.

29    Different names for God are often seen as a suitable criterion for the isolation of different literary sources according to Pentateuchal criticism.

30    See J. Barton, *Reading the Old Testament: Method in Biblical Study*, 2nd edn, London: Darton, Longman and Todd, 1996 on this problem of sources/redactor interrelationship.

31    M. Noth, *History of Israel*, London: A. & C. Black, 1958 (German 1950).

32  For example, G. E. Wright, *God Who Acts: Biblical Theology as Recital*, SBT 8, London: SCM Press, 1952.

33  G. von Rad, *Old Testament Theology*, Vols 1 and 2, Edinburgh: Oliver and Boyd, 1962; London: SCM Press, 1975 (German 1958–61).

34  As W. Schmidt writes in his *Old Testament Introduction*, New York: Crossroad, 1984: 'The Old Testament came into being in the course of a history and most of what it says has to do with history. At the same time, however, its presentation of history is in the form of a testimony to faith; it does not preserve the tradition in its originally "historically pure" form, but relates it to the present and in the process alters it' (p. 9).

35  K. Whitelam, *The Invention of Ancient Israel: The Silencing of Palestinian History*, London: Routledge, 1996, p. 69. Whitelam's contention is that ancient Israel, as constructed by the scholarship from biblical texts, is an invention, that it is 'ideologically loaded' and that it represents the outlook of an elitist group. His agenda is a political one relating to the dispossession of Palestinians and the creation of the modern state of Israel that rests on the assumption of an imagined entity that was ancient Israel.

36  Whether or not the exodus happened is on the agenda in the current debate. See discussion in G. I. Davies, 'Was there an Exodus?' in *In Search of Pre-Exilic Israel*, ed. J. Day, JSOTS 406, London: T. & T. Clark International, 2004. This is a useful, multi-authored volume that attempts to redress the trend to date all Old Testament texts to the post-exilic period.

37  W. M. L. De Wette, *Beiträge zur Einleitung in das Alte Testament*, Halle: Schimmelpfennig, 1806–7.

38  M. Noth, *The Deuteronomistic History*, JSOTS 15, Sheffield: JSOT Press, 1987 (German 1943).

39  For example, J. Gray, *1 and 2 Kings*, Old Testament Library, London: SCM Press, 1964 (3rd edn, 1985).

40  Even if we see these details as the work of redactors, it is clear that at some point in its development the text has been given a historical context.

41  See D. M. Gunn, 'A Man Given over to Trouble' in *Images of Man and God: Old Testament Short Stories in Literary Focus*, ed. B. O. Long, Bible and Literature Series 1, Sheffield: Almond Press, 1981, pp. 89–112; and *The Fate of King Saul: An Interpretation of a Biblical Story*, JSOT Supplement 14, Sheffield: JSOT Press, 1980.

42  Scholars have argued for pro- and anti-monarchic sources in this section. Some of the incongruity of the stories in comparison to the harsh judgements on Saul may be due to this disjunction.

43  For example, E. M. Good, 'Saul: The Tragedy of Greatness' in his *Irony in the Old Testament*, Philadelphia: Westminster Press, 1965, pp. 56–80, does a fascinating study of the Saul cycle noting the irony in the portrayal of Saul and of his interaction with God and other characters. This is part of a wider study of irony in the Old Testament, as the title of his book indicates.

44  Traditionally regarded as a witch, but feminist critics have sought to redeem the woman (who is essentially a professional medium) from this terminology.

45  John Bright, *A History of Israel*, London: SCM, 1960 (3rd edn, 1981). There is considerable continuing interest in archaeology today, although its ability to prove anything about the Bible in a decisive way is severely questioned in some scholarly circles.

46   M. Noth, *A History of Pentateuchal Traditions*, Englewood Cliffs, NJ: Prentice-Hall, 1972.

47   An inscription on a Victory stele mentioning 'the house of David' was found at Tel Dan. The inscription tells how Hazael, King of Aram, killed seventy kings, among them Yehoram, King of Israel, and Ahaziahu, King of Judah, whose names appear in partial form. It corresponds to the biblical account in 2 Chronicles 22 which describes the war between Hazael and these kings of Israel. However, it contradicts 2 Kings 9 which relates the murder of two allied kings by Yehu. This is the only monumental inscription from the First Temple period (ninth century BCE) ever found in Israel.

48   The scholarly debate over whether Ezra and Nehemiah are to be included in the work of the Chronicler is an involved one. See H. G. M. Williamson, *1 and 2 Chronicles*, New Century Bible Commentary, London: Marshall, Morgan and Scott, 1982; S. Japhet, *1 and 2 Chronicles*, Old Testament Library, London: SCM Press, 1993.

49   Wellhausen is often seen as the 'father ' of Old Testament study in his definitive statement of the four-source documentary theory in relation to the Pentateuch – see his *Prolegomena to the History of Israel*, Edinburgh: A. & C. Black, 1885 (reprinted by Scholars Press, Atlanta, in 1994), from which this quotation is taken (p. 182). He also had interesting views on other topics, such as this one. Thus his chapter on Chronicles contains a good discussion of the differences between parallel accounts in Samuel/Kings and Chronicles.

50   Grace Emmerson, '1 Chronicles', *Guidelines* 21/3, ed. J. Duff and K. J. Dell, Oxford: Bible Reading Fellowship, 2005, p. 7.

# Chapter 3 How to 'Open' the Old Testament for Ethical Guidance

## Authoritative Texts?

There has been a sea change in biblical studies in the last twenty years and it has been in the area of appreciating the reader. The recognition is that the text of the Old Testament speaks to us differently than to someone else, depending on who we are and on our historical, cultural and geographical location. Of course, the text itself does not change, but the 'audience' does.[1] So in particular when we look back over history, as we shall do briefly later in this chapter, we see immense differences in how our predecessors read texts and in the message(s) they took from them. And as we shall explore in chapter 5, even in our modern world different 'readers' – be they men or women, black or white, rich or poor – read texts differently and may well find nourishment from a selection of texts that is different to our own.[2]

All this has raised questions about the authority of the text. This emerges in particular when we open the Old Testament for ethical guidance. For example, how far are the Ten Commandments timebound – revealed at a particular point in history for a particular people? How far are they some kind of absolute moral imperative with abiding authority for all people? Are some texts – such as laws – more authoritative than others? And who decides on the selection of authoritative texts – the church or the synagogue? This brings us back also to the canon, because the original 'selection' of texts was done in the first century CE.[3] Is that selection just as authoritative for us today?

In the last chapter we focused on the historical 'story' of Israel. Does that 'story' of Israel have modern relevance? We might answer that parts of it

LIST OF WRITINGS
Psalms
Job
Proverbs
Ruth
Song of Songs
Ecclesiastes
Lamentations
Esther
Daniel
Ezra-Nehemiah
1 and 2 Chronicles

clearly do, such as the great tale of liberation from slavery, but that there are elements of Old Testament ethics that are most distasteful, such as vengeance upon enemies. In fact we saw that the 'grand narrative' of Israel is made up of many individual stories, many of them about families. An interesting characteristic of the Old Testament is that it is built up into a grand narrative by these building blocks of individual tales. Take the book of Ruth, for example (discussed in chapter 5). This is a family tale of a daughter-in-law who chooses to go to Bethlehem from the land of Moab with her mother-in-law. It is about her gleaning in the fields and meeting the man who will become her husband, integrating her – a foreigner who nevertheless has embraced the Israelite God – into their society. It appears to be unconnected to the story of Israel and one wonders why it is there, apart from being a heart-warming story that speaks of conversion to faith in God. We discover however right at the end of the book how it is linked to the grand narrative and possibly why it is there.

Many stories illustrate moral points. The book of Ruth, for example, keeps reiterating that Ruth and others did 'good deeds' which appear to be rewarded by God. It seems here that right actions – even from foreigners – are highly valued by God. Some stories are perhaps slightly more immoral – one thinks of the 'texts of terror' isolated by Phyllis Trible (see chapter 5) that concern women who are violated in various ways that would be totally unacceptable morally to us today. There is a whole range of individual stories in the Old Testament, many of them contained in the Writings, like Ruth, but also within the Pentateuch and elsewhere. The Israelites clearly enjoyed telling stories, not just because they were true, or just because they were good yarns or even had an important theological point to convey, but because, importantly, they also had a moral point to make. We dwelt largely on the history/story nexus in the last chapter.

In this chapter I wish to move on to two other genres found in the Old Testament, those of law and wisdom.

## The Ten Commandments

Perhaps the most famous place to begin a discussion of ethical guidance in the Old Testament is with the Ten Commandments. There seems to be an endless fascination with these ten prescriptions. They are seen to provide universal ethical standards relevant to a wider society than simply a religious one. Their authority almost transcends the two faiths, Judaism and Christianity, in which they find an important voice. They have perhaps been taken out of their context and elevated too much and hence often interpreted in rather more far-reaching terms than they actually represent. There is a historical dimension to the way they are now regarded in such universal terms. Because of the religious roots of our society, these ten principles have found their way into the making of laws within what we might term today as a secular context. In medieval times, for example, the religious and secular were so intertwined that this was a natural direction to go in for those compiling laws. In modern times this connection has been questioned and the religious aspect of the Ten Commandments – in many ways a symbol of morality and devotion to God – emphasized in considering the true nature of their universal application.[4]

---

THE TEN COMMANDMENTS
1   *I am the LORD your God . . . you shall have no other gods before me*
2   *You shall not make for yourself an idol, whether in the form of anything that is in heaven above, or that is on the earth beneath, or that is in the water under the earth. You shall not bow down to them or worship them; for I the LORD your God am a jealous God*
3   *You shall not make wrongful use of the name of the LORD your God*
4   *Remember the sabbath day, and keep it holy*
5   *Honour your father and your mother*
6   *You shall not murder*
7   *You shall not commit adultery*
8   *You shall not steal*
9   *You shall not bear false witness against your neighbour*
10  *You shall not covet your neighbour's house; you shall not covet your neighbour's wife*

Exodus 20:1–17

---

**Figure 3.1**  Code of Hammurabi. The top of the Stele shows Hammurabi, King of Babylon (1792–1750 BCE), receiving the law from the Sun God. The laws are written below and this code is perhaps the most famous parallel to Israelite law from the Ancient Near East. © akg-images/Erich Lessing.

John Barton in his book *What is the Bible?*[5] points out that in fact the Ten Commandments are 'not quite such a useful basic moral code as people think'. We might be surprised to read that. He explains that most of them have a negative tone, condemning immorality rather than commending good behaviour – 'Thou shalt not' resounds throughout the text. Barton writes, 'Most of them could be kept by staying in bed all day and avoiding any human contact' – surely not their real point at all! Barton goes on to note that they belong to a very different cultural context to our own, one in which the adult male householder is the dominant addressee (and in one version of the Ten Commandments wives are part of his property). We need therefore to translate their message into a modern situation, which may be easier with some commandments (e.g. 'Thou shalt not kill') than with others (e.g. coveting neighbour's maidservants). Barton also points out that people tend to generalize from the Ten Commandments, largely extracting positive duties (e.g. respect others; practise honesty and loyalty) from the negative prohibitions, rather in the same spirit that Jesus summarized them in Matthew 19:16–22 (love God and your neighbour),[6] and clearly focusing on the basic message of the commandments, thus detaching them from any particular cultural context. There is probably nothing wrong with doing that, as long as we realize that's what we are doing!

So perhaps the Ten Commandments have some inadequacies as a universal moral code. If we go back to their original context, they are firmly placed within the relationship between God and the people of Israel, with a concern to exclude any other gods who might threaten that relationship. As a purely moral code one could therefore ignore the first four commandments that speak of God – and yet that would be to 'humanize' them too much. They are about *relationship*, first with God (and included in that is certain observances such as sabbath-keeping in commandment four)[7] and then with each other within society. Their character is quite different across the ten commands – there are just two positive commandments about keeping the sabbath day and honouring parents;[8] the last five are more 'absolute' in character. Some are quite terse, others more explanatory. They really form quite an untidy text. As Barton writes: 'It is clear that the Commandments are not the text we should produce if we were trying to provide a summary of ethics for our society.' Perhaps we might add that because of their very general nature as a summary they are open to many interpretations (and sometimes misinterpretations).[9] Because they are terse, they need further explanation.

Furthermore, it is often forgotten that there are two versions of the Ten Commandments in the Old Testament which differ slightly – one version is contained in Exodus 20 and the other in Deuteronomy 5. Maybe the repetition is due to their importance within the tradition. They very likely have oral antecedents – ten commandments are easily remembered on the fingers of the hand and would be likely to have represented ten rules on which a nomadic community might have based its community life – and then been 'written up' by those writing these books.[10] But it is interesting that there are variations in these texts, particularly if they were so authoritative.

It is important to be clear that the Ten Commandments are ethical demands rather than a 'lawcode'. They are expanded upon in many of the lawcodes of the Old Testament that surround them (e.g. Exodus 21–3; Leviticus 19–26; Numbers, Deuteronomy).[11] They are assumed by prophets in their critique of Israelite shortcomings (e.g. Hosea 4:1–2; Jeremiah 7:8–9). They are more of a summary than a specific set of laws, since they consist of general principles rather than detailed cases.[12] They also do not specify any punishments and only imply that those breaking the commandments would incur God's wrath and that of the community in a general way.[13] They are presented within their Old Testament context as the words of Yahweh to Moses,[14] which the Israelites accept as their side of the covenant relationship. They are essentially an act of grace on the part of God, freely accepted by Israel as the chosen people.

At the heart of the Ten Commandments is respect – for God on the one hand and for one's 'neighbour' (i.e. any other human being) on the other. The first four commandments list negative prohibitions in relation to God which can be reinterpreted as positive duties. The second six concern right conduct within the community, presented in terms of the individual and his or her obligations – largely what a person *shouldn't* do, rather than what they *should* do – the first of these six being in the specific religious context of the **sabbath** day and its nature.

---

The **sabbath** is the seventh day, when God rested from the work of creation. It is kept as a day of rest by Jews and Christians.

---

## Exodus 20

Let us take a closer look at the texts. I will focus on Exodus 20 as the better-known version, but note the variations with Deuteronomy 5. It is interesting that the first 'commandment' is really a statement of who God is and of God's uniqueness. We are brought back again to the grand narrative of Israel's historical identity; back in fact to liberation from slavery in the exodus. In the historical context of the law-giving on Mount Sinai this event would have just happened to the people. The immediate concern is to legislate in a negative tone that no other gods are acceptable. We know of the incident with the golden calf soon after this account and the second commandment anticipates that event with its prohibition of images. This has always been a keynote of Israelite faith – the prohibition of any image of

God. This distinguishes the religion from surrounding nations in which idols of gods were commonplace (e.g. the Canaanite god Baal depicted by a bull) and were thought to capture something of the essence of those gods. No image is acceptable – no divine image or human, animal or fish. Making an idol would impose a limitation on God's freedom and sovereignty that would be unacceptable. It appears to be the nature of God and how God is to be appropriately worshipped that is of primary concern here, rather than polemic against other religions and their idols, until, that is, the secondary command: 'You shall not bow down to them or worship them.' This denotes a shift from prohibition of forming any image of God to prohibition of the worship of other gods. The reason given is Yahweh's jealousy, which has a twofold reference that corresponds to the rest of the commandment: God is jealous of the exclusivity of the relationship with Israel first and foremost, yet also jealous of other gods in that they pose a threat to that exclusive relationship.

An expansion of the second commandment shows God as remembering wrongdoing for a long time – for generations, we are told here.[15] Converse rewards apply to those who love God and keep these commandments. Of course, we haven't yet been told precisely what those commandments are! However, this places the rest of the commandments within the context of the covenant relationship. In that sense commandments one and two are introductory. Arguably, commandment three is too in its concern with the 'name' of God. However, one difference is that while the first two commandments are in the first person in reference to God, as if God is speaking, we find a shift in the third commandment to reference to God in the third person. We had the revelation of the divine name Yahweh to Moses in Exodus 3 at the burning bush. This is his special name (unable to be spoken in some circles). This commandment could be interpreted as condemning blasphemy and swearing. But actually within this context it is more about God's character and uniqueness and demand for respect from the chosen people.[16]

The fourth commandment concerns the keeping of the sabbath on the seventh day of the week and is positive, although it contains some negative prohibitions. On that day no one shall do any work, not even livestock, and it applies outside the bounds of the people of Israel to any resident aliens in the area.[17] Here we come across one of the main differences between the Exodus and Deuteronomy accounts. The reason given for keeping the sabbath in Exodus 20 is that God rested on the seventh day of creation. This takes us back to Genesis 1 and the creation of the world and gives the commandment a universal tone that the Deuteronomy account lacks. For in Deuteronomy 5 the reason given is remembrance of how God brought the people out of slavery in Egypt.[18] This, of course, links up with the way God is introduced in the first commandment. We don't really know how this variation occurred.[19] Certainly, both reasons are good ones and the tradition has combined them into one great act of redemption.[20]

The fifth commandment is the second positive one about honouring your father and your mother. It is interesting that this is given such pride of place. The reason given is so that 'your days may be long in the land that the LORD your God is giving you.'[21] This provides an interesting link-up with the patriarchal promise of land that was so strong in the Abraham tradition. In many ways this seems an odd juxtaposition. Why should respecting one's parents have anything to do with occupying a land? The link is again in the area of good behaviour which leads to good reward (as indicated in commandment two). However, it does seem a strained connection – almost as if a more general precept has been deliberately linked up with Israel's specific promise. When we generalize about the Ten Commandments and try to extract universal principles from them, the second part of this commandment is generally ignored!

The sixth, seventh and eighth commandments prohibiting murder, adultery and theft are fairly straightforward. As Barton notes, they do beg other questions. For example, if adultery is wrong, what about other types of sexual behaviour that might be similarly condemned (e.g. bestiality)? Murder is a straightforward category, but what about extreme violence in other forms and with drastic, if not such final consequences? And theft does not cover attempted theft. Other lawcodes in the Old Testament do expand things for us, and yet here in many ways the terseness begs more questions than it answers.

The ninth commandment is about bearing false witness. This sounds old fashioned to our modern ears and we may not be sure of its meaning. In a legal context it would be to falsify evidence. It might carry the wider connotation of loyalty towards your 'neighbour', whoever that might be. The tenth commandment concerns covetousness. One might argue that this is scarcely a crime as one can covet from afar, but that is not the same as actual theft. It may be a sin of the heart or mind, but it is in a different category to the crimes of commandments six, seven and eight. Perhaps nine and ten belong together as being more about good behaviour towards others than actual crimes, although bearing false witness would be seen in a court of law as a crime, and while covetousness could be a motive for crime, it is not a crime in itself.

In this final commandment we note another difference from Deuteronomy. Here the individual is enjoined not to covet his neighbour's house, his wife, slaves or animals. The house is placed in order before the wife, as the wife is regarded as part of the property. In the Deuteronomy version the wife is placed first and separately from the house, slaves and animals. Perhaps this tells us something of the changed status of wives by the time of Deuteronomy.

This commandment, perhaps more than the others, gives us a picture of the cultural context in which these commandments find a place – it emphasizes the priority of the adult male householder over his 'property', including his wife. We can extract the general principle of covetousness being a bad thing, but we may find the social structure revealed more difficult to engage with. This brings us back to the problem of the Ten Commandments being in part culturally timebound as well as having originated (and finding their emphasis in commandments one to four) in a particular faith.

So how universal and absolute are the Ten Commandments? They are a pointer in the right direction for most people and most societies, but we might wish to widen our search for a morality in the Old Testament that is less prescriptive. If we were to turn to the lawcodes of the Old Testament we would find them more specific and prescriptive than the Ten Commandments, which are statements of general principle. We might also find other laws on rituals even more culturally timebound.[22] Even though we separate out the Ten Commandments from their context, we cannot deny that they are part of a special relationship of a covenant between God and Israel. We have seen that the nature of many of them is specific to that religious commitment. Perhaps we need to move away from laws given in the context of Israel's particular story to look at texts that have a broader, more universal relevance, such as the wisdom literature.[23] Wisdom is a system of morality, but derived through perception, deduction and experience. Let us turn to its seminal book, Proverbs, to see if there is any mileage in considering this literature under our ethical heading.

## A Broader Ethic from Proverbs

Ethics is the science of morals in human conduct. The term is used within the discipline of theology to denote a particular area of study. Old Testament ethics is a subject in itself, too.

Many people come to the Old Testament looking for some kind of moral or ethical guidance – sometimes people with no religious faith still acknowledge the valuable contribution of the Bible to **ethics**. They may fear that some of it is out of date – and of course we need to reinterpret for our own time – but perhaps the best place to start for 'timeless' advice is in the book of Proverbs. Here we find 'pithy sayings' on all kinds of topics, from attitudes to work to how to handle money, from difficult wives to lazy servants. This is the wisdom of experience, passed down in the tradition from one generation to another. Such proverbial wisdom is found in many cultures around the world and seems to be a natural human preoccupation.[24] We find the image in Proverbs of life as a path which needs to be trodden: we all have a choice in how we follow our own paths in relation to our decisions at various turns and in our ethical choices.

Many temptations are out there – how do we steer a successful course? The answer given by Proverbs is that it is all about being 'wise'. Two women represent alternative paths: woman wisdom the path of upright behaviour and woman folly that of the wicked. One might object that life isn't quite as black and white as this, and that such a division may only be true in terms of totally good people and totally wicked people – and probably neither of them exists. However, there *is* something black and white about behaviour. We normally know – and our conscience reminds us – when we are stepping outside the bounds of acceptable behaviour. We *do* have a strong sense of right and wrong in our everyday lives.

Interestingly, in Proverbs as in the Ten Commandments, we find mention of adultery and theft, the honouring of parents and the dangers of envy. But the difference that a wisdom context makes is underlined by the way the topics are treated. For example, in Proverbs, while adultery is acknowledged as an enticement for a young man, it is described as a senseless act leading to destruction and the path to death with inevitable punishments – but it is advised against rather than legislated against. It is dealt with in Proverbs 6:24–35, for instance, alongside theft, which is mentioned in verses 10–11. In addition, theft itself is relativized here – stealing is not so bad if it is only to satisfy hunger – and yet inevitable punishment is acknowledged. There is a hint here that theft is not as bad as adultery.

Many topics are covered in the Proverbs. While the tone is sometimes admonitory – 'Do not!' – it is not quite 'Thou shalt not'. These are not edicts but choices, advice rather than laws. Each proverb stands alone and the treatment of certain key topics has a cumulative effect. However, sometimes the cumulative advice is contradictory because of the individual nature of each saying. Some proverbs are pure observation; some exhort; some state truisms, facts even; some draw unlike parallels say between human and animal behaviour or between human emotions and the natural world. There is a rich diversity of imagery and illustration. I suggested earlier that the best way to open the Old Testament in many ways is to launch straight into the text. But Proverbs may be an exception in that its character as lists of maxims can be somewhat wearying. Maybe that is why sections of Proverbs are seldom chosen for lectionary readings, because of their indigestible randomness. A thematic presentation would be more palatable to our modern sensibilities.

Particular favourite topics of the wise are work and money. Work is commended over laziness, not simply in relation to making money but in terms of a purposeful life. And work need not mean paid work, but any kind of fulfilling activity. Money is of importance to the wise as it gives security – they don't advocate excess, but they are very aware of the dangers of falling into poverty and of the threat that posed. Other major themes include the importance of planning ahead and the essential place of good communication. Neither of these topics are really moral judgements, but they are simply sensible and very true advice. The wise are interested in the whole range of human emotions – pride, anger, gladness, sorrow and hope – and in human relationships such as that of parent and child, husband and wife, friends and neighbours. Issues of authority, discipline, training of a child and care and respect for elderly parents all get an airing.[25]

## Proverbs 20

Perhaps launching at random into a chapter will give us a glimpse of the kind of text that Proverbs is. Despite the piecemeal character of any one chapter, such an approach will help us to appreciate the diversity of topics and styles of presentation – from moral exhortation to friendly advice, cheery observation and insightful sayings. Let's take chapter 20. It begins with a very familiar topic, as relevant today as it ever was – the dangers of drink.

We read in verse 1, 'Wine is a mocker, strong drink a brawler, and whoever is led astray by it is not wise.'[26] Many of us will have seen a drunken person out of control of their actions, perhaps shouting and picking a fight. Drink leads to a false confidence and anything done under its influence can be regretted later. The wise path is decidedly not taken by the drunken person. There is a lesson here for binge drinkers of both sexes today. Whilst this is essentially an observation, it contains an implicit exhortation not to overindulge!

The next proverb is about the anger of a king, which is likened to the growling of a lion.[27] This is really about anger and its effects, but anger is more frightening when it comes from someone in authority, so it is also about power. If a king – and for king read president, prime minister or anyone in authority – gets angry, he has clout and can make life very difficult for anyone who has provoked him! In past times such anger might have cost someone his or her life. The comparison with a creature from the animal world is lively and vibrant – the shouting that accompanies anger resembles the lion's roar. This is also an observation rather than an exhortation, although it may make us think twice about letting anger get out of control.

The third verse introduces us to a related topic – that of strife. Anger and strife often go together.[28] Here we are told that it is more honourable to avoid strife where possible – fools are quick to pick arguments and get into quarrels.[29] This is part of a wider communication theme in Proverbs – it is better to restrain oneself and keep a guarded silence than to get embroiled in a hasty and pointless argument. This is good advice for all.

The lazy person is featured in verse 4 in an agricultural image. Good farming depends on harvesting at the right time and that is often very hard work. The lazy person who doesn't do that is empty-handed. The consequences of this are not spelt out here, but the inference is that this is the road not only to stupidity and folly but also to poverty. No planning for another year would mean that no seed would be available to plant. Neglect leads to loss. The wider application of this proverb is the need for careful preparation and hard work in order to achieve one's goals. One might have one's mind fixed on certain goals, but getting there needs a good deal of hard work which cannot be shirked. Planning to achieve such goals rather than a vague hope that good things will come our way is a key message here.

Verse 5 by contrast strikes a more profound note – the human mind is complex and people's reasons for doing things are often impenetrable. The human mind is likened to deep water,[30] but the optimistic note struck is that the intelligent person can draw out (as one draws up water) these deeper purposes. This brings to mind the work of psychologists trying to draw out the profundities of a disturbed human mind. There is a practical aspect even to what is primarily a comment on human nature.

Verse 6 is a 'things are not what they seem' type of proverb: 'Many proclaim themselves loyal, but who can find one worthy of trust?' It is easy to say things such as 'trust me', but are we really trustworthy? There is a difference between having or nurturing a reputation for a virtue and actually practising it when the chips are down. This is food for thought – it is an observation, but one that challenges each of us to ask whether we are in category *a* or category *b*. The potential of human nature for hypocrisy is aired here. The next proverb in verse 7 provides a contrast to this pessimism about the human condition. It is made clear that there are people of integrity around, who set good examples for their children.

In verse 8 we are back to the king who sits in judgement over others and sees evil (probably in the form of evildoers) before him. The king or any leader is in a special place of authority, privy to information that others do not have and with responsibility to perpetuate justice.[31] The reference to winnowing refers to separating chaff and grain, driving them off in different directions. This proverb, again using agricultural imagery, is essentially a statement of fact.

The next proverb in verse 9 is phrased in terms of a question: 'Who can say, I have made my heart clean; I am pure from my sin?' It is a rhetorical question because the answer is 'no one'. No one is completely pure.[32] This may link up with the previous proverb in that the king sees evil before him and no one is completely without sin.

Verse 10 launches into the very different subject of diverse weights and measures. This is the oldest trick in the book – to sell someone a stated amount of goods, but actually to weigh less than the required amount in order to make money. Interestingly here God comes into the picture and this kind of practice is regarded as a direct abomination to him.[33] Honesty was highly regarded by the wise; dishonest communication and behaviour are condemned in the severest terms. Perhaps in these more religious admonitions we are starting to draw closer to the atmosphere of the Ten Commandments, although this is arguably aimed at a specific group of traders, demanding more honesty from them.

Verse 11 harks back to the theme of purity – even children are accountable for right behaviour and 'actions speak louder than words', to quote a well-known aphorism. Clearly, children need guidance – early formation and training along the right lines – as is evident from elsewhere in Proverbs, but once a sense of right and wrong is instilled in them, they are obliged to act upon it. This reminds me of crimes perpetrated by young children – sometimes even murder. One wonders whether such children have indeed been given any kind of moral framework as they have grown up. The proverb states that even children can sin – perhaps with the inference, how much more an adult?

Verse 12 is a truism – God made eye and ear – and is really a note of praise to God for the wonders of the human body. The right use of eye and ear may also be implied – the 'hearing' of wisdom is often enjoined in Proverbs.

Verse 13 returns us to the laziness/poverty nexus. A contrast is drawn between sleeping during the daylight hours when work needs to be done and hence ending up in poverty, and alert, open eyes that are awake during the day, leading to prosperity and abundance. Too much sleep is clearly a bad thing![34] This observation has a clear practical outworking.

Verse 14 reminds us of the diverse weights – another old haggling trick is to pretend that the goods are bad and get them for a knock-down price and then go away and boast about the bargain one has made. This practice is not commented upon here in moral terms, but I can't imagine the wise approving of it. Perhaps this proverb is essentially a warning to look out for crafty tradesmen, or maybe it is just a reflection of human nature that one person will try any range of tricks to outdo another, especially where making money is concerned. Maybe such wheeling and dealing is rather cynically presented as a simple fact of life.

Verse 15 comments on the plentiful nature of riches, but we can't buy knowledge. This might remind us that education more easily leads to social advancement, not simply wealth. This proverb doesn't disparage wealth, but it sets it in the wider context of education, which is perceived to be more precious in the long term (cf. Proverbs 3:15). Again the contrast within the observation suggests moral choices to the reader.

Verse 16 refers to the ancient practice of taking a garment as a pledge. This is rather like a deposit on goods or services. In this case the addressee is enjoined to take the garment of the person who has acted as surety for a foreigner. In a modern context this is comparable to loan companies taking some security, such as a house, on a loan. The second half of the sentence basically repeats the thought: the point is not to avoid the transaction completely – although the wise clearly thought that it was risky to underwrite the financial liabilities of another person – but to guarantee security for oneself.[35] There is a certain 'looking out for number one' mentality to a lot of these proverbs – here you need to secure yourself when dealing with someone who might have bad debts because of their dealings with outsiders.

Verse 17 could well be continuing the thought that failure to protect oneself leads to bad repercussions. The topic here though is deceit – one might feel rather clever at having got something for free such as bread, but it turns to gravel in the mouth as we start to feel guilty about it or we get caught – the precise outcome is not specified, although it is clear that there are going to be consequences. Generally, it is not a good thing to deceive others – that is the message of the wise here.

Planning is another important theme in Proverbs. In verse 18 the need to take advice from others is emphasized. This is particularly important when planning to wage war. This looks like primarily advice to kings and other leaders who would be in such a position, but it could have a metaphorical application to anyone confronting hostility. Strategy is also needed in daily life – planning and consulting are always key to any decision.

Another key theme of Proverbs is communication, which appears in verse 19 with a warning against gossips. Your secret is not safe with a gossip who enjoys spreading information[36] – this is advice, not a law, but phrased in the strongest terms of 'do not'! We have all at some time regretted telling someone information that has then been spread abroad by a gossip. Here the advice is to avoid such people.

Verse 20 echoes and reverses the commandment about honouring father and mother. The warning is that cursing either parent is a shameful act (cf. Leviticus 20:9). The imagery of a lamp going out is a powerful one, indicating misfortune and even untimely death. This proverb could be linked to the next in that the reason for cursing parents could be to do with wishing to inherit prematurely. Verse 21 airs the theme of wealth – the wise were against wealth acquired quickly (cf. Proverbs 13:11; 15:27). Here the referent seems to be one who lays hands on the family fortune prematurely. Inheritors can often be too eager to claim their prize. Divine blessing will be removed from such a person.

Verse 22 echoes the 'eye for an eye, tooth for a tooth' mentality known to us from elsewhere in the Old Testament[37] and emphasizes caution in repaying evil too quickly. Hastiness in thought and deed is warned against by the wise. Thoughtful waiting on the Lord (i.e. faith) is recommended.

Verse 23 goes back to the subject of false weights and scales in a virtual repeat of verse 10. It provides a possible motive as to why one might want to repay evil in the previous verse, if the two are linked.

Verse 24 returns to the thought of verse 22 in seeing our lives controlled by God who holds the real key to knowing ourselves – this echoes verse 5, but the interesting difference is that verse 5 is confident that humans can understand human purposes, whereas this verse prefers to trust that to God. The imagery of steps, paths and ways is found here, indicating the way God can give direction to one's life. It is sometimes said that the proverbs are rather secular in their concerns, but here we can see that there is mention of God behind the scenes, directing action and involved in human lives. The religious worldview permeates this book in a less 'historical' mode than elsewhere in the Old Testament, but it is there nevertheless.[38]

Verse 25 warns against false religious activity – hastily making vows before reflecting on what one is doing. Religion needs to be practised with spiritual concerns uppermost (cf. Amos' indictment of his society for going through the rituals of sacrifice without the accompanying heart, e.g. Amos 4:4–5). Calling something holy without thought is impetuous and unhelpful. In verse 26 we are back to the king who, as in verse 5, sees evil and acts in punishment against the wicked.[39] Again, haste is not recommended. These verses are presented as true observations in usual proverbial style which usually contains some moral bite!

In verse 27 we are back to God's direction of the human spirit, seeing everything, including the human body, inside and out. In verse 28 the king is praised – he is the figurehead of all that is good about society. There is perhaps an implication that God is behind the scenes giving him these gifts and upholding him. Verse 29 addresses youth and old age. The wise saw the benefits of being grey-haired in relation to experience of life – something we would be wise to acknowledge in our own time where the cult of youth is dominant. This proverb praises the strength of the young person and contrasts that with the beauty of grey hair. This is not to say that one is better than the other, but to stress the mutual dependence of the generations. This praising reference to grey hair is ironic in an age in which many grey-haired people dye their hair to look younger! The chapter ends on a rather disciplinary note which we might find unpalatable today – the idea that we are cleansed by a good beating (v30). Perhaps we should emphasize the fact that punishment in any form can be a cleansing experience in the long term, however hard it is at the time.

While we have noted the miscellany of sayings just within one chapter, quite a few of them are connected in subject matter, and with the occasional repeat. One would almost like to reshuffle the pack and put them in a more logical order. Some scholars have found more pattern in the chapters than others.[40] We have also noted the different styles of proverbs. Most of them are quite definite in tone, offering advice, taking their starting point from repeated observation and the experience of others, often with an admonitory tone such as 'Do not' or 'Take', sometimes pointing out the dire consequences of actions. The religious element is not lacking either – God is in control and understands the deep workings of the human psyche. Trust in him and you won't go far wrong. A good deal of the proverbs reflect the society of the day with its pledged garments and false weights, yet they are easily translatable into modern terms.

Proverbs provides quite a complex collection of advice that has a definite moral edge without being prescriptive. There is a certain 'take it or leave it' attitude – although you would be most unwise to leave it! This kind of presentation speaks to our modern world quite profoundly in an age when the individual and individual choices are prized. It is therefore a profound source of guidance for ethical choice – guidance based on ever repeated human experience.

## Solomon and the Queen of Sheba

Our famous character in this chapter is the wise man *par excellence* Solomon, together with his traditional sparring partner the Queen of **Sheba**. Traditionally, Proverbs is ascribed to him – we read in the first verse of the book, 'The proverbs of Solomon son of David, king of Israel' (Proverbs 1:1). We might wish to take this claim with a pinch of salt, as we did the ascription of all the psalms to David. Proverbs is widely acknowledged to be made up of various collections from different periods of Israel's history. There is mention in Proverbs 25:1 for example of the 'men of Hezekiah', a later king to Solomon, who 'copied' Solomon's proverbs. Another section (Proverbs 22:17 – 24:22) has very close similarities with an Egyptian Instruction (Amenemope), which suggests possible borrowing. This is interesting as the Instruction was copied within an educational context and might suggest a corresponding educational context for all or part of these Proverbs.

> **Sheba** is thought to be a country in south-west Arabia, possibly the Sabaen kingdom.

Nevertheless, Solomon must have had some connection with the wisdom enterprise.[41] It is likely that he opened Israel up to her ancient Near Eastern neighbours, so there may well have been Egyptian cultural influence in his court (cf. stories of the patriarch Joseph as the wise counsellor in Genesis 39–50). There would perhaps have been a blossoming of intellectual life which enabled 'wise men' to function at the court, possibly even a kind of 'enlightenment' as some scholars have termed it. This

**Figure 3.2**    Stone head of a woman from Sheba with her name written on her brow in the Sabean script. © Z. Radovan, www.BibleLandPictures.com.

**Figure 3.3**   Papyrus from the Egyptian Instruction of Amenemope (or Amenemopet). © The Trustees of the British Museum.

foreign contact might explain the visit of the Queen of Sheba to Solomon, about which we shall read in a moment.

The 'historical' stories about Solomon are contained in 1 Kings 1–11, with parallels in 2 Chronicles. I put the word historical in quotation marks because we have already noted the tension between history and story. There is a consensus of scholarly opinion that the account of Solomon's reign has been idealized by those writing it up.[42] We need to bear this point in mind as we approach the account. A great deal of this material concerns his building of the temple and setting it up in a proper way. This is not the part of the text that we will look at here, however. I want to focus on Solomon's reputation for wisdom and on his riddling with the Queen of Sheba. We will begin by looking at 1 Kings 3, 4 and 10 and then turn (in line with what we did in chapter 2) to the parallel account in the work of the Chronicler in 2 Chronicles.

Solomon's links with Egypt are made clear at the beginning of chapter 3 when he makes a marriage alliance with Pharaoh and marries his daughter. We are also told that the temple was not yet built, so that the people had to sacrifice at the **high places** around the land – former Canaanite shrines that often became hotbeds of either Canaanite or a mixture of Yahwistic and Canaanite ritual. We are told significantly in verse 3 that Solomon loved the Lord. In the language of the Old Testament this expresses his loyalty. In loving the Lord he is fulfilling the first of the Ten Commandments.

The **high places** are former Canaanite shrines, usually on high hills or mountains.

We are given a picture of a model king, walking in the statutes of his father (in fact, God's statutes according to David's charge, cf. 1 Kings 2:3) and sacrificing at high places to some excess. It is at one such high place, **Gibeon**, that God appears to him and asks what Solomon wishes to be given. Solomon asks for wisdom or understanding: 'Give your servant therefore an understanding mind to govern your people, able to discern between good and evil; for who can govern this your great people?' (1 Kings 3:9). This is a model prayer. God is pleased with this request. Solomon has not asked for wealth, as many might have done, or for longevity, but for wisdom. God grants the request: 'I give you a wise and discerning mind; no one like you has been before you and no one like you shall arise after you' (1 Kings 3:12). God then gives Solomon those very things for which he has not asked: wealth, honour and long life. When Solomon wakes up it has all been a dream – a pleasant one nevertheless.

> **Gibeon** is a city in the central hill country, south of Bethel and north of Jerusalem.

Immediately, at the end of chapter 3, we are given an example of Solomon's exercise of his God-given wisdom. Two women bear children, but then one of the babies dies and they both claim the remaining child as their own. One woman accuses the other of tricking her while she was asleep by placing the dead baby at her breast, which was not in fact hers at all, and taking her baby away as her own. It is Solomon's task to solve the problem. He calls for a sword and proclaims that the easiest solution is to divide the boy down the middle, giving the women half each. This drives the real mother of the living child to ask Solomon to give the boy to the other woman rather than kill him. The other claimant agrees to the king's decision. Solomon proclaims that the first woman is certainly his mother and that she should be given the child. This execution of justice stuns the people by its wisdom. Interestingly, this display of Solomon's God-given wisdom is not without guile – sometimes wisdom involves playing one's cards cleverly and carefully!

Moving into 1 Kings 4, we find an opening list of high officials for the organization of the kingdom which need not concern us much here, except that it shows the extent of Solomon's power and wealth and the sheer size of the state establishment he has set up. We will fast forward to verse 20 and the vision of contentment and prosperity of the united kingdoms of Judah and Israel – the people were numerous, 'they ate and drank and were happy'. We are told that Solomon was sovereign over the kingdoms from the Euphrates River to the land of the Philistines, up to the border with Egypt. This incorporated small kingdoms which were in a state of vassalage to Israel and hence had to bring tributes to the king. The food provision just for one day, as described here, is immense. This all shows Solomon's wealth, based on economic power over neighbouring states as well as over Israel. It was a time of peace and safety. Solomon had horses, chariots and horsemen – all adding up to considerable military might. We are returned to Solomon's wisdom at the end of the chapter, where it is described as 'vast as the sand on the seashore so that Solomon's wisdom surpassed the wisdom of all the people of the east and all the wisdom of Egypt' (1 Kings 4:29–30).

Egypt was the real centre of wisdom at that time, from whence many of our parallel wisdom documents – notably 'Instructions' – come.[43] There was also a wisdom tradition in Mesopotamia, which may be one of the 'peoples of the east'. We are told here that Solomon composed three thousand proverbs – many more than in the book of Proverbs (and hence an exaggeration perhaps) – and a thousand and five songs. He had a knowledge of nature, of fish and animals, birds and reptiles, and people would come from far and wide to hear him speak. This suggests that he had a kind of encyclopaedic knowledge of types of plant and animals (resembling Egyptian lists known as onomastica). It is implied that all this is the manifestation of God's gift to him. There is no criticism of him at all. All is rosy about his reign. It only remains for him to build the temple, which is the topic of the next few chapters.

We jump to chapter 10, which lists more of Solomon's great acts, including his commercial activities. We are now introduced to the Queen of Sheba who comes to test the king. She too is wealthy – she is very much his equal, which is unusual for a woman at that time. Solomon passes the test of answering all her questions. She is overwhelmed not only by his wisdom, but by

**Figure 3.4** Stevens's reconstruction of Solomon's Temple, showing pillars, vestibule and side storage chambers. Taken from *New Bible Atlas*, ed. J. J. Bimpson, J. P. Kane, J. H. Paterson, D. J. Wiseman and D. W. Wood. © 1985 Leicester Universities and Colleges Christian Fellowship, used with permission of InterVarsity Press, PO Box 1400, Downers Grove, IL 60515.

his temple and by his opulence. She tells him that he far exceeded her expectations and she blesses his God's choice of this magnificent king. She gives him gold, spices and precious stones (not that he needed them!), gold from Ophir along with almug wood,[44] musical instruments and so on. In return Solomon granted her every desire[45] and gifts in return. Then she went home. Her visit is chiefly intended to underline Solomon's wealth, power and beneficence, as well as his continuing and unsurpassed wisdom. We are then told of his riches – gold and ivory, some of which goes into building a throne. Gold seems to be the most highly prized metal here – even his drinking vessels were of gold. We are told that 'Once every three years the fleet of ships of Tarshish used to come bringing gold, silver, ivory, apes and peacocks' (1 Kings 10:22). Solomon seems to have been the first lover of exotica! Year by year his wealth accumulated – precious commodities such as silver and cedar wood became everyday items in Jerusalem. We are almost glutted with this description of his wealth – and does he never put a foot wrong?

Well, if we were to go on to chapter 11 we would see that one of Solomon's downfalls is his foreign wives, who lead him into worship of foreign gods, which is roundly condemned by God. We turn now however to the Chronicler, in which any criticism of Solomon is carefully avoided.[46] The account of Solomon's reign in Chronicles is dominated even more than the Kings account by temple-building, the direct fulfilment of the preparations made by David.[47] In 2 Chronicles 1 we read a similar tale of God's appearance to Solomon at Gibeon to ask him what gift he would like, together with Solomon's wise reply.[48] Interestingly, it is not presented here as a mere dream.[49] The story of Solomon's judging the two mothers is also omitted – perhaps because the Chronicler prefers to see the gift of wisdom with which Solomon has been endowed as channelled into temple-building and wise rule rather than spent on such trivialities! We are also given a few verses on Solomon's military and commercial activities, but in nothing like as much depth. Of course, for the Chronicler, the main focus is on Solomon as temple-builder – in which direction the military and commercial activities are channelled – and we launch into this description from chapter 2.[50] If we fast forward to the visit of the Queen of Sheba described in 2 Chronicles 9 and to the description of Solomon's great wealth, perhaps surprisingly we find an account almost exactly parallel in every detail to the Kings account.[51] The Chronicler chose here not to change very much – unlike his portrayal of David.

In some ways the Chronicler is our first commentator on scripture, even though his 'history' is itself part of scripture. This author is self-consciously using pre-existing sources, rearranging material, adding his own theological slant and shaping material according to his particular literary interests.

We start to find in the later books of the Old Testament more emphasis on quotation of earlier material. For example, in the book of Jonah there is much quotation of other texts, in particular in Jonah's psalm in chapter 2, spoken ostensibly from the belly of the whale.[52] Indeed, had there not been a canon that drew a line under additions, expansions, new books and so on, that process might have gone on and on. And in one sense it did go on and on outside the canon. The New Testament contains much material that is commentary on the Old and the apocryphal texts often take their inspiration from a canonical text. Fresh translations of the Bible in turn were a chance to interpret afresh – and some translations were closer to the original than others. Oral tradition expanded on stories, notably on the details that seemed to be missing. Within emergent religious traditions of Judaism and Christianity new ways of commentating on scripture and expounding its meaning for a new generation were found. This brings us back to the point I made at the beginning of this chapter about context – as time went on, the Old Testament was read and read again in ever changing contexts as history unfolded. And it goes on being interpreted afresh today. It is to that process that we shall now turn and continue to discuss in subsequent chapters.

## The Story of Job in the History of Interpretation

Over the centuries people have turned to the Bible for ethical guidance. While many Christians believe that New Testament ethics have relativized those of the Old Testament, parts of the Old Testament have continued to be read and followed. The Ten Commandments are a prime example. They are still found in service books today and are often written on the walls of churches.[53] In synagogues, they are usually depicted as two tablets, as indicated by the biblical account of Moses coming down the mountain of Sinai with the law (Exodus 34:28–9). The experiential wisdom of Proverbs has also passed into the folklore of many cultures.

However, people don't just come to the Old Testament for laws or maxims. Its stories are read over and over again as 'example stories' – those of faith, those of interaction with God and other people, those of interaction with the environment in which we live. Some Old Testament figures become examples that we might strive to emulate or people we might come to admire. One such is the character of Job as found in the wisdom literature of the Old Testament. The book of Job contains experiential wisdom like that of Proverbs, but it is presented in a completely different way, by means of a character who gradually learns through his experience of suffering and who is in a profound relationship with God. This is not just a good story about an Old Testament character – although it might be that too. It is a story that has rung down the ages as that of every person who has ever suffered and tried, in the light of that suffering, to hold on to a meaningful relationship with God. The suffering that we experience may be very different to that of Job, but in the end the questions we might ask are the same – Why me? Why should I continue to believe in a God who does these things? How am I going to cope with this burden?

Thus the Old Testament speaks to us, not just as a system of ethics, but as stories that teach us truths about life. The story of Job is one such example. Let us look at how it was treated at key points in the history of interpretation.[54] This will help us to get a feel of how our ancestors read the very same texts that we are reading today and what they hoped to get out of them.

In many ways the story of Job is about good behaviour. The piety of Job is stressed in the opening chapters – he was 'blameless and upright, one who feared God and turned away from evil'. He is in fact held up by God, in conversation with Satan, as a model of piety who loves God 'for nothing' (Job 2:3). At the end of the book this good behaviour is rewarded with the doubling of Job's possessions, a new family, longevity and many offspring. This story then would seem to be straightforwardly upholding ethical principles known from elsewhere in the wisdom literature and in the wider Old Testament. It is what happens in between the opening and the conclusion that throws a spanner into the works! Despite this good behaviour Job is put through trials (as a result of a heavenly wager between God and Satan) that test his faith to its limit. No longer does good behaviour lead to rewards, but simply leads to more misery, as one calamity follows another in rapid succession. First, Job's possessions and then his children are swept away in a moment. Job's reaction is most interesting: at first he seems to accept everything thrown at him by God (and Satan). He goes into mourning and says, 'Naked I came from my mother's womb, and naked shall I return there; the LORD gave and the LORD has taken away; blessed be the name of the LORD.' But then in chapter 3 he starts to rail against God for this bad treatment, cursing the day of his birth and the night that he was conceived. Three friends – and later in the book, a fourth – who ostensibly come to comfort him, tell him that he must have sinned and consequently is being punished by God, but Job insists that this is not the case and that he is blameless of any wrongdoing. The climax of the book is the appearance of God himself in a whirlwind. Although God appears in response to Job's plea, God does not answer any of Job's questions directly, but rather speaks of the wonder of the creative acts. It is enough however to humble Job, who says, 'I despise myself and repent in dust and ashes'. This prepares the way for restoration in the epilogue.

**Figure 3.5** Job comforted by his friends – an illustration of Job 2:13. Byzantine manuscript illumination, Vatican, Rome. Unusually, the fourth friend, Elihu, who does not appear until Chapter 32, is depicted here below the other three friends. © Biblioteca Apostolica Vaticana, Vat Gr 749, f30.

There was no question that this book should be part of the canon of scripture and so no debates raged about its inclusion during the first century CE when the Old Testament canon was finalized. It seems that early translators of the book were somewhat embarrassed by some of Job's more impious remarks in the dialogue with his friends and toned down some of the sentiments. The Septuagint – the translation of the Bible into Greek – takes the opportunity to do so and expands some omissions (for example, it plays up the role of Job's wife, giving her a name and expressing her sorrow at the loss of her children).[55] This expansion of the characters themselves and the filling in of 'gaps' in the text became widespread in Jewish and Christian circles, especially where knowledge of biblical characters was largely oral. Few people had access to the texts themselves and so their contact with Job would be through the liturgy or through folk tradition. We find an extensive 'Job tradition' that almost takes on a life of its own and starts to bear little resemblance to the actual book of Job itself. The most interesting aspect of this Job tradition is that it focuses on the story part of the book (in Job 1–2; 42:7–end) and generally ignores the dialogue. Thus the story becomes much more positive than the outline I have just given. The upright, pious Job is tested by God by the calamities that rob him of property and children, but Job's response, as in the prologue, is essentially a pious one: 'Shall we receive the good at the hand of God, and not receive the bad?' (Job 2:10). This response is then rewarded in the epilogue with the doubling of property and a new set of children. Thus Job becomes known for his patience in the face of suffering, as seen in the New Testament reference in James 5:11: 'You have heard of the endurance of Job, and you have seen the purpose of the Lord, how the Lord is compassionate and merciful.' This is supported within the Old Testament itself in Ezekiel 14:14, 20, in which Job is referred to as a 'righteous man' alongside Noah and Daniel.

Some past commentators seemed to have valued the Job tradition more than the original Hebrew text. Theodore of Mopsuestia, for example, disciple of Diodorus of Tarsus and teacher in the theological school of Antioch (died 428 CE) wrote about 'an outstanding and much esteemed history of the saintly Job, which circulated everywhere orally', a true history which he contrasted with the Hebrew book, which he thought a fiction composed by an author who wished to gain a reputation. He clearly battled with Job's speeches in the dialogue and found them unworthy of a man (i.e. Job) 'who governed his life with such great wisdom and virtue and piety'. We see here an early 'reading' of Job that disliked the unpalatable parts and so went as far as to reject the original text for a more favourable oral history. This shows us how selective people are about texts – they read the parts they like and cut out those they don't!

**Figure 3.6**  Statue of Sophia (Wisdom), from the ancient library at Ephesus.
© Iva Villi/Stockphoto.com.

An influential document on the Job tradition was the Testament of Job (probably written in the first century BCE), now found in the Pseude-pigrapha. This presents the story of Job as a last will and testament in which Job relates his trials to his children. Like the Septuagint, the Testament of Job embellishes some features of the original story, such as the role of Job's wife. More significantly, Job understands the reason for his trials from the start – there is no wager between God and Satan; rather, Job brought the suffering upon himself by antagonizing Satan. Job knows that while his body suffers his soul will stay intact and he learns from an angel that he will be rewarded in the end. Job's rebelliousness disappears and is replaced by patience and endurance. The roles of Job and his friends are reversed in the Testament, with Job advising them, upholding divine justice in the face of their doubts.[56] Job's charity towards others is stressed and he even becomes a musician in his efforts to cheer others up! At the end of the biblical book of Job, Job gives an inheritance to his sons and daughters. The Testament of Job gives it just to the sons, but adds the embellishment that each of the daughters receives a magical band, the very bands which God gave to Job from the whirlwind when he was healed (also an embellish-ment). This notion of magical bands and hence secret knowledge of God adds a new dimension to Job's wisdom.[57]

This image of Job as the just sufferer was a popular one throughout the Middle Ages and beyond. The rebellious Job was largely ignored or glossed over. The ecclesiastical Job tradition supported this emphasis, often seeing Job as a prefiguration of Jesus, the one who suffered for the sins of humankind but who was blameless within himself. One influential work from the Middle Ages is Gregory the Great's *Moralia in Iob*, a commentary on almost every verse. Here we find interpretation on various levels – a literal and historical one, and an allegorical one or a moral one. The alle-gorical level took the verse to refer to Christ or to the church. For Gregory, 'Job' signifies 'the sufferer' and so is easily referred to Christ. His exem-plary patience is the moral focus, while difficult verses are ingeniously explained away.

People had access to Job through the liturgy of the church. An abbrevi-ated version of Job, known as Little Job, became popular and is found in service books in the later Middle Ages in Britain and France, for example. Nine passages, all spoken by Job, are selected and there is no narrative. Here we have a first glimpse into the 'real' Job who laments in the dia-logue. In the first set of passages Job confesses that he has sinned and prays for remission of his sins. In the second, Job complains that he has not sinned and that God has been unfair in thinking so (close to the complaining of the original, although we find some toning down in translation into Latin (the Vulgate) here). In the third set the mood is one of repentance again, added psalms between the readings also stressing penance and trust in God's justice. There is then a hint here of Job's accusation of God, but within the overriding context of penance leading to God's grace.

Even by the time of the Reformation when there was greater access to the written texts themselves, the rebellious Job did not come to the forefront. Luther translated the book into German and argued that its theme was whether misfortune can come to the righteous from God. For him, God alone is righteous, but some people are more righteous than others. Job is a model of piety and even such saintly figures can stumble. Job is a man tempted by God, who nonetheless passes the test and is rewarded in the end. Calvin wrote many sermons on Job and so extracted from the book lessons for current morality. If a saint like Job needed to be rebuked by God from the whirlwind, how much more ourselves? A sinful person needs to recognize his or her inferiority and trust in God's goodness; humans should not presume to answer God, rather they should listen in fear to God's word.

Such emphases have changed radically in modern times, with Job the protesting, rebellious sufferer being at the forefront of interest. Carl Jung famously wrote of a God 'who does not care a button for any moral opinion and does not recognize any form of ethics as binding.'[58] He thus puts the blame for Job's suffering onto an immoral and unprincipled God. The focus here is on the God speeches that are seen simply to demonstrate the arbitrariness of God who is not really meting out justice and is scarcely in control. Karl Barth takes up this point about the character of the deity being open to question. He sees the issue as the apparent change in God – Job and his friends had expected a certain form of divine justice and Job receives something very different. Job is thus railing against the change in God, which leads to his being exposed to the blows of misfortune.

These kinds of interpretation have found a voice in the modern age when the mood has been one of questioning accepted values, questioning the existence and benevolence of God, wondering about humanity's place in the universe and so on. Job has thus inspired an existential play called *J. B.*[59] and other profound and questioning pieces. Each age has found inspiration in different emphases in the book. In the modern age, fascination with the relationship between God and humanity has dominated the discussion and opened up the real profundity of the book of Job. It is fascinating the way that different generations address different questions to the text and come up with different answers. Each reader of the text comes to it with different presuppositions – I read a piece recently that sees Job in the light of third world debt.[60] Feminist readings have taken a renewed interest in the role of Job's wife[61] and liberationist readings have seen Job as representative of the poor who suffer in a South American context.[62] Job has inspired playwrights, artists and musicians over the centuries and continues to do so today.

Each biblical book has its own 'story of interpretation' and we could have focused on any one. The interesting aspect of Job is that it has been read as an exemplary book in many contexts – but then in the modern age, it becomes exemplary of the questioner, even the atheist. There is thus a very wide range of differing interpretations of this book – more than you would find of most. The text itself is timeless, sufficiently profound to lend itself to many and varied interpretations. It can be seen as addressing the ethical question of 'good behaviour' on one level, but its ultimate challenge is much more profound – questioning the basis of the relationship between God and human beings in the light of suffering. Job asked 'Why me?' and he didn't really get a satisfactory answer. That may well be true for those suffering today.

## Job 14

I want to end this chapter with a taste of the text of Job, with an eye to later interpretation of the work. Let us 'open' Job at chapter 14. We may find the opening verses reminiscent of the funeral service in which they are quoted: 'Man that is born of a woman hath but a short time to live, and is full of misery. He cometh up, and is cut down, like a flower: he fleeth as it were a shadow, and never continueth in one stay' (Job 14:1–2 as cited in the 1662 Book of Common Prayer). Here Job is bewailing the fate of humanity in general, rather than just himself in particular. The context of the opening sentiment is that humankind is so insignificant and each individual life so short, why does God even trouble to take any notice? This is part of Job's complaint: he cannot get away from God's surveillance. The images of the flower and the shadow are conventional illustrations of life's brevity.[63] Verse 4 speaks of clean and unclean and was cited more frequently than any other verse in Job by the church fathers who wished to discuss original sin. The inference is that nothing is without sin and that hence no 'cleanness' is possible. Verses 5 and 6 go back to the theme of life's brevity with the added thought that God has determined the lifespan of each individual. Again, Job asks, why pay us this much attention? Why not leave us alone to enjoy our days?

The rich image of a tree is used in verses 7–12 with which to contrast human life. Unlike a tree, which, although felled, shoots again, we only have one chance at life and death is final. This has often been interpreted as discussing the issue of life after death. Perhaps as there is hope for a tree, there should be hope after all for humanity after death? We find images of dried up rivers and lakes as a parallel to a finished human life.[64] Verses 13–17 return us to Job's particular situation. He speaks of Sheol, the land of the dead where, it was believed, all went and there was nothing but a shadowy existence apart from God. Job wishes he could be hidden there until God stopped being angry or indeed until God remembered him. He raises the question of the possibility of life after death, but with the expectation of the answer 'No'.[65] Job then muses on how wonderful it would be if God were to release him from his suffering, call to him, long for him and not dwell on his sins. This perhaps reminds us of the Christian understanding of forgiveness in which sins are forgiven and forgotten. This is nothing but a dream though – the reality is that everything in nature is ultimately destroyed, and so are human beings. Even great mountains and rocks are eventually eroded away with the passage of time. He presents a very negative assessment of human life here – people do not live to see their children succeed, people suffer and who is there to care? Death itself can involve much suffering; dying can be protracted and painful and, above all, lonely.

## Wisdom and Law

In this chapter we have focused on the genres of law and wisdom in the Old Testament, those to which one would most naturally turn for self-help or ethical guidance. The essential difference between wisdom and law is perhaps that wisdom offers guidance based on experience but without obligation; law, on the other hand, makes specific demands of those within the covenant relationship. The law has a greater authority and affects how a person leads their daily life, and yet wisdom gives a richness that is lacking from simple ethical admonitions and a grounding in the reality of human experience.

We focused on the Ten Commandments as perhaps the most famous part of the law, maybe even as the best-known part of the Old Testament as a whole. We unpacked the nature of the commandments and their continuing relevance. We then turned to proverbial wisdom and its maxims, noting their range and diversity within a broader ethical context.

We considered the most famous wise king of Israel, Solomon (also credited with these writings), and we went on to look at another famous wisdom book, the book of Job, and its influence through the centuries. We see more clearly the richness of the Old Testament's literary heritage as seen in particular in some of the Writings. Diversity really is the keynote of this ancient collection of books.

## Notes

1 This recognition was described by Paul Ricoeur as the 'hermeneutical circle', whereby text and reader are in constant tension. See P. Ricoeur, *Hermeneutics and*

*the Human Sciences: Essays on Language, Action and Interpretation,* ed. J. B. Thompson, Cambridge: Cambridge University Press, 1981.

2  Thus we find certain texts favoured by different generations of readers that might be termed 'canons within the canon.' For example, in recent times a feminist 'canon' has emerged as a result of the viewpoints of this particular reader of texts.

3  Brevard Childs spawned the 'canonical approach' which prioritized this period of the selection of authoritative texts that would form the 'canon' and which argued for canonical readings that took into account interpretations from across the canon rather than simply in one text alone. See his *Old Testament Theology in a Canonical Context,* London: SCM Press, 1985.

4  See the fascinating discussion of the 'reception history' of the Ten Commandments in Scott M. Langston, *Exodus Through the Centuries,* Oxford: Blackwell, 2006, pp. 186–220. This Blackwell series focusing on the history of interpretation of biblical books illustrates well the renewed interest in 'readers' of all generations and how they interpreted texts.

5  J. Barton, *What is the Bible?* London: SPCK, 1991. Quotations are from pp. 94 and 95.

6  In Christian interpretation Jesus' summary of the commandments has often been seen to be an 'update' of the Ten Commandments, leading to a certain ambivalence towards them as an essential code. Luther apparently remarked in the introduction to his *Large Catechism* that whoever knows the Ten Commandments perfectly knows all scripture, but this was mixed with a certain ambivalence in his struggling to separate what was of universal relevance from the particularism he also found there.

7  On the varying approaches to the keeping of the sabbath over the centuries in both Jewish and Christian circles, see Langston, pp. 218–21.

8  The reason given in the text for honouring parents is 'so that your days may be long in the land'. This links the commandment specifically with the promise of land that forms the covenant with Abraham. This shows that the original context was quite a particular one, but that in the universalizing of the commandments such connections have been lost.

9  Langston (pp. 210–11) cites a disturbing 'expansion' of the Ten Commandments by white supremacists in the twentieth century, seeking to justify their racist stance. For example, 'Honour thy father and mother' is supplemented by 'at least enough to preserve the racial purity they have passed down to you'.

10  Source theory posits that the account of the Ten Commandments in Exodus 20 belongs to source E, the Elohist, with P, Priestly, additions, notably in the sabbath command; the account in Deuteronomy 5 belongs to the D or Deuteronomistic source. The original list of Ten Commandments was probably shorter than either of the present accounts, without the additional explanations found in some commandments (which often account for the variants between the two accounts, e.g. the reason for the sabbath commandment).

11  This is the usual view that most other lawcodes 'presuppose' the Ten Commandments, thus highlighting their status and antiquity. However, some modern scholarship has questioned this, arguing that they were a supplement and reinforcement of other laws and deal with matters such as sabbath-breaking that are difficult to legislate against. The individual emphasis placed the burden of obedience on each and every Israelite. If this is the case, it might suggest that the laws are not so primary as generally thought. R. E. Clements, Old Testament Guide to

*Deuteronomy*, Sheffield: Sheffield Academic Press, 1989, sees them as the product of the Deuteronomists in the seventh century BCE.

12 In both versions they are carefully 'placed' in order to form an introduction to other laws – in Exodus 20 they introduce the book of the covenant which contains detailed laws of both a religious and social nature and in Deuteronomy 5 they are used as a prologue to the Deuteronomic law, the first two commandments being particularly emphasized. Their loose connection to their wider context indicates an independent original (e.g. the Decalogue in Exodus 20 is only loosely joined to the narrative of the Sinai theophany by a general introductory sentence, 'Then God spoke all these words').

13 Anthony Philips, *Ancient Israel's Criminal Law: A New Approach to the Decalogue*, Oxford: Blackwell, 1970, argues that the Ten Commandments are indeed a lawcode, notably ancient Israel's criminal law. He argues that since the authority of God lay behind the demand implied in each commandment there was no need for the precise penalty for breaking the commandment to be specified (as would be usual in a lawcode). He argues that originally each of the issues covered by the commandments would have carried a capital penalty. Alt, on the other hand, believed that no special penalties for infringement of the commandments were listed because it was believed that God himself would act against the wrongdoer. See Albrecht Alt, 'The Origins of Israelite Law' in *Essays in Old Testament History and Religion*, Oxford: Blackwell, 1966 (German: 1953).

14 There is scholarly debate concerning whether the Ten Commandments originate with Moses. They seem to indicate a settled society rather than the nomadic one that would most naturally be associated with Moses. A distinction probably needs to be made between oral tradition which may go back to earliest times and the continuing relevance of these ten commands that led to their written form.

15 This is reversed in the exilic prophets, notably Ezekiel, who goes to great lengths to stress that sin is not transferable from one generation to another (Ezekiel 18), nor is 'righteousness' (Ezekiel 14).

16 Ezekiel goes to great lengths to emphasize God's concern for his name, which is one of the grounds of the desire to restore the people to their homeland after Exile. God is also concerned for his name in terms of reputation among other nations in the world (e.g. Ezekiel 37:28).

17 Mention is made in both accounts of 'the alien resident in your towns', which indicates a settled environment, not the nomadic days of the wilderness wanderings. This is one of the indicators that at least the written accounts of the Ten Commandments postdate the events that produced them and that they have been expanded from an original core that did not contain such references.

18 It is also interesting that Deuteronomy 5:12 reads, 'Observe the sabbath day and keep it holy, as the LORD your God commanded you', which uses 'observe' rather than 'remember' and also suggests that the commandment has already been made in the past by God (as reiterated again at the end of the command) during the actual exodus events (or is this an indicator of a later hand?). There is also more emphasis on the resting of slaves in the Deuteronomy command, which fits in with the general ethos of the book of Deuteronomy which advocates good treatment of slaves and which also fits with the emphasis on release from slavery as the reason for keeping the sabbath.

19  Probably source writer variation – if creation is a later tradition in Israel it could be that this is a P addition to the commandment. P would have been responsible for Genesis 1, too.

20  For Deutero-Isaiah the division of the firmament at creation and the parting of the Red Sea are seen as one event (Isaiah 43:15–17).

21  Interestingly, there is a slight variation in the Deuteronomy version which reads 'so that your days may be long and that it may go well with you in the land that the LORD your God is giving you' (Deuteronomy 5:16). This has the effect of detaching a long and fulfilled life from life in the land.

22  Barton notes that we tend in the Christian tradition to reject ritual laws and food laws, seeing them as having a place within Judaism but not within Christianity. He also points out that in an age where respect for the natural world is more to the forefront of our concern, there may be more relevance in some of the food laws than we had previously thought.

23  There was a widespread neglect of wisdom literature in the scholarship until the mid-twentieth century. See discussion in Katharine J. Dell, *The Book of Proverbs in Social and Theological Context*, Cambridge: Cambridge University Press, 2006, ch. 1.

24  Proverbial sayings are a worldwide phenomenon, with Norse and African proverbs particularly well documented. We also have many English proverbs that are still widely used and can be mutually contradictory (e.g. 'Too many cooks spoil the broth' but 'Many hands make light work').

25  For a full analysis of the main themes of Proverbs, see Katharine Dell, *Seeking a Life that Matters*, London: Darton, Longman and Todd, 2002.

26  Wine and strong drink (or beer) are personified here. They usually occur together as a pair. Elsewhere in Proverbs wine is a symbol of prosperity (e.g. 3:10; 9:6), although it is also seen in a negative light at other times.

27  Cf. Proverbs 19:12.

28  Maybe there is a deliberate juxtaposition of these two verses – anger and forbearance being opposites.

29  More honourable to whom? To society or to God? The message is 'better humility than revenge'. Cf. verse 22.

30  Some scholars see negative overtones here indicating a conniving mind. This would be more likely if the verse were part of a list of foolish types, but as an individual phrase it does not, in my view, contain such overtones.

31  Some scholars argue that heavenly authority is implied here.

32  With the possible inference that only God is completely pure.

33  This is true in all proverbs on this topic (e.g. 11:1; 20:10, 23). God is represented on earth by the king who actually sets standard weights and measures.

34  There is a link with the previous verse with the mention of the eye, perhaps linking up with the thought of the proper use of the eye in life. Sleep is often seen in negative terms in Proverbs, although it is also a gift (3:24). This reminds us of John Barton's comment that the Ten Commandments could all be kept by staying in bed all day. Sleep leads to the omission of life-giving words and deeds, although none of us could do much without it!

35  Some scholars see this proverb as sarcastic, actually saying that it is stupid to be responsible for a stranger's debts, but I see it as affirming the need for some kind of financial comeback.

36  The gossiping may be careless and compulsive rather than malicious, but it still indicates unfaithfulness to your secret.

37  Exodus 21:23–4; Leviticus 24:19–20; Deuteronomy 19:21.

38  For a full discussion of this point, see Dell, *The Book of Proverbs*, ch. 4.

39  The agricultural image of a wheel indicates a threshing cart that cut sheaves and separates the chaff and husks.

40  In general I prefer to take the proverbs individually, noting possible associations, particularly in style and language, but not being restricted by too much pairing and thematic association. Other scholars think differently. For example, see K. Heim, *'Like grapes of gold set in silver': Proverbial Clusters in Proverbs 10:1–22:16*, BZAW 273, New York: Walter de Gruyter, 2001. In my view, such linking tends to narrow their frame of reference and sometimes leads to seeing sentiments that are not there.

41  Solomon is also connected to authorship of the book of Ecclesiastes, the Song of Songs and the Wisdom of Solomon. The rabbis, in the Babylonian Talmud, regarded the Song of Songs as the product of Solomon's youth, Proverbs as from middle age and Ecclesiastes as a product of his old age (Baba Bathra 15a).

42  However, as these stories are part of the Deuteronomistic history, there are notes of criticism emanating from that particular redaction. See the discussion in Walter Brueggemann, *Solomon: Israel's Ironic Icon of Human Achievement*, Columbia: University of South Carolina Press, 2005.

43  See the discussion on wisdom in the ancient Near Eastern world in Katharine Dell, *Get Wisdom, Get Insight: An Introduction to Israel's Wisdom Literature*, London: Darton, Longman and Todd, 2000, ch. 7.

44  A fine wood, but it is not precisely known what type of wood it is.

45  There is a Jewish tradition that there was a child as a result of this meeting, so that 'granting her every desire' might have had sexual overtones.

46  For example, 1 Kings 1–2 and 11:1–40. Such omission is to stress Solomon's obedience to God's commandments (cf. 1 Chronicles 28:7) (something which Saul failed to do, hence his downfall). The reference in 1 Kings 3:7 to Solomon's youth and inexperience has been moved by the Chronicler to 1 Chronicles 22:5 and 29:1. The reference to not knowing how to go out or come in has been made into part of the request for wisdom and knowledge in 1 Chronicles 1:10. This is a good example of the ingenuity of the Chronicler in using his source.

47  Completion of the temple is one of the major conditions of the everlasting nature of the Davidic line. See H. G. M. Williamson, *1 and 2 Chronicles*, New Century Bible Commentary, London: Marshall, Morgan and Scott; Grand Rapids, MI: Eerdmans, 1982. Interestingly, the account of the building of Solomon's palace (1 Kings 7:1–12) is omitted here, perhaps to shift the focus even more onto temple-building. Small asides such as 2 Chronicles 1:9 ('let your promise to my father David now be fulfilled') make key connections between the two reigns.

48  The prelude to this account in 1 Kings 3:4 is here amplified into four verses (1:2–6) in which the king leads all the people in an act of worship involving sacrifice at an altar (cf. the temple), linking back to the depositing of the Ark in Jerusalem in David's reign (1 Chronicles 16:39; 21:29). The request for wisdom in 1 Chronicles 1:7–12 is considerably abbreviated from the 1 Kings account. Is this because the Chronicler was working from a shorter version of 1 Kings, was he was working from memory, or is there a more subtle reason for his treatment? These are the kinds of issues with which scholars working on Chronicles are wrestling all the time.

49   This omission may reflect later times in which such types of revelation were less acceptable (cf. Jeremiah 23:25ff.). The closure of the dream and Solomon's sacrifice in 1 Kings 3:15 are also omitted by the Chronicler.

50   Chapter 2:12 indicates that even Solomon's wisdom and wealth are most significantly channelled into temple-building – here, the royal palace is mentioned in half a sentence. In fact most of the Chronicler's rearrangement of material has that emphasis in view.

51   Small variations could simply be due to the mechanics of transmission of texts. Emphasis on 'Israel' is a Chronicler's theme and may account for changes in verse 8. There is also emphasis on Solomon's international esteem in verses 13–28. Critical material from 1 Kings 11 is again expunged in 2 Chronicles 9:29–31.

52   See Katharine J. Dell, 'Reinventing the Wheel: The Shaping of the Book of Jonah' in *After the Exile: Essays on Biblical History and Interpretation in Honour of Rex Mason*, ed. J. Barton and D. Rymer, Macon, GA: Mercer University Press; Kampen: Kok Pharos, 1996, pp. 85–101.

53   Whether or not to display the Ten Commandments publicly has been a debate in recent times engendered by the church/state tension. See the discussion in Langston, p. 217. Speaking about the American context, Langston notes that some believe that the public display of the Ten Commandments will help to strengthen morality, oppose evil tendencies in society and divert possible divine anger.

54   I shall focus here on Christian interpretation. For an excellent coverage of Jewish interpretation in general terms, see the chapter by Philip Alexander in *The Oxford Illustrated History of the Bible*, ed. J. W. Rogerson, Oxford: Oxford University Press, 2001, pp. 256–77.

55   It is the Septuagint version that seems to lie behind the 'Job tradition'. Many Christian churches would possess only the Septuagint version of Job. For a fuller discussion, see chapter 1 of Katharine J. Dell, *The Book of Job as Sceptical Literature*, BZAW 197, New York: Walter de Gruyter, 1991.

56   Elihu, the fourth friend, is demonized, almost replacing the role of Satan.

57   Cf. mantic wisdom, a branch of wisdom in which there is knowledge of hidden things, dreams and magical happenings.

58   C. Jung, *Answer to Job*, London: Routledge and Kegan Paul, 1954, p. 10.

59   Archibald MacLeish, *JB: A Play in Verse*, London: Secker and Warburg, 1959. In this play Job and his wife are the central characters. It is interesting how MacLeish has found it appropriate to emphasize the role of Job's wife and her equal part in the suffering along the lines of the earlier 'Job tradition'.

60   See *The Global Bible Commentary*, ed. D. Patte, Nashville: Abingdon Press, 2004. The article on Job is by B. A. Ntreh, pp. 141–50. I would criticize it for departing too much from the substance of the text of Job itself, using it as a platform for a wider grievance.

61   For a lively reinterpretation of the original prose tale, see Ellen van Wolde, *Mr and Mrs Job*, London: SCM, 1997.

62   Notably Gustavo Guttierrez, *On Job: God-talk and the Suffering of the Innocent*, Maryknoll, NY: Orbis, 1988.

63   The flower may also represent youth, which is short-lived too!

64   Possibly also a reference to the 'drying up' of the functions of the body in old age.

65   The Septuagint turns this question into a statement 'and will live' – a subtle, but consequential change.

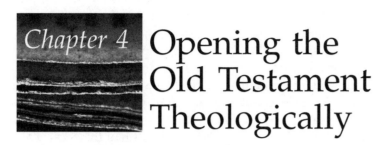

# Chapter 4 Opening the Old Testament Theologically

## Major Theological Themes

The Old Testament has its own distinctive theological themes. Whether it has one overall theology is debated and most attempts to find a key to this theology fail.[1] In this chapter I want to explore two of the major theological themes of the Old Testament, both of which relate to the God-human relationship, not forgetting the relationship with the non-human world, too.[2] I then wish to turn to the genre of prophecy, in many ways the most overtly 'theological' genre of the Old Testament, concerned with the ongoing and evolving relationship between God, the nation Israel and all human beings.

We have seen how a key aspect in approaching the Old Testament is recognizing that understandings developed over time, often in conjunction with the historical and social changes that were also taking place, but not limited by them. It is perhaps all too easy to extract the theological themes of the Old Testament away from their historical/cultural moorings and to consider them in abstraction. I shall attempt to stay grounded in the historical/social context of the unfolding of key themes, rather than treating them in any abstract, systematic way. Reading a text 'theologically' is to look at it with concerns about 'the word of God' foremost. Hence the focus is on what any text has to say about the nature of God and his revelation of himself to human beings and to the created world as a whole. Such a reading is informed by historical and literary concerns, but not confined by them.

In this chapter I will restrict the discussion to two major theological themes in the Old Testament, but one could easily consider others. These two are arguably at the centre of emphasis in the Old Testament itself and most sub-themes relate to either one or both of them.[3] When one starts to look into this issue, one sees how closely interconnected all such themes are and even separating out one or two themes is somewhat false. In a sense, theological themes are coming out the whole time as we consider the various literary genres of the Old Testament and as we consider its history – once again, we are back to the trio of literature, history and theology. However, if we are to be true to reading the Old Testament theologically, the one theme that we need to draw out is the God-human relationship. The theme of covenant does to a large extent cover that in both historical and theological terms, but we have already encountered the more personal engagement with God as found in psalms and the more rational encounter with God in the wisdom literature that indicates the potential breadth of this topic. One could focus just on 'God' and the Old Testament view of God in various guises as 'warrior' or 'hidden'; or indeed issues such as whether there was always one God or whether the Israelites ever believed in a pantheon of gods.

One might focus just on humanity, not simply in terms of being created in God's image, but also in relation to the human view of the world, as found in the wisdom literature, or in relation to experience of God through dreams, visions and angelic intermediaries. Alternatively, we might look at the relationship between God and the created world (and in some ways our focus on creation brings that into view), yet one could discuss this issue too in a wider selection of genres of material.[4] We might wish to draw out sub-themes that are important theologically. We might consider, for example, alongside covenant, the theme of election of the people of Israel to special privilege, a theme which draws out the particularity of much Old Testament thought and could lead us into problems when we consider the nationalism that this kind of stance generates. This might lead us instead to wish to consider universalism, a theme also aired in parts of the Old Testament.

Alternatively, we could look at a theme such as suffering, either of nations or individuals. As Job wondered, as we saw in chapter 3, is all suffering deserved?

I have chosen to follow a more genre-based procedure which may sideline some themes, but my attempt in this book is not to be exhaustive but to give the reader a taste of the Old Testament in its richness and diversity.[5] One might cover many topics, but that would lead to a much heavier tome than this one!

---

**Mount Sinai** is the holy mountain where God was believed to dwell. It is also known as Horeb. It is most likely to be equated with modern-day Jebul Musa ('Mountain of Moses') in the southern Sinai peninsula, by St Catharine's monastery, although there have been other suggestions as to its location.

---

## Covenant

We considered the Ten Commandments in the last chapter. They, of course, form an essential part of the narrative of the covenant-giving to Moses on **Mount Sinai** as related in Exodus. The Ten Commandments represent the 'agreement' of both parties. In the ancient world, we find examples of covenant treaties (e.g. from the Hittite civilization, in which master and servant would each hold a copy of the laws and seek to abide by them in order to ratify the agreement). Could it be that the two tablets of stone containing the Ten Commandments did not contain five on each tablet, as usually portrayed, but actually contained two full copies of the ten? Covenant is of course a bigger concept than a set of laws, but this expression of a relationship in this context between God and the people is fundamental to their understanding of their 'chosenness', which is manifested in keeping a particular set of laws and adopting a particular way of life.

It is often forgotten that God instigates covenantal relationships of various types. There is not simply one covenant in the Old Testament, but four and arguably five with the vision of a new covenant after the Exile. Each covenant has a different character and each of them unfolds in a particular historical situation, as presented in the text, and to that extent the concept is historically linked. However, the theological implications of covenant extend well beyond the boundaries of the historical events that generated them and the concept becomes a fundamental of Old Testament theology, a formal expression of relationship with God.

We have seen that there is a difference between how the Old Testament presents the order of events and how scholarship believes that they happened.

**Figure 4.1**   Mount Sinai (Jebel Musa), on the southern Sinai peninsula. The Arabic name means 'the mountain of Moses'. It stands at 7455 ft/2273m. © Kazuyoshu Nomachi/Corbis.

I shall begin here with the Old Testament's presentation of the covenant relationship and then consider what scholars have thought. The first covenant presented by the Old Testament is with the whole of humanity and the created world. It is the covenant with Noah in Genesis 9, the manifestation of which, after a few stipulations which can hardly be called laws, is the rainbow. This section of the Old Testament (known as the primeval history) in Genesis 1–11 describes the days before the start of Israelite history proper. Its stories have a legendary and didactic character that differs from the arguably more 'historical' presentation of much of the rest of the history. However, we have seen how relative 'telling history' is, and we are led to ask how far these stories differ in reality from those of the patriarchs, which we also saw to be selective and fairly symbolic at times. While we might not wish to take the account of the **garden of Eden** and the flood literally, they

> The **garden of Eden** (meaning 'delight' or 'luxury') is an ideal place, probably not to be identified in geographical terms, although some have tried to do so. The main suggestions are in Armenia in the north or Babylonia in the south. It represents an ideal place in which the man and woman are to live, tending the garden with light work and with a natural interrelationship with nature. There are comparable myths from the ancient Near East of an ideal land or garden (e.g. Dilmun from Sumerian culture).

certainly express profound and symbolic truths about the relationship of God with the created world and with human beings. These truths deserve to be taken as seriously as we might take other parts of the Old Testament.

## The Covenant with Noah

First, let us consider the covenant with Noah. We have just had the flood as a punishment for the sin that human beings have perpetuated (and it is interesting to note that the whole of nature suffers as a result). The survival of species in an ark is symbolic of the grace that God shows to animals alongside human beings. We need to open our Old Testament at Genesis 8:20, where we read of God's promise to Noah. This is the beginning of the covenant – it is entirely an act of God's grace that God promises never to 'curse the ground because of humankind . . . nor . . . destroy every living creature.' The rhythm of nature is to be maintained: 'seedtime and harvest, cold and heat, summer and winter, day and night, shall not cease.' There is a recognition here that the flood impinged on the right of the earth to exist as an independent entity quite apart from human actions – we might remember this as we dominate and destroy our envir-

**Figure 4.2** Mount Ararat, the traditional landing place of Noah's Ark. ©
Blickwinkel/Alamy.

onment. There is a recognition too that 'the human heart is evil from youth'.
There is a note of despair here that human beings are never going to be perfect
– they are fallen and sinful, as described in the account of the fall in Genesis
2–3. The promise to Noah is made in the context of sacrifice – the sacrifice
of animals leads to a promise to the animals and to the earth as a whole.

When we turn to Genesis 9, and to the covenant with Noah in particular, the blessing is first to him and his family. The promise of progeny is
high on the list, foreshadowing the promise to Abraham of descendants
in Genesis 12. Here we have a rather different slant on the relationship
between Noah – and by implication all humanity – and the created world
to the one we found at the end of Genesis 8. This passage stresses the
subservience of the animal world to humans and allows humans to eat
animal flesh. It is interesting that this is perceived as a falling away from
the previous state in the garden of Eden in which human beings were
vegetarians. This represents perhaps the gradual falling away from an ideal
– a recognition of the sinful nature of humans and an allowance of
domination of nature that wasn't the case in the harmony of Eden.[6] The
human control over nature is acknowledged here and from a modern
standpoint emphasizes our duty to use that responsibility well.

**Kosher** laws refer to the edict about meat in Genesis 9, which should not be eaten with the lifeblood still in it. There are also rules about not mixing meat and milk products.

From verse 4 of chapter 9 we start to get into the detail of the way meat should be eaten – without its blood, hence the **kosher** laws in Judaism today. We are told that this is because the lifeblood is sacred to God. This dictum is extended also to human beings – the lifeblood belongs to God, who expects something in return for it. We are not to take the gift of life for granted. When a human being takes the life of another, this will in turn lead to a corresponding denial of life to the perpetrator – this is the beginnings of the 'eye for an eye and tooth for a tooth' (Exodus 21:24) mentality that we find in the Old Testament. God is seen as a God of justice, demanding a 'reckoning' for life-giving gifts. The idea of reciprocity and relationship is here introduced. It is not only through an act of grace that God makes promises. God wishes allegiance in relation to respect for the creation of human beings. The climax is perhaps the repetition of the thought that God made humanity in God's own image (cf. Genesis 1:26–7). To spill the lifeblood of another is to offend against God whose image is found in each and every one of us. Verse 7 returns us to the command to Noah and family to multiply – God wishes human beings to fill the earth and use it to their benefit.

From verse 8 we come to the covenant proper. Here the focus shifts again to the animal world, which seems to be on an equal level to humans in this promise, despite the previous paragraph. The covenant is established with Noah and his descendants – the whole of the known human world at that time (or a symbolic representation of it). Then it is also made 'with every living creature' – birds, domestic animals and all animals. The covenant is with humanity that will never be destroyed again in its entirety by a flood, but also with the earth that will never again be destroyed, echoing Genesis 8:22. The sign of this covenant is the rainbow – a natural phenomenon rather than any human institution. This is to show its universal nature. The 'bow in the clouds' is to be the sign of the covenant between God and the whole earth.

Of course, we can explain the phenomenon of a rainbow scientifically nowadays and so it is only a symbolic covenant act. Yet there is a recognition here that it is at times when clouds come that the bow is seen. There is a primitive understanding of the processes of nature – ancient humans would no doubt have marvelled at the phenomenon of a rainbow and seen it as an act of God, just as the clouds and rain were sent by God. The rainbow is an act of remembrance by God of the covenant that has been made with 'all flesh' and is therefore the visible sign of God's covenant with the creation. Of course, the symbolic implications of this covenant extend well beyond the context of Noah and the flood. Given the likely legendary nature of the story, it is arguably the theological message that is contained in this covenant that is the most important factor. The message is that God has made a fresh commitment to the world. God created the world in the first place and then there was the fall and the recognition of sinfulness in the nature of humankind. In a sense this was a false start which then led to the flood as a punishment of that human sinfulness. Here, however, God is saying that never again will human transgression be a cause of their destruction. Perhaps the message is that God was putting humanity too much at the centre of God's universe, almost as if expecting too much from this creature made in God's image. Now it is as if the world is on a stronger footing with a proper recognition of the rights of animals and plants. They are still under human power, but God has made a fresh commitment never to allow their destruction (almost despite what human beings might try to do). The sign of the rainbow is a constant reminder of that everlasting commitment – it is thus a powerful sign or symbol of God's grace and of God's continuing watch over the world that God has made.

## The Flood Story in the Ancient Near East

Before we turn to other Old Testament covenants, let us pause for a moment to consider the parallels to the creation story in the Old Testament from the ancient Near Eastern world, in the Epics of Gilgamesh and Atrahasis. It is often forgotten that the writers and thinkers whose work came to be recorded in the Old Testament were influenced by the stories and legends that they heard around them. The flood story is not only contained in our Old Testament, but is attested to in various forms throughout the ancient Near Eastern world at that time. There must have been some kind of deluge for this image to have become so powerful. However, the ancient Near Eastern parallels, while fascinating in their closeness to the biblical account, particularly in the details, are also interesting in their differences – there is no covenant resulting from the flood and no moral obligation either. This opens up another issue of the relationship of the Old Testament with the world in which it emerged – many parts of the Old Testament are enlightened by such comparison and it is particularly illuminating in this area of primeval, symbolic happenings that illustrate fundamental truths about God, human beings and the world. And yet sometimes it is the differences that highlight particular elements of importance in the Old Testament understanding. Perhaps the biggest difference is the belief in one God as creator of the world versus the attribution of different elements to different gods within a pantheon.

In the Epic of Gilgamesh, a tale told from earliest times in ancient **Sumer** and Babylonia, there is a

**Sumer** is the plain that was the homeland of the Sumerians, north of the Persian Gulf. It is sometimes identified as the setting of the garden of Eden in Genesis 2–3.

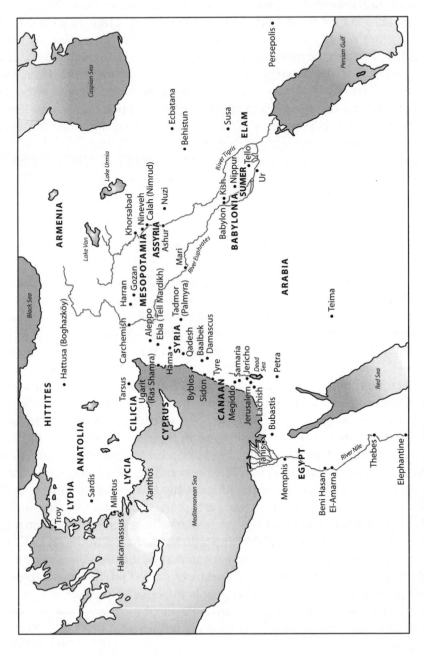

**Map 4**  The region of the ancient Near East.

pantheon of gods. There is a god responsible for sending the flood, for example. The Epic is much longer than simply a flood account. It tells how the ancient king Gilgamesh tried to win immortality. After many adventures he reached a distant land where there lived the only man who had ever become immortal, a man named Utnapishtim, the Babylonian equivalent of Noah. He told Gilgamesh about the flood to explain why the gods gave

**Figure 4.3** Tablet 11 of the Babylonian Epic of Gilgamesh containing the Babylonian version of the flood story. It is written in Babylonian cuneiform script and was found in the library of the Assyrian king Ashurbanipal (669–631 BCE) at Nineveh, along with thousands of other cuneiform tablets. © akg-images.

| SUMERIAN | BABYLONIAN | YAHWIST | PRIESTLY |
|---|---|---|---|
| Enlil decrees destruction of mankind because of their noise | Gods decree flood | Yahweh decrees destruction of man for his wickedness | Elohim decrees destruction of all flesh for its corruption |
| Nintu (Ishtar) protests | Ishtar protests | | |
| Ziusudra (Akkadian Atrakhasis) hero of Flood | Utnapishtim hero of Flood | Noah hero of Flood | Noah hero of Flood |
| Ziusudra's piety | | Noah finds favour with Yahweh | Noah only righteous man before Elohim |
| Ziusudra warned by Enki (Ea) in dream (by Ea through reed hut) | Utnapishtim warned by Ea through wall of reed hut | | Noah warned by Elohim |
| Ziusudra's vessel a huge ship | Ship a cube: 120 by 120 by 120; 7 stories; 9 divisions | Instruction to enter ark | Ark: 300 by 50 by 50; 3 stories |
| | All kinds of animals | 7 pairs of clean, 2 of unclean animals; Yahweh shuts Noah in | 2 of all animals |
| Flood and storm | Flood from heavy rain and storm | Flood from rain | Fountains of great deep broken up, and windows of heaven opened |
| | | | Exact date of beginning and end of Flood given |
| Flood lasts 7 days | Flood lasts 6 days | Flood lasts 40 days, retires after 2 (33) periods of 7 days | Flood lasts 150 days, retires in 150 days |
| | Ship grounds on Mt Nisir | | Ark grounds on Mt Ararat |
| | Utnapishtim sends out dove, swallow, and raven | Noah sends out raven and dove | |
| Ziusudra sacrifices to Sun-god in ship | Utnapishtim offers sacrifice on Mt Nisir | Noah offers sacrifice on altar | |
| | Gods gather like flies to the sacrifice | Yayweh smells sweet savour | |
| Immortality given to Ziusudra | Immortality and deification for Utnapishtim and his wife | Yahweh resolves not to curse the ground again for man's sake | God makes covenant with Noah not to destroy the earth again by a flood |
| | Ishtar's necklace of lapis-lazuli as sign of remembrance | | God gives rainbow as sign of remembrance |

**Figure 4.4** Chart of similarities between flood stories from S. H. Hooke, *Middle Eastern Mythology*, Harmondsworth, Penguin Books, 1963.

him his eternal life. After the story was told, he showed Gilgamesh that he could not hope to become immortal and sent him home.

Several details and oddities suggested to scholars that the Babylonian flood story did not begin as part of the Epic of Gilgamesh. Thanks to the discovery of another poem, known as the Atrahasis Epic, the story can now be seen in a different setting. Like Genesis, the Atrahasis Epic tells of the creation of humankind and its history to the time of the flood and the new society that was set up after it. In this story, Atrahasis is the 'extra wise' man who built an ark and saved mankind from destruction – he becomes Utnapishtim (which means 'He found life') in Gilgamesh, in which immortality is his reward. Here the reason for the flood is clear, which it is not in the Gilgamesh Epic: mankind made so much noise that the chief god on earth could not sleep. The gods, having failed to solve the problem in other ways, therefore sent the flood to destroy these troublesome humans and their overpopulating tendencies and to silence them for ever. According to Atrahasis, humans were created out of clay mixed with the blood of a dead god and their purpose in life was to relieve the gods of hard labour.

The similarities between flood stories (see figure 4.4 which amalgamates features from different epics) are striking. The Sumerian version seems closer to the biblical account (itself divided into sources J and P) and might suggest that this is the older common source, although the Babylonian version contains some startling similarities too (such as the detail of the types of bird sent out after the flood). One important difference however is the basic monotheism of the Hebrew account (i.e. one God, rather than many gods). The moral attitude is different, too. In Genesis, God punishes humankind for its wickedness. The reason for the flood in the Sumerian version (in the Atrahasis Epic) is simply the noise humans are making. Similarly with the creation of humanity, which has interesting echoes in the Genesis story. Their purpose is to give the gods a rest, while in Genesis God creates human beings to be in God's own image, to be fruitful and multiply and to enjoy life as given by God. It is only later that the element of hard toil comes in as a form of punishment for having tried to become like God. Mention is made in Genesis 3:22–4 of the tree of immortality, which is out of bounds forever. This perhaps has overtones of the quest for immortality by Gilgamesh.

## The Covenant with Abraham

The next covenant is that with Abraham as related in Genesis 12 and reiterated elsewhere. (We have already considered these texts in chapter 2 and so do not need to repeat them here.) We saw before how the two main elements of the Abrahamic covenant are descendants and land, which were important to these ancestors who needed to establish themselves, literally 'to multiply' and become a strong clan with a home of their own. God responded to such needs with an assurance of God's presence with Abraham and his family and in covenant relationship with them. God had no real reason to choose a particular family or a particular people to favour, but it became an important means of revelation of God's name, character and purpose. One might wonder how the God of the universal stage of the world and the God who made a covenant with the whole world via the rainbow in Genesis 9 suddenly, at least as the Old Testament presents it, becomes limited to a personal family deity.[7] This personal covenant could be seen to smack of exclusivism, but it is how the Old Testament presents the progression. One might say that it shows how God is both big and small – how God acts on a cosmic scale and on a very personal one. Perhaps God

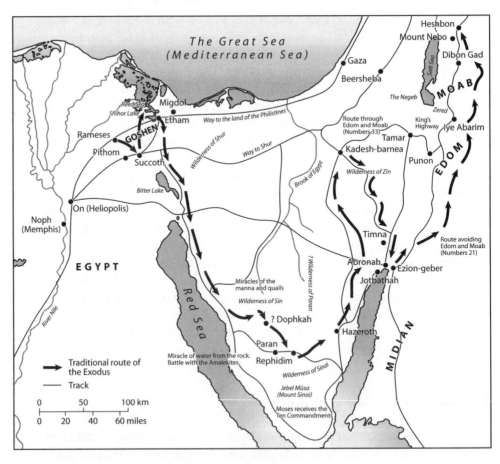

**Map 5**  Possible route of the Exodus from Egypt.

simply makes different types of covenant with different people at different times and we are wrong to seek unity in the concept.

## The Covenant with Moses

When we looked at the Ten Commandments we didn't consider the surrounding narrative of the law-giving on Mount Sinai. We will consider here the longer account of the event in Exodus rather than the terser version in Deuteronomy 5. Our account begins in Exodus 19 when the people of Israel reach Mount Sinai. This account reflects a fairly primitive belief in God residing on a mountain. Moses goes up and down the mountain to receive God's word. The first time God reminds the people, through Moses, of the actions of liberation on their behalf in defeating the Egyptians, saying, 'I bore you on eagles' wings and brought you to myself' (Exodus 19:4). This is a wonderfully rich image of God's protection and yet releases the people to a new-found freedom in relationship with God. Here we find an element of conditionality about the relationship – the people need to keep the covenant in order to remain the chosen people.

This has overtones of the lifeblood argument in the passage about the covenant with Noah, even though it is more particular to the Israelite situation. Mutual agreement and respect are the order of the day. An important part of this account is that the people be holy – 'a priestly kingdom and a holy nation' (Exodus 19:6). This is thought to be a post-exilic, priestly emphasis that has found its way into the account. The next section emphasizes the consecration of the people, washing ceremonially so as to prepare for the coming of God in theophany on the holy mountain. There are also rules about not going near the mountain on pain of death. We are given a frightening account of the theophany of God – thunder and lightning, thick cloud and a trumpet blast that made the people tremble, followed by fire and heavy smoke.

Moses still leads the talking with God and in fact is described as going up to the top of the mountain.[8] Moses is told at this point that no one can see God or they will die, even priests. Moses is then given the concession of bringing Aaron (who later becomes a priest and founder of a dynasty of priests) up the mountain with him, but no one else. This is the context of the Ten Commandments recorded in Exodus 20, followed by the law of the altar, laws about idols and sacrifices and by other sets of laws known as the book of the covenant in Exodus 21–3. It looks as though the narrative framework has been used for adding a number of early laws, in fact formulated once the people were settled in the land, reflecting an agricultural society and a primitive cult. Putting the laws into the framework of the Sinai narrative lends them authority and gives the desired impression of a historical 'moment' of authoritative law-giving.

At the end of the laws the promise of land in Canaan is reiterated (Exodus 23:20ff.) and then we are returned to the narrative. It seems from Exodus 24 that Moses goes up the mountain three more times – or perhaps this repetition is better explained by Pentateuchal source theory that suggests that three different writers wrote of one event from three different angles, hence the three accounts (in 24:9–11 (source E), 24:12–14 (source J) and 24:15–18 (source P) according to traditional designations by scholars). In the light of such a theory, Exodus 24:1–2 looks like an attempt by a redactor seeking to harmonize the chapter to explain the disagreement of the three accounts as to who goes up the mountain. One account (24:9–11) suggests that Moses, Aaron, Nadab and Abihu and seventy elders of Israel go up; another that Moses accompanied by Joshua went up (24:12–14) and the third that just Moses went into a cloud alone (24:15–18). The redactor therefore tells us that although many went up the mountain, only Moses came near the Lord.

Thus, verses 9–11 state not only that a whole party went up, but that they 'saw' the God of Israel – this contradicts what was said previously about not being allowed to see God or else they might perish. We are told that they saw with clarity a pavement of sapphire stone at his feet. It is stressed that God did not touch them, but the 'chief men' of Israel saw God and ate and drank together with God in hearty companionship. In verses 12–14 the LORD (note the change from the God of Israel)[9] asks Moses to come up (seemingly again) specifically for the tablets of stone. Joshua accompanies him. Moses tells the elders to stay where they are (presumably at the foot of the mountain) and lead the people. Then from verse 15 we have a third trip up the mountain and this time the cloud covering the mountain for six days is emphasized. On the seventh day (perhaps recalling the sabbath day) God calls Moses out of the cloud and we are given details of the strange fiery presence of the Lord on the mountain. Moses duly enters the cloud and we are told he remains on the mountain for forty days and nights (thought to be symbolic numbers).[10]

The covenant with Moses is essentially about the giving of the law, but there are other important elements in the Sinai account. One of them is the **theophany** of God and the nature of God's presence with the people. Another is the prescription concerning fitness and holiness and readiness to receive the presence of God. This relationship is not simply with one man – although Moses has the special honour of seeing God and being in close conversation with God. We are reminded of Exodus 3 where he 'saw' God in a burning bush and God revealed his

---

**Theophany** is a manifestation of God, often expressed in the Old Testament in terms of God's appearance in burning bush or whirlwind.

name, Yahweh. The special relationship is with the people of Israel in their state of nomadic existence in the wilderness, and yet it transcends that historical situation to become norm-ative for the people in their later life in the land – hence the laws that pertain to that later period. The element of conditionality is interesting – God acts out of grace. God set the people free from Egyptian tyranny out of grace, and yet demands something in return. If God does not receive the allegiance and obedience desired, there may be consequences. This becomes important later on as the people seek to understand why they were sent into Exile.

## The Covenant with David

The next covenant in the Old Testament is with King David, recorded in 2 Samuel 7.[11] This covenant is really about the final establishment of kingship in Israel under David. There had been a false start under Saul and now some stability is needed for the institution, which, after all, was somewhat of a 'test' in Israel, which had formerly been ruled by Judges and prophets such as Samuel (1 Samuel 8). There were elements of opposition to the establishment of the institution in the first place. In 2 Samuel 7 the Davidic covenant joins the others to be ratified by God in establishment of David's line. It is thus a promise to David and his descendants in much the same manner as the Abrahamic covenant, but here with the duty of rule.

We are told that only when David is 'settled in his house' and at rest from his enemies that the covenant moment arrives. This is mediated through God's prophet Nathan, which is perhaps symbolic of the transfer of power, just as Samuel originally anointed Saul. It is clear from David's opening question that he is concerned about the building of the temple, and this of course is an essential part of the establishment of a kingship – that it should be accompanied by a suitable and permanent temple. The Ark, which represents the presence of God, resides in a tent while the king enjoys the benefits of settled living in a 'house of cedar'.[12] God responds that David has rightly sensed his desire for a proper dwelling place. Then we move swiftly on to God's election of David. Again, we get a sense of God's gracious purpose – God took David 'from following the sheep to be prince over my people Israel' (2 Samuel 7:8; cf. Amos 7:15). God stresses the gracious care of David and his guidance of events so that David has had nothing but success in overcoming his enemies.

God promises to make David's name great. But David's role is as king of his people and so the promise to David is equally to the people – they too will be established, settled and free of fear of enemies. We are given a reminder of the time of the Judges when the Philistines were constantly posing a threat. The next promise is of not only descendants as to Abraham, but a dynasty or 'house' for eternity. This is some promise! The context of relationship is quickly spelt out, however. 'I will be a father to him and he shall be a son to me' (2 Samuel 7:14). Kingship is the closest thing to being God's son – God's representative on earth and in the closest relationship to God.[13] This is election to a great privilege and yet the note of caution is not far behind: iniquity will be punished. However, this time, unlike for Saul, any iniquity will not break the covenant. This is a major difference to the covenant with Moses, which we noted was conditional. The Davidic covenant, like the Noachic and Abrahamic, is forever and nothing David and his descendants will do – and some of them are a pretty 'heathen' crew – will overturn it. Of course, when the dynasty did effectively end at the Exile this posed a problem for the people – that is perhaps why Davidic hopes were kept alive and became merged with messianic ones.

David's response is one of humility and he wonders why such favour has been placed upon him. He quickly takes up the task of temple-building. He reasserts the greatness of God, a God above all other, the guardian of a nation like no other in the way God has saved them from their enemies. He states the everlasting nature of the relationship between God and the people of Israel. David speaks many laudatory words here, but he is almost overcome by the situation and doesn't know what more he can say. He is overawed by God's generosity in the choice of his dynasty and his people.

## Covenant as Relationship in the Prophets

There are other expressions of 'covenant' in the Old Testament in terms of relationship.[14] For example, Hosea the prophet speaks of a marriage between God and Israel that has been seen as formative of the richer understanding and outworking of the covenant idea.[15] Perhaps most famously, the exilic prophets Jeremiah and Ezekiel speak of a 'new covenant' arising out of the ashes of the old. 'They shall be my people and I will be their God', says Jeremiah (7:23). At the Exile the old institutions were lost; there was no longer a monarchy or a temple, and seemingly no covenant. These prophets stressed that God had judged Israel and sent the leaders of the nation into exile just because they had not kept their side of that fragile, conditional bargain. But as the Exile progressed and hope started to flower that maybe that was not the end of the relationship, these prophets started to speak of a new covenant, one that would not be written on tablets, but directly on the heart of each and every person (Jeremiah 24:7). This would be a covenant of pure grace – not because of any good in the people that might lead God to want to restore them, but simply because God wishes after all to maintain that relationship. Former covenants are displaced by this new covenant – and yet the Davidic one stays a distinctive promise to a particular dynasty and so survives in a rather different form.

## Scholarly Evaluations of Covenant

We have looked at the actual covenants contained in the Old Testament. Now we might want to ask how scholars have evaluated them. In relation to times of writing, we have just seen in the context of the covenant with Moses how some elements of the account of the ascent of Mount Sinai seemed to indicate the concerns of a later age – and in fact how there was little attempt to cover that up. If scholarship is correct in positing a Priestly strand in the Pentateuch – a kind of post-exilic redaction (or source) wishing to update older material for a later audience – then that might explain some of those additions, notably the emphasis on holiness and on priesthood.

Rather as we saw the Chronicler rewriting history from his own perspective, so too the Priestly author/redactor may well have added his own material and perspective.[16] In this context it is often thought that the covenant with Noah – the first covenant, as the Old Testament presents it – is probably later and from the Priestly pen. There may well have been an ancient story that lies beneath the account (part of the flood account is attributed to an earlier source writer (J) possibly from the early monarchic period), but the stipulations about meat-eating and the universalism of the covenant may well belong to a time when those perspectives were becoming more widespread. This would in some ways give us a better explanation of that 'jarring' we noted when we considered the transition from the universal covenant through Noah and the rather particularistic covenant with Abraham.

What if the covenant with Abraham came first and the notion of relationship gradually deepened and widened to include first the whole people at Sinai, then the king as leader of a nation, and finally the whole world? This development in its gradual opening out would seem to make sense.[17] Scholars also believe that although early Israel did have ideas about God as creator, a kind of full-blown working out of God as creator and what that meant for Israel may have been a later development. If that is the case the Noachic covenant might well find its most significant point of development in the post-exilic period when Israel was a vassal to a larger power and started to realize that its God was not just the God of one nation but the God of all nations, with a universal purpose for the world.

## Creation

The covenant with Noah and the created world shifts our focus to another great Old Testament theme, that of creation. The Old Testament famously opens with an account of creation and those opening chapters have been the most influential in thought about this concept over the centuries. However, there are also other types of literature in the Old Testament that mention God's creative act: wisdom literature, for example, portrays God as creator above any other depiction and provides us with a rival set of chapters to Genesis 1–2.

A particular example is the account contained in Job 38–9 where God appears in a theophany to answer Job and speaks of the wonder of the acts of creation, first the created order but then, notably, the creation of all different kinds of animals – mountain goats, wild oxen and asses, ostriches, horses, hawks and eagles. There are some psalms too that are dominated by the thought of creation, notably Psalm 104 and parts of Psalms 74 and 89. Creation features in some prophets alongside the salvation history, as we shall note below. However, the most famous passages are in Genesis 1–2, which are still discussed today in arguments about creation and evolutionary theory. We need also to bear in mind the ancient Near Eastern background of creation myths that may have influenced the formulation of this Israelite version of how the world was made (see figure 4.4).

What we have in the opening chapters of Genesis is creation by word. God speaks and the different creative acts come into being. God is seen to pre-exist the created world – it is a formless void until God causes a wind to sweep over the face of a watery chaos.[18] God creates order out of disorder, imposing form on chaos. There are eight creative acts performed over six days.[19]

First there is light versus darkness, day and night. Then there is the separation of the waters of chaos into sky and sea. The appearance of dry land is next, followed by vegetation. The creation of sun, moon and stars is then described. This account is all about distinction between opposites. There is a poetic quality to the piece with the repetition of 'let there be' and 'there was evening and there was morning'.[20] The goodness of creation is also stressed by the repeated phrase 'And God saw that it was good'.

Next come the living creatures in the sky and in the sea, followed by land animals. Finally, at the climax to the account, is the creation of humankind 'in our image'. That humans are made in the image of God is repeated. We also find the differentiation between the sexes: 'male and female he created them' (Genesis 1:27).[21] The humans are to have 'dominion' over the animals, rather as in Genesis 9. However, dominion does not mean exploitation, but is rather to be seen as election to a responsibility for all living creatures.

Following the creation of man and woman is the charge to 'be fruitful and multiply', rather along the lines of the covenant with Abraham. Progeny and descendants are very important for the Old Testament writers. At this point it is just plants that are given for food – an edict that is to change later on after the Flood, as we have seen. At the climax of creation we are told that everything was 'very good' and God was able to rest from the work of creation on the seventh day, which was especially blessed.

We have now moved into Genesis 2. In most Bibles you will find a break here in verse 4 and even occasionally a heading such as in the NRSV: 'Another Account of the Creation'. This reflects the consensus of scholarship that there are actually two accounts of creation contained in the early chapters of Genesis, suggesting two different source writers and (perhaps more significantly) two different worldviews. The account that we have just looked at is actually thought to be the later of the two, with the one in Genesis 2:4bf. as the more primitive. Many scholars believe that a fully developed view of creation might have been a later development in Israelite thought. If this first account is from the exilic period, for example, it would represent a later reflection on the way creation happened. It would also explain the contradictions between one account and another.[22]

The second creation account begins with 'the day that the Lord God made the earth and the heavens' before there was any vegetation on the earth. There is no overcoming of the waters of chaos. Rather, the earth is dry until God causes rain to come and vegetation to come to life.[23] There is no one to till the ground until God forms man. The man is formed from dust and God breathes life into his nostrils.[24] Place then becomes important as a garden is created in which the man can live. This is the garden of Eden, full of lush trees. We are told here that there are two particular trees: the tree of life and the tree of the knowledge of good and evil. This sets the scene for what is to happen later on at the fall, when the tree of the knowledge of good and evil will come centre stage as the cause of temptation. The tree of life represents eternal life, which we are told later on is especially guarded after the fall in order to prevent the human beings from seeking to attain it. It is interesting that such a desire is in humanity even now and that the biblical authors recognized it.

In the parallel creation accounts from the ancient Near East, eternal life features more strongly than in the Old Testament account (e.g. in the Epic of Gilgamesh). This second account of creation is much more localized in scope and less cosmic. It centres on human beings in relation to their immediate environment – in this case, an ideal garden.[25] At this point there is just one human being, who is a man. A river is described as going through the garden and then opening out into the four great rivers of the local area.[26] This account is also more geared into storytelling, which we have seen is a keynote of the presentation of Old Testament history. We have another mention of the tree of the knowledge of good and evil – on being given the garden to till. It is important to note that living in Eden is not just about putting one's feet up! Adam is instructed that he should not eat from that tree or else he will die. God then decides to create a 'helper' for man, but before doing so God allows the man to name all the animals. We are told that none of these was a suitable partner for him and so God created woman from Adam's rib. On seeing the woman Adam recognizes his own kind and he names her Woman. We are then given the reason that a man leaves his father and mother and is married – they are 'one flesh together', i.e. united in a bond of flesh.[27] There is a lack of equality in this account that possibly reflects a patriarchal bias.[28]

We all know how the story continues with Adam and Eve, tempted by the serpent, eating of that forbidden tree. The serpent tells them that they will not die but their eyes will be opened.[29] The first sign of this opening of their eyes is in fact their shame at being naked. God is described in Genesis 3 (and indeed in Genesis 2.4bf.) in quite anthropocentric terms. God places the man in the garden. God is concerned for man's loneliness. God puts the man to sleep and performs the rib operation. God walks in the garden at the time of the evening breeze and calls to the man and the woman. God speaks to them freely. However, the result of eating the tree is disastrous. First, the serpent is condemned. We are then given the reason that women suffer pain in childbirth, the reason for their subservience to men, the reason men have to toil in an inhospitable earth in the quest for food to keep alive, and the reason that human beings die. This is a string of explanations for why human life is as it is – and animal life in relation to serpents. But then at the end of this condemnation God shows grace in clothing the pair. It is at that point that there is mention of the tree of life – that other tree that would make human beings live forever. This tree is then carefully guarded by the cherubim.

This second account has many differences from the first. God is portrayed in much more human terms, and the whole scene is more local and more human-centred without the cosmic scope of the other account. The name for God is LORD God, whereas in Genesis 1 it is simply God. These differences have led to a widespread consensus that what we have here is the tradition remembering creation in two different ways and presenting both versions. This seems to be the style of the writers or editors of the time – they tend to conflate two accounts rather than merge them or cut one out as we might do. This gives us a unique insight into how the text probably came to be as it is today. These two accounts do not detract from the fact of creation, but they probably show that ideas did develop over time, just as with covenant. If the 'full blown' creation doctrine is later, then the first account in Genesis 1, thought to be from the Priestly writer at the time of the Exile, would make sense in that line of development. The earlier account (Genesis 2:46) – probably written by J (the Jahwist) in the monarchic period[30] – would then belong to a stage in which God's actions in relation to the creation of humanity and the earth were the focus, with a particular interest in explaining the reasons for human hierarchies and facts about human life such as death, toil, pain and so on.

This distinction between accounts done on a literary level – but with the thought that earlier traditions might well be contained in each of the 'sources'[31] – raises the question of historicity. This question is raised more sharply in this section of the Old Testament in that it is a kind of pre-history before history proper begins, supposedly with Abraham. There is much in Genesis 1–11 about genealogies – trying to trace the generations from Adam to Abraham and see it all as a continuity, with world history and Israelite history thus united into one story and creation brought into line with salvation history. This is an attempt to place a historical pattern upon the material, and yet the character of the material is more legend and origin story than actual historical information. The parallels with the ancient Near East highlight that impression and yet, as with the flood, the differences also show the distinctiveness of the Israelite view of God as one and of God's relationship with the world that he made.

The evidence from the Old Testament of a quite widespread interest in creation indicates to me that ideas about God as creator circulated from earliest times. This was the understanding of God shared by the cultures around Israel, albeit in terms of many gods. It seems inconceivable that in turn Israel would not have had her own ideas about God as creator. The understanding of what that meant particularly in relation to Israel's own salvation history seems to have developed over time, but we would be wrong to deny creation its proper place alongside covenant as a formative doctrine in the Old Testament thought-world. The wisdom literature demonstrates that from earliest times people were maxim-making about the world and saw God as creator within that framework.[32] They were also expressing human relationships in terms of animal behaviour (e.g. sluggards and ants) and even expressing the call to young men to gain wisdom through the medium of a female figure who was present during God's creative act, so linking wisdom to creation itself (Proverbs 8). Such descriptions come to a climax in the book of Job with the awe-inspiring description in the speeches of God (chapters 38–41) of the wild creatures that God has made. These included the Behemoth and the Leviathan, which may denote the hippopotamus and crocodile, or may refer to mythological beasts which God defeated in primeval times, according to the pattern of other primitive creation texts from surrounding cultures. Creation therefore takes its place alongside covenant as a major and formative theological theme of the Old Testament. Both themes feature strongly on the thought of the prophets of the Old Testament to whom we shall turn in the next section. Particularly at the time of the Exile, when new theological understandings were called for at a time of crisis, prophecy came into its own in shaping such fresh ideas.

## The Prophets as Theologians

The prophets are perhaps the greatest theologians of the Old Testament. They provide us with a good example of messages that arose in particular historical contexts, but which were not bound by those contexts.[33] The message of each prophet lifts off the historical plane onto a theological one which makes the message timeless and relevant to differing historical and social situations and to ethical concerns.[34] There is a literary dimension to this too, because those who preserved the prophetic books realized that ongoing relevance and before the closing of the canon shaped older material and added material from their own time to the prophecies themselves. We also have examples of one prophecy being added on to another, for example in the case of Isaiah in whose book we have at least two prophecies dating from different periods and with completely different theological emphases (possibly even three).

   Prophecy first emerges with great figures such as Samuel (who is both priest and prophet), Elijah and Elisha. We can learn about them from the books of Samuel and Kings, which is why these books (along with the rest of the Deuteronomistic history) are traditionally known as the former

| LIST OF MINOR PROPHETS (THE BOOK OF THE TWELVE) |
| :---: |
| Hosea |
| Joel |
| Amos |
| Obadiah |
| Jonah |
| Micah |
| Nahum |
| Habakkuk |
| Zephaniah |
| Haggai |
| Zechariah |
| Malachi |

prophets. Moses has also traditionally been seen as a prophet, although it is arguable that this was an honorific title for him assigned by a later time that wished to stress his authority and significance. We also find in the Old Testament a number of prophetic books (these would each have a match-box on our colour scheme). We find a number of long prophetic books – Isaiah, Jeremiah and Ezekiel – and also twelve 'minor prophets', all of which are considerably shorter.

The prophets – especially the long books – can be a little indigestible at times, largely because of long tracts about judgement. It is perhaps these sections of the Old Testament that most readily deserve the criticism of 'blood-thirstiness'. The prophet Ezekiel is a good example because he is not at all squeamish in likening Israel (in chapter 16) to an unwashed baby, covered in blood, whose umbilical cord has not yet been cut, or when he speaks of child sacrifice. We will go on to consider such accusations in the next chapter. However, many of the prophets have a particular concern with social justice, notably the minor prophet Amos, who preached in the eighth century BCE to a corrupt society that had forgotten how to worship Yahweh and how to behave as true recipients of the elected status they had received. His call to correct behaviour from all levels of society – especially from the idle rich and from judges and others in positions of authority – rings down the centuries as a reminder to all societies of the dangers of corruption.

There is also a concern (particularly in the eighth century BCE) for proper religious conduct and practices in the face of threats from other religions, notably Baalism. This is addressed briefly by Amos, but much more developed in the prophet Hosea, who points out that such is the intermingling of Yahwistic worship with Baalism that people are forgetting which is which and calling the Israelite god 'My Baal'. This is a reminder to us when we celebrate Christian festivals to be mindful of the true nature of the event we are remembering (think of the encroachment of Santa Claus on the true meaning of Christmas, for example).

The prophetic word was a word of power, able to change situations and to will judgement or salvation. The chief concern of the prophets was with the relationship of God to the people, for which a whole range of metaphors is used. We find images of God as creator; we find God differently portrayed as husband or as father, one who suffers anguish at the waywardness of the people. Perhaps the overriding image of God in the Old Testament prophets is of a God of judgement who is to mete out punishment on the wayward people, although there are also some more hopeful, restorative images.

A combination of the historical events through which the prophets lived, their theological understanding of God, and the relationship with Israel and from Israel to the world, led to the particular character of Israelite prophecy.

Most prophets receive some kind of call to prophesy God's word, even if it is profoundly unpalatable. Jeremiah is called and protests that he is too young (Jeremiah 1:4–10), but God doesn't take much notice of that excuse. Taking on the prophetic role proves to be a great burden for him – after all, anyone who preaches judgement upon the nation is unlikely to be popular, particularly with the ruling classes. He suffers humiliation and imprisonment for his message. In his confessions (e.g. Jeremiah 20) we have a unique insight into his personal torment, passages that sound very much like lament psalms or like parts of the book of Job (compare Job 3 with Jeremiah 20 for example).

The call to prophesy for God took over a person's whole life. Jeremiah preached at the time leading up to the Israelite Exile – a moment of real catastrophe for the nation when its leaders were sent to Babylon and the country came under foreign control. Indeed, the nation of Israel effectively ended. This is what Jeremiah foretells. As the Exile unfolds he continues his words about an all-powerful God who had to send the people into exile as a punishment for sins committed, for the breaking of the covenant. He feels God's pathos at having to punish God's own beloved people, alongside his own anguish at the prophetic task.

## Exilic Prophecy in Ezekiel and Deutero-Isaiah

In many ways the Exile, although a painful historical event for the people of Israel, was a time of great innovation in theological thought. Ideas about God were challenged on the one hand and developed in new and interesting ways on the other. God was no longer simply the God of the nation – questions were raised about God's presence elsewhere . Questions were raised about God's power – how could God allow another nation to take control of the promised land? Questions were raised about God's nature – was this God simply a harsh God of judgement?

The prophet Ezekiel also belongs to this context. He lived in exile in Babylonia by the river Chebar and had his prophecy there. His prophecy is very unlike Jeremiah's in that he receives much of God's message through powerful visions, such as that which opens the book. This is a vision of God's heavenly throne, which is 'on the move' – leaving the temple in Jerusalem and going into exile with the people (Ezekiel 10). This is an interesting type of religious experience, not seen before in the prophets. He uses colourful and metaphorical language to describe Jerusalem, the unfaithful, harlotrous wife (Ezekiel 16), in order to convey God's disgust with the people's behaviour and hence their punishment with the Exile. He also experiences translocation (being transported from one place to another, either

**Figure 4.5**    Relief: 'On the Shores of Babylon.' © Tower of David Museum of the History of Jerusalem.

just in the mind or physically as well) as he sees pagan rituals defiling the temple in Jerusalem.

The prophecy takes over Ezekiel's life: he supposedly lies on his side for a year to symbolize the length of the Exile (Ezekiel 4) and he parts his hair into three and cuts it off to symbolize the major powers threatening Israel (Ezekiel 5). He must have seemed a curious character. He too makes some profound theological strides. Like Jeremiah, he sees that God is powerful and has punished the people deliberately because of their wayward behaviour. His vision of hope for the future is stronger than that of Jeremiah in that he sees the only hope of eventual restoration being the fitness of the people to receive God's grace and in that context stresses ritual purity and holiness. This fits in with his former role as a priest and his interest in the temple, which links up with concerns known to have existed among priestly groups.

A third prophet of the Exile is the unnamed second prophet in the book of Isaiah. The conclusion that Isaiah should be divided into at least two prophecies has been widely held by scholars for over a century. The historical context of each is clearly different by a number of centuries. While the second prophet may have been inspired by the first or even have edited the first, the style, message and theology are very contrasting. It might be that this second prophecy was added to the first simply because of extra space on the original Isaiah scroll, or perhaps this second prophet was also called Isaiah.

We do not know why this prophecy is entangled with Isaiah 1–39, but there it is in Isaiah 40–55. It belongs to the period of the Exile and actually mentions the Persian King Cyrus who delivered the Israelites from Babylonian domination and exile in 539 BCE. This second Isaiah is known as Deutero-Isaiah and in contrast to first Isaiah, and indeed his forerunners as exilic prophets, his message is entirely one of hope. A nice change for the persevering reader of the Old Testament! We are given few details of the person. The theological message is dominant and although the historical event of Cyrus' deliverance of the people is mentioned (Isaiah 44:28; 45:1), little else in the historical arena features.

His theological message is of a God of love who is about to restore the people to their homeland. There is exuberance and joy at this announcement which comes across in his language, as in 'Comfort, O comfort my people, says your God. Speak tenderly to Jerusalem, and cry to her that she has served her term' (Isaiah 40:1–2a). He also expresses God's power and reminds the people of both creation and liberation from slavery in almost the same breath. This emphasis on God as creator and redeemer at one and the same time is particularly fresh in this prophecy.[35] God has redeemed the people in the past and is about to do so again. This time the return home

**Figure 4.6**   The Cyrus Cylinder. This clay cylinder, covered in cuneiform writing, is only 23 cm long. The text records the capture of Babylon in 539 BCE by Cyrus, King of Persia (549–530 BCE) and mentions his policy of returning exiled people to their homeland. Cyrus is mentioned in Isaiah 44:28–45:4; 2 Chronicles 36:22–33 and Ezra 1:1–4. © Trustees of the British Museum.

will be even greater than the original exodus event. Israel will also be a beacon to other nations who will see their return and acknowledge God's power. Cyrus will simply effect the deliverance – he is a pawn that God uses to carry out God's purposes. But because of that role, Deutero-Isaiah exalts him, using language usually reserved for the Davidic kings. Cyrus was not a particularly religious man[36] – he was more of a conqueror, fighter and political opportunist. His significance for the people of Israel was enormous though because he enabled their restoration to their homeland and was the instrument of God's redeeming grace. He is hailed as the redeemer of Israel as chosen by God ('I surname you though you do not know me', Isaiah 45:4b), expressed in the language of kingship.

One very enigmatic feature of Deutero-Isaiah's prophecy is his vision of the servant who will redeem Israel. Often in the prophecy Israel is described as 'my servant', but in four passages (Isaiah 42:1–4; 49:1–6; 51:3–9 and 52:13–53:12) the servant seems to be a male individual who will bring salvation to Israel and suffer on their behalf. Much scholarly ink has been spilled over who this character might have been. He is described as powerful in one passage and yet as the victim of abuse in another. He almost seems like a combination of a kingly figure and a prophetic one. If he was a historical figure living at the time of the Exile, the precise details of who he is eludes us. In the fourth passage he is described in very moving terms as a lamb who went to the slaughter and who suffered death on behalf of the nation. We may pick up the resonance here of language that has commonly been used of Jesus. And yet this is the Old Testament. Could this have been a long-range forecast of Jesus' death and resurrection?

## Christian Engagement with the Servant Image

This raises the issue of Christian interpretation of the Old Testament. Christians have searched the Old Testament for texts and ideas that relate to Christ and that demonstrate the essential continuity between the two testaments. We find many examples of 'proof texts' in the gospels and in the letters of Paul. It is also possible that the Old Testament prophets were reaching out towards a long-distance prediction of events, although Old Testament scholars generally prefer to see the Old Testament on its own terms and the prophets as being short-range forecasters rather than long-term ones.

However, in the very elusiveness of this particular image of the servant it may be that the prophet himself was speaking of things he didn't fully understand that would come to fulfilment in a different age and time. This is certainly how Christians have traditionally treated the Old Testament, as pointing forward to Christ. In fact, it is perhaps surprising that we don't have more of Deutero-Isaiah's servant in the New Testament itself. We would think it was a gift image to use, yet there are only three direct quotations (in Matthew 8:16f. from Isaiah 53:4; Matthew 12:18–21 from Isaiah 42:1–4; Luke 22:37 from Isaiah 53:12), the last of which is the only passage quoted by Jesus (thus showing Jesus' self-consciousness of servanthood). It was only taken up later on in church tradition in a much greater way. Perhaps that suggests that those who wrote the New Testament were aware that the servant image originally related to something else. That would be intriguing, but a question to which we will probably never know the answer (as is the nature of many questions relating to the Old Testament!).

Much more popular with the writers of the New Testament is the original prophet Isaiah (as found in Isaiah 1–39). His prophecies are well known to us from the Christmas liturgy, in the foretelling of Christ's birth and life (e.g. the 'young woman shall conceive' 'Immanuel' prophecy of Isaiah 7 and 'the people that walked in darkness' 'Prince of Peace' prophecy of Isaiah 9). We also see the view expressed in the Christmas liturgy (e.g. in the Nine Lessons and Carols) that creation itself was pointing to a fulfilment in Jesus in the citation of Genesis 3, the fall of humankind overturned in the death and resurrection of Jesus Christ. Jesus is seen as the second Adam – rather like life after the flood, God promises that through belief in Christ humanity's sinful nature is overcome. (See chapter 5 for a discussion of the relationship of Old Testament and New Testament.) It is interesting to look, as we shall now do, at 'First Isaiah' (henceforth Isaiah) in his historical context, in terms of the way his 'book' has evolved in literary terms and in relation to his theological message – both for his time and as it was 'read' by those after him. All these aspects go hand in hand as we approach any text and lead us to appreciate the richness of any attempt to 'open' the Old Testament.

## First Isaiah

Isaiah lived in the eighth century BCE, a contemporary of Amos, Hosea and Micah (and so these prophets are collectively known as the eighth-century prophets). This means that he was prophesying in the 700s BCE (precisely 745–701 BCE) in Jerusalem and primarily to the southern kingdom. He was probably a politician or adviser in the royal court – he seems to have access to kings (notably Ahaz and Hezekiah in 7:13–17; 37:2–7, 21–35), to be in the role of giving advice and he is particularly concerned with foreign affairs. He was an educated man, possibly trained in a court wisdom school if such existed in ancient Israel and possibly a professional 'wise man' at court. His message is particularly related to the historical events of his time, which included making alliances with other small states (a move that he opposed) and becoming a vassal state to **Assyria**, which he regarded as a defeat. In these situations he advises anxious kings such as Ahaz to 'Take heed, be quiet, do not fear' (Isaiah 7:4). He advocates trust in God and not in human alliances. He opposes human pride in its own achievements and failure to listen to God's word and purposes. When the Assyrians failed to capture Jerusalem and there was great rejoicing, Isaiah did not approve, regarding such rejoicing as complacency on Israel's part. Although other parts of his book contain some prophecies of deliverance, notably of Zion the holy hill, it is unclear whether these events are being referred to or whether this tradition post-dates Isaiah himself.

> **Assyria** was the dominant large nation of the era, a major Mesopotamian civilization, at times extremely powerful, demanding vassal payments from smaller states such as Israel, something that happened in Isaiah's time.

On a theological level, the message of quiet trust in God and return to God is at the heart of Isaiah's message (see Isaiah 30:15). His vision of God in his call is also a momentous experience for him (Isaiah 6) (see discussion below). Like all the eighth-century prophets, he is also concerned with social justice and has a vision of an ideal society in which people deal with each other fairly and with respect for societal hierarchies. In fact chaos ensues when people behave above their status or when the rich fail to protect the poor in the way that they should. He opposes foolish pride and misplaced confidence, not just in alliance-making but in worshipping idols instead of God and in failing to see God as directing all human activity in a divine order that pervades both the political and the ethical spheres. Although he preached within a historical arena his message of trust in God is timeless and in many ways idealistic, conveying a profound awareness of the way the God-human relationship should work.

The book of Isaiah also needs to be engaged with on a literary level since it is made up of many layers of editing. Chapters 1–12 and 28–31 are seen by scholars to contain the kernel of material from the historical Isaiah, although even within that there are additions and rearrangements (e.g. introductory oracles in chapter 1 from different periods in the prophet's life). Chapters 13–23 contain oracles against other nations, a well-known genre from prophecy – people enjoyed hearing their enemies being bad-mouthed! These too are probably from different periods but are gathered together under the heading of the genre 'foreign oracles' rather than under any chronological scheme.

Chapters 24–7 form what is known as the Isaiah **Apocalypse** and may be much later than the prophet – possibly as late as the third century BCE. These chapters are probably an indication of how the book of Isaiah was starting to be 'read' by a later generation – as prophecy of a future time.[37] Chapters 32–5

> **Apocalypse** (meaning revelation) in this context refers to a genre of writing which concerns visions or prophecies of the future end-time. The most famous example of this genre in the New Testament is the book of Revelation.

again contain a mixture of earlier and later oracles on different topics. Chapters 36–9 are distinctive because they are in the third person and represent narratives about Isaiah, while the rest of the book is in the first person. This section also overlaps with 2 Kings, the end of the Deuteronomistic history, which is interesting and may suggest some overlap in authorship or borrowing.

These conclusions about literary layers in Isaiah do not detract from his historical persona, which still rings out from the pages of the prophecy. They illustrate how the message was worked over, reapplied, expanded and so on in the light of unfolding situations and new theological insights. It shows that a prophetic book almost had a life of its own – the book might never have stopped evolving had not the canonizers of the Old Testament not stopped the process at a particular point in time.

## Isaiah 6

Once again, we can analyze the book of Isaiah on the various levels of historical, theological and literary, but to really 'open' the book we need to look at some carefully selected passages. One passage that gives an interesting insight into the prophet and his message is his call in chapter 6. This is the account of how Isaiah came to be a prophet of God (see the calls of other prophets, such as in Jeremiah 1:4–10 and Ezekiel 1:3–3:15). The setting of the call may have been the temple in Jerusalem – possibly during an act of worship – as he sees God sitting on a throne and hears the phrase 'Holy, holy, holy', although the whole experience may have been a visionary one.

The description of God is awesome. In verse 2 'the hem of his robe filled the temple', which suggests that God was conceived to be wearing a robe so large that its train occupied the whole space of the main hall of the temple. Maybe God was regarded as a figure of giant proportions or maybe it is simply a statement of God's incomparable splendour to point to his garments rather than his person. Also in verse 2 we read, 'Seraphs were in attendance above him'. The **seraphim** were of serpent form, but possessed of three pairs of wings and hands and feet like a human. Such creatures of mixed form were popular in Egyptian royal symbolism where the winged cobra was a widely used symbol for a divine protective spirit guarding the king. It appears pro-minently both on royal headdresses and as a throne adornment. The seraphim are probably guardian deities, or servants, protecting the way to the throne of Yahweh, and comparable to the **cherubim**,

---

**Seraphim** are angels or heavenly beings which make their appearance in the call-vision of Isaiah. They may have been winged serpents of some kind.

---

**Cherubim** are also heavenly beings and winged creatures, possibly larger creatures such as bulls. They are mentioned many times in the Old Testament, notably in Genesis 3:24 where they guard the way to the tree of life.

images of which as winged lions stood in the inner sanctuary of the Jerusalem temple (1 Kings 6:23–8). There is no indication that any images of seraphim were set in the sanctuary of the Jerusalem temple, although a bronze snake had been set there and was removed in Hezekiah's reign (2 Kings 18:4). The experience was clearly quite frightening. We read in verse 4, 'The pivots on the thresholds shook'. The smoke which filled the house may have derived from the smoke of incense and offerings in the sanctuary, though it has become linked as part of the visionary accompaniment of a theophany.

In the second part of the call account we find the act of cleansing and preparation of the prophet for his task. The prophet feels inadequate and speaks of unfitness to use his mouth in the service of God and there is in this a very real understanding that he was being called upon to become the spokesman of God's word. The fact that he lived in the midst of a people of unclean lips refers to his consciousness of the prevalence of sins of speech among the people generally (cf. Proverbs 10:18ff.). In verse 6 we have the ritual of cleansing the lips of the prophet, which is otherwise unattested in the Old Testament. It may be that Isaiah was familiar with a practice from the ancient Near East of touching the lips with a live coal as a ritual of cleansing. With the cleansing of the lips the whole being of the prophet is assumed to have been purged from sin, and thereby made ready for the service of Yahweh as his prophetic messenger.

This is followed in verse 8 by a dialogue which may be taking place in the heavenly court among members of a divine council, or it may simply be between God and the prophet. With this verse, the commissioning of the prophet begins. He says, 'Here am I! Send me.' The prophet's response indicates his acceptance of the commission to take God's message to the people. Up to this point no indication has been given of the content of the message the prophet will be called upon to take. It is clear from the way that the account has been constructed, however, that the prophet's special purging from all guile and deceit has been stressed in order to prepare the way for the disclosure that the message will not prove to be a popular or readily acceptable one. It is in verse 9 that the addressees of the message are made known, and it becomes evident from the manner of Yahweh's describing them as 'this people' that he will no longer lay claim to them as constituting 'his people'.

In verse 9, 'Keep listening, but do not comprehend; keep looking, but do not understand' is somewhat enigmatic. The saying is in part full of irony, for the prophet undoubtedly did, very passionately and sincerely, want the people to hear and to understand. It may be that the prophet has (or others have) written down this report of his call at some interval after the actual experience on which it was based. Or it may be that it simply describes the tension that we find in his thought that despite his calls to trust God the people are unable to listen to him. It may be then that these verses incorporate the reception of his message only known afterwards, or it may represent a prediction by him of the deep-seatedness of the nation's sin. The effect of these verses in this position in the call is to imply that God knew very well that the people would not respond to the message, but God offered them a choice nevertheless.

In verse 10 we read, 'Make the mind of this people dull'. The seat of reasoning and intelligence in Hebrew psychology is to be dulled so that the people become incapable of making intelligent and rational decisions. Isaiah makes it clear to them that their refusal to listen to his words, and to act accordingly, is an action of the grossest irrationality. 'So that they may not look with their eyes' shows that the prophet nevertheless delivered his message with a firm hope that it would enable his hearers to turn to Yahweh 'and be healed'.

Verse 11 changes key when the prophet asks a question: 'Then I said, "How long, O Lord?"' The cry 'How long?' is regularly used for the opening of laments (cf. Psalm 89:46). The picture that then follows in the verse 'Until cities lie waste without inhabitants' pictures the devastation that would be caused by war. The reference intended by 'the land' must primarily have been to Judah and Jerusalem, which would suffer as a result of the threatened judgement.

Verse 12 – 'until the LORD sends everyone far away' – is a threat, but may be a reflection from a position of hindsight about how the judgement had taken effect in the deportation of many from the land. In verse 13 too, 'Even if a tenth part remain in it' is a threat: just as the stump or trunk of a tree may be burned after the tree is felled, so will the survivors of Israel and Judah suffer further punishment, when they already feel that they have suffered more than enough. The final words of verse 13c – 'The holy seed is its stump' – elicits an element of hope that even the stump of a felled tree may regrow, again probably with the hindsight of deliverance. It is likely that the holy seed refers to the survivors of Judah in general, the **remnant**, rather than to the royal seed of the house of David, although there are echoes of both senses.

The **remnant** is that part of a tribe or nation that survives catastrophe, most commonly used of the remnant who returned to the land of Israel after the Exile.

So from the call narrative we get a sense of the divine nature of Isaiah's commissioning and hence of the seriousness with which he took his prophecy. From the moment of cleansing with the coal the words that came from his mouth were not his but God's. We also get a sense of the frustration that the prophet experienced, that his words fell on deaf ears from a people that were ill-equipped to listen to him. Perhaps there is a sense in which we are called to listen afresh in each generation, hence the reinterpretations that have given the book its continuing life.

## Isaiah 7, 8 and 9

The chief feature of Isaiah 7 and 8 is the mention of sign-names given to children. The three names are all sign-messages from God in connection with their immediate context in the Syro-Ephraimite war, the first of the 'alliance' crises to beset Israel, yet they were seen to have ongoing theological relevance even within the confines of Isaiah's own message. The names are Shear-jashub in 7:3, Immanuel in 7:14 and Mahershalalhashbaz in 8:1, 3. There are small interpretive sections added to each to make plain what they mean, interpretations that may well be added by the prophet himself or an immediate circle (7:7–9; 7:16–17; 8:4). We also have some later redaction from the exile in 7:17 and 8:4 making explicit reference to the king of Assyria.

The message in the crisis via the names Shear-jashub ('a remnant shall return'), Immanuel ('God with us') and Mahershalalhashbaz ('the spoil speeds, the prey hastens')[38] was first that the attempt to depose Ahaz and replace him with a puppet king would fail; second that the siege of Jerusalem would have to be relinquished; and third that both Damascus and Samaria would be plundered by the Assyrians, so that the aim of the anti-Assyrian coalition would prove to be disastrous. Ahaz therefore should maintain his neutrality and have nothing to fear from the threat. However, there is a more theological aspect, too: the message that God can be trusted (Immanuel, 'God with us') over against human alliances is all too familiar from other parts of Isaiah. In the Immanuel prophecy also the tension between judgement and salvation comes out – 'God is with us' would seem to signify a sure salvation and deliverance and yet the people refuse to trust God, hence God is about to strike. Isaiah 7:8–15, immediately following, contains oracles of judgement.

The three children could easily be seen as children of Isaiah, except that the chronology is complicated – the first child is already born, the second is only just conceived and the third is just born all within a three-year period. It has been argued that the second child may not have been from the same woman as the other two. Who is the young woman mentioned in 7:14? It could refer to any young woman, or to 'that woman over there'. It could refer to a royal queen (possibly Ahaz's wife who gave birth to Hezekiah and so secured the line) so that the king would be assured of an heir or maybe the young woman was the wife of the prophet. The third suggestion is often thought the most likely and yet it seems to me that these kinds of discussions miss the point of the symbolism. It is the message that is primary, a message not necessarily only for its time, but with enigmatic qualities that have enabled later generations to read them in new ways, as in particular with the Immanuel prophecy.

With the third name there is reference to the writing of the name on a tablet, which links up with the end of chapter 8 where the message is to be sealed up: 'Bind up the testimony, seal the teaching among my disciples' (Isaiah 8:16).[39] The idea of this action by the prophet's contemporary disciples is mainly to prove that the prophet spoke before events happened in order to confirm the genuineness of the predictive quality of the prophecy. However, later in the passage the further idea is expressed that at some future time, instead of consulting the dead through mediums, the message should be reread. These sentiments are often thought to come from the exilic age, on the assumption that only in times of despair would people consult mediums. But this a weak argument and in my view it is better to take these words in the same context as verses 16–18. These words suggest that the message was not to be restricted to one generation alone and that when the time was ripe, the words would have meaning once again.

If such sentiments at least originate with Isaiah himself, this passage would put an interesting slant on what he is saying in his own present and might suggest that the reinterpretation of his prophecies that has gone on was part of his own original intention. In this light we could interpret his veiled language as a note of indeterminacy on his own part – a reaching out for meaning in the present from the word that he has received, but a recognition that this may not be the full story.

This argument that the prophecies of Isaiah can be read on more than one level has been propounded by some scholars in the interests of a Christian interpretation. Kaiser, in particular, comes down strongly against such ideas. He writes (in reference to Isaiah 7:10–17):

> As long as we suppose the scene to be historical, it is impossible to adopt the expedient of either making the prophet look towards an *unknown future* or making him look upon it as a *mystery hidden* even from him, that one day the recipient of *salvation*, or the *bringer of salvation*, Immanuel, will be born as representative of the remnant that is returning. (Kaiser 1975: 158–9; his italics)

However, biblical interpreters may have swung too far in the other direction, disallowing any futuristic element in the prophet's message. As we have seen when considering Isaiah's message, thoughts about the remote future were not outside his concern.

With this in mind we turn to Isaiah 9. It may be that the juxtaposition with the end of chapter 8 is deliberate and provides us with a way of reading 9:2–7, one of the most difficult of Isaiah's prophecies. This has been variously interpreted as an original Isaiah prophecy about Hezekiah in the not-too-distant future, or even about Josiah, or as a post-exilic messianic prophecy of the coming of a Davidic ruler. In fact, the latter is often rejected since there is no explicit mention of restoration of the Davidic monarchy after an interval in which it had ceased, which of course was the case at the Exile and after. Isaiah 9:2–7 has many connections with the psalms – overtones of a royal psalm or of a song of thanksgiving. It perhaps expresses an ideal rather than a reality, since in fact the promises of the ending of warfare in verse 5 and a vast international rule for the house of David in verse 7 were not realized.

The contrast of the darkness with the light symbolizes the transition from judgement to promise and the saving action of God. Is the birth of a son to be taken literally or is it a reference to a king as in Psalm 2:7, when on the accession of the king God says: 'This is my son, today I have begotten you'? If it was a royal occasion it might have inspired new throne names which may be represented by 'Wonderful, Counsellor' etc. The hope for the Davidic house recalls the covenant with David in 2 Samuel and the reference to 'the people' suggests the ideal of a united kingdom as in the days of David and Solomon. There are overtones of the restoration of order – that ideal after which Isaiah so strived, the two foundation stones being justice and righteousness. This may well be part of Isaiah's utopian vision of an ideal society, rather than merely a royal prediction. We find in the wisdom literature the theme of the king as the determinant of the health of the whole society. Again, its veiled nature may be deliberate – a vision of hope for an unknown future as well as an oracle into which meaning could be read for the generations that immediately followed its utterance. It has become a famous prophecy for Christians of the coming of Christ and is read in the Christmas liturgy year by year.

## And so to the New Testament

Perhaps it is hardly surprising given the above discussion that the most quoted prophet in the New Testament is Isaiah. In chapter 5 I shall turn to the relationship of the Old Testament to the New. The New Testament uses texts such as these from Isaiah as fulfilment texts from prophecy to show the New Testament as in essential continuity with the Old. It is more about seeing the New Testament as a fulfilment of the Old than actually a comment about the nature of the Old Testament. In Christian circles we have been used to seeing the prophets as long-range forecasters of Christian events, but I hope that this study of Isaiah has shown that any prophet is a product of his or her own time and place first and foremost. Isaiah's theological message may transcend the particularities of his own situation and far extend beyond the boundaries of its first utterance, and Isaiah's book itself may represent a continuing and evolving tradition, but he also lives on as a man of the eighth-century BCE who opposed human pride, advocated trust in God and no other, and who spoke of a deliverance and a future for Israel and her representatives.

## Notes

1  W. Eichrodt, *Theologie des Alten Testaments*, Leipzig: J. C. Hinrichs, 1933–9 (English, Vol. 1, 1961; Vol. 2, 1967) found 'covenant' to be the key; others have made alternative suggestions, e.g. C. Westermann, *Blessing in the Bible and the Life of the Church*, Philadelphia: Fortress Press, 1978 (German 1968). Scholars have attempted to find central books or themes, but such attempts usually fail by being too one-sided. The historical salvation scheme has often been seen as the dominant one, although recent scholarship has questioned that emphasis.

2  I prefer to see the dynamic as three-way – God, humans, the world – as represented by the Noachic covenant rather than two-way – God, humans – as found in the covenants with specific representatives of Israel and in that with the people of Israel as a whole.

3  For example, the theme of 'the promise of land' relates to covenant in relation to Abraham in particular, to Deuteronomic themes about covenant and to the relationship of God with the natural world, which links up with creation themes.

4  See Katharine J. Dell, 'The Use of Animal Imagery in the Psalms and Wisdom Literature', *SJT* 53/3 (2000), pp. 275–91. The Earth Bible project is a good example of how this kind of approach is now finding favour in mainstream scholarship.

5  For more comprehensive and exhaustive introductions to the Old Testament, see the list of further reading.

6  Compare futuristic prophecies of harmony such as that in Isaiah 11:6 of the lamb and the wolf living in harmony together.

7  See below how scholars have reconstructed the development of theological ideas rather differently to how the Old Testament actually presents it. Cf. J. Rhymer, *The Bible in Order*, London: Darton, Longman and Todd, 1975, discussed in chapter 2.

8  This could be a conflation of two sources in that all the people are present at one moment and then suddenly Moses alone goes up.

9  Different names for God are an important criterion for source theory.

10  Scholarship has long regarded this passage as a good example of source theory, with verses 9–11 being attributed to E, verses 12–14 to J and verses 15–18 to P. It is possible that they represent different strands of tradition if not sources *per se*, but it is hard to account for this variation historically without recourse to a literary theory.

11  1 Chronicles 17 also records this in an identical account. The emphasis on the building of the temple and on the honour afforded to the Davidic dynasty fits the Chronicler's concerns admirably, so he clearly saw no need to doctor the account.

12  Cedar being a rich wood, used for palaces, suggests a place of grandeur.

13  Cf. other texts (e.g. Psalm 2). In the New Testament there is representation of Jesus 'the son' as 'king'.

14  We discussed in chapter 1 the possibility of a covenant renewal festival from early times in the worship of Israel.

15  A point noted by scholars is that although Hosea seems to formulate a covenantal idea, he rarely uses the Hebrew word *berit*, 'covenant', nor does the word generally appear in the eighth-century prophets. This might suggest that the concept did not really develop until after the eighth century BCE and so the early relational understanding was gradually more formalized and seen in covenantal terms. On this model there is the possibility of a 'P' shaping of the Abrahamic, Mosaic and Noachic covenants.

16  Of course, when one brings in the distinction between the time that events happened and the time in which they were written down, all kinds of possibilities open up. Some recent scholars have placed much of the 'writing down' of all the Pentateuchal sources at the Exile or after. We might ask how far the various covenants are ideological pictures from a later generation who had lost such certainties.

17  Developmental views of religion have come in for some criticism among scholars. See in relation to wisdom, Katharine J. Dell, 'On the Development of Wisdom in Israel', *Congress Volume: Cambridge 1995*, ed. J. A. Emerton, Leiden: Brill, 1997, pp. 135–51.

18  Some have seen echoes of ancient Near Eastern chaos dragon myths in the idea of a pre-existent 'deep'.

19  This account can be likened to a Babylonian eight-day creation account. If there is any such influence it is possible that an eight-day account has been made into a six-day one with eight elements, with the climax placed on the seventh day for the sabbath.

20  This has suggested to some that Genesis 1 might have pre-existed as an independent hymn.

21  The simultaneous creation of male and female in the first account of creation is to be noted, and is particularly stressed by feminist scholars seeking to rectify the 'women in second place' argument that long held the field.

22  Criteria for positing different sources include variant names for God and some places, repetitions and contradictions. Perhaps more significant are the theological differences, each source being seen to have a consistent theological outlook.

23  This could reflect a dry desert background where water was not plentiful, while the first account might reflect a background in which water was available in abundance.

24  Human beings are formed from dust mixed with the blood of a dead god in the Babylonian Creation Myth, tablet 6. The god Kingu is slain for misbehaviour and from his blood humankind is created expressly for the service of the gods.

25  Dilmun is a parallel ideal garden described in the literature of ancient Sumer in the Epic of Emmerkar. Later on it becomes the dwelling place of the gods where Utnapishtim, the hero of the Sumerian flood story, and his wife were allowed to live after the flood.

26  The Tigris and Euphrates are two of these rivers, now in modern Iraq. The others, Pishon and Gihon, are of uncertain location.

27  This is an aetiology – the nature of these stories is as 'origin stories' explaining phenomena in human life.

28  Feminist scholars have been concerned about this. P. Trible in 'A Love Story Gone Awry', chapter 4 of *God and the Rhetoric of Sexuality*, London: SCM Press, 1978,

pp. 72–143, made the suggestion of an 'earth creature' before the differentiation into male and female.

29  The talking serpent is perhaps the most obvious indication of the legendary nature of this account. The serpent was associated with immortality in the ancient Near East because of the regular shedding and renewal of its skin.

30  This source writer is known as J because it was named the Jahwistic source by Wellhausen. It is because of the use of Yahweh rather than Elohim, which is a simple way of distinguishing this source.

31  Some scholars think that J is also exilic but contains older material that may well have circulated orally.

32  See discussion in Katharine J. Dell, *The Book of Proverbs in Social and Theological Context*, Cambridge: Cambridge University Press, 2006.

33  Most prophetic books have a core of material that relates closely to events of their own time and so attempts to deny their historical actuality generally fail. Some scholars have seen prophetic books as primarily literary products – ideological constructs of later ages – and hence not necessarily reflecting the words of any actual historical prophet (see R. P. Carroll's Old Testament Guide on *Jeremiah*, Sheffield: JSOT Press, 1989). While the words of prophets were later cherished and often supplemented a great deal by those wishing to understand fresh situations in the light of original prophecies, this does not deny a historical kernel to the prophecy itself embodied in a prophetic figure.

34  Through the process of literary embellishment the prophetic books gradually emerged over time, through redactors and editors, as rich theological sources in themselves, far exceeding the bounds of their original intentions.

35  This emphasis has contributed to the thought that a doctrine of creation emerged fully integrated with that of salvation in the exilic period (cf. the P account of creation).

36  The Cyrus Cylinder indicates that Cyrus espoused the Babylonian God Marduk in order to capture Babylon without much of a fight and so suggests religious allegiances were for him secondary to political expediency.

37  These chapters of Isaiah provide us with a good example of how books were 'updated', which might have continued had it not been for the closing of the canon. It also gives us an insight into how a later generation was reading texts, in this case in a futuristic manner.

38  The reference of this strange name is clarified by the context of the prophecy: 'for before the child knows how to cry "My father" or "My mother", the wealth of Damascus and the spoil of Samaria will be carried before the king of Assyria' (Isaiah 8:3).

39  H. G. M. Williamson, *The Book Called Isaiah: Deutero-Isaiah's Role in Composition and Redaction*, Oxford: Clarendon Press, 1994, makes a point of such passages in showing links between the different prophets that make up the book. Perhaps Deutero-Isaiah saw himself as living at the time when the testimony of first Isaiah was to be opened up and reinterpreted for a fresh generation.

 *Chapter 5* Opening Difficult or Liberating Texts

## Selecting Texts

The Old Testament is more often than not read in church alongside the New Testament in a thematic way. This means that we get a 'pick and mix' of stories or theological points that fit in with the theme of whichever part of the Christian year we are in. If an Old Testament text is preached on, it is generally one which aligns itself fairly naturally with central tenets of the New Testament and it will often be brought into conjunction with a New Testament text. This is the case with the **Lectionary** which selects suitable pairings of texts throughout the church's year. Occasionally, whole chunks of books will be read over a period (e.g. at **Evensong** over a month), but it is rare that one gets the whole book – it is usually edited highlights. Even in Bible studies conducted in groups there is often no time to go through a whole text – and frankly there are tedious and repetitive parts of most texts – and it is more sensible and profitable to select highlights. While books of the New Testament are read and preached upon systematically, Old Testament readings are used to illuminate the New Testament. Thus, many texts in the Old Testament are ignored completely.

The **Lectionary** is the official guide to the prescribed readings to be used from week to week in church. Different denominations of the church have different lectionaries and they are revised from time to time.

**Evensong** is the last service of the day, traditionally sung and featuring readings and sometimes a sermon.

One side-effect of missing out texts is that quite often the more unpalatable or difficult texts are not read. The difficulty is on two levels. The first is the cultural difference between ourselves and the Old Testament world. Detailed rituals for sacrificial worship and long lists of genealogies might be the first contenders for curing insomnia at night (as we might struggle to get through Leviticus). Many texts need a wider context and one just

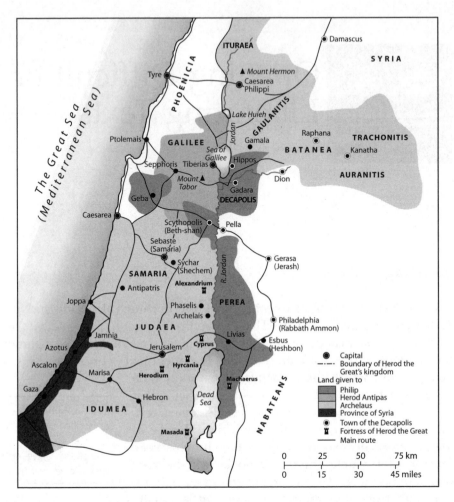

**Map 6**    Palestine in the time of Jesus.

---

**Pericopes** is a scholarly term for recognizable chunks of text, sometimes a story but sometimes a section chiefly denoted by its distinctive style or form.

---

gets a snippet and fails to grasp its meaning. Second, the way we read texts is as self-contained 'stories' or **pericopes**. We have seen how in many ways this is true to the character of the text as 'story' and indeed may well have been how the texts were first shaped in the oral tradition. Yet this is not in fact how the texts themselves were written down in their final form – they were written continuously in long books.

One of my aims in this book has been to give a sense of that wider context which is so hard to grasp when hearing an account of a battle or a list of names. The difficulty is also one of unpalatability – some texts are quite abhorrent to our modern sensibilities. A few years ago I wrote a piece on 'Hospitality in the Old Testament' for *Guidelines*[1] and I had a letter from a reader who was shocked to find the story of Lot and the men of Sodom in Genesis 19 in the Bible at all. Phyllis Trible also drew attention to some shocking texts about women in her *Texts of Terror*,[2] which drew attention to Judges 19 among others – not a text you would normally find in your lectionary.

Perhaps here we have stumbled across the reason that some difficult texts are left out of lectionaries – they are unpalatable and relatively unedifying compared to other more nourishing parts.

## A Bloodthirsty Old Testament?

In chapter 1 we saw the problems of the difficult verse in Psalm 137. Difficult texts such as this lead to the accusation that the Old Testament is bloodthirsty. Let us briefly consider this accusation. There are plenty of examples of bloodthirstiness, many of them springing, as in Psalm 137, from the fact that God was perceived to be on the side of Israel in fighting battles against foreigners. War leads to acts of terrible cruelty. The view of God as a warrior as a theological theme comes to the fore here.

It is a fact that there is in the Old Testament a good dose of blood and guts, of wheeling and dealing, even of sheer cruelty. Jael and the tent peg in Judges 4:17–23 is a good example. The enemy, Sisera, comes into Jael's hands, believing her to be trustworthy, but she takes the initiative and drives a tent peg into his temple while he is sleeping. The traditional role of the woman as carer is turned on its head here. For the Israelites, this is triumph over an enemy, and the means justifies the end. We might find it an unpalatable text to read as 'the word of the Lord', as is often said at the end of a lesson in church. Of course, one can explain it in its cultural context – this is war and the survival of the nation is of prime concern. We can also argue that there was development in understanding as the religion became more sophisticated and that a very nationalistic concern gradually gave way to a much bigger picture of God and of God's activity on behalf of many nations. However, that God should condone such behaviour so that a story like Jael's became part of 'holy scripture' seems incredible!

Walter Brueggemann in his book *The Bible and Postmodern Imagination*[3] stresses that in a postmodern age we need to find fresh and challenging, even subversive interpretations of texts. We need not simply choose difficult texts, but we might want to find challenging interpretations of texts that we thought we knew all the answers to. He writes, 'It is my judgment that church interpretation . . . has tended to trim and domesticate the text not only to accommodate regnant modes of knowledge, but also to enhance regnant modes of power' (p. vii). He is suggesting that it is in the interests of those in authority to perpetuate certain interpretations – the church could be accused of that in relation to the submission of the Old Testament to the New in the lectionary. Brueggemann calls for an act of counter-imagination in which texts are used to challenge the reader and lead to the possibility of real change and growth. This kind of model opens up new doors of interpretation and fresh approaches that keep scripture alive and new. This has perhaps helped to inspire some of the new approaches that **postmodernism** has spawned and which are mentioned later in this chapter.

**Postmodernism** is a philosophical development, used in biblical studies to describe the interest in readerly interpretation and diversity of perspective in relation to any text.

In fact, the picture that the Old Testament paints of God is a good way of seeing the diversity that is the Old Testament and also of appreciating the problem of very different conceptions of God within its pages. The bloodthirstiness is part of the portrayal of God as warrior. It was important for the writers of the Old Testament to state that God was powerful, more powerful than other gods and able to win wars on behalf of the Israelites. The great period of united monarchy under David and Solomon was hard-won – the result of many military exploits in which no doubt many innocent foreigners were killed.

Deuteronomy 7 takes delight in the demise of Israel's enemies and is just one of many possible examples. God is seen to clear away the inhabiting peoples of the land as Israel comes to enter it. We read: 'when the Lord your God gives them over to you and you defeat them, then you must utterly destroy them. Make no covenant with them and show them no mercy' (Deuteronomy 7:2). Of course, one could argue that this is more about God's promise of land to the Israelites and a stable settlement than about destroying enemies. The destruction is a by-product of a great promise – and yet dispossessing and destroying existing inhabitants is a very difficult issue, as we see in today's world. It is a primitive view of God, one that does open up into a broader picture in other parts of the Old Testament, notably where God is viewed as Creator of the world (such as in Genesis 1–11), universal redeemer (as in Deutero-Isaiah) and so on.

While one could argue for a gradual development away from more primitive to more sophisticated, it is still true that we go on reading texts, often very formative, important texts such as Deuteronomy, with this very unpalatable view of God. It should not be forgotten that Deuteronomy contains some of the most famous statements of Old Testament belief, some of which were cited and taken up by Jesus: 'You shall love the LORD your God with all your whole heart' (Deuteronomy 6:5); 'the LORD is our God, the LORD alone' (Deuteronomy 6:4), etc. It is perhaps the inconsistency that causes most problems – there is not an unchanging picture of God, but a very varied one, at times palatable, at times not. Is it right to pick and choose? Is it right just to read those texts that fit into a New Testament conception of a God of love? Or should we simply dismiss Old Testament understandings of God as preliminary and hence less valuable? It seems that the richness and diversity of the Old Testament with all its different genres – something we had previously seen as a strength – is a weakness when it comes to finding a satisfactory and unified picture of God.

## A Legalistic Old Testament?

Another way the Old Testament is often undervalued is by being carica-tured. For example, the legalism that characterized parts of later Judaism is often seen as the norm, so that the whole of the Old Testament is regarded as oppressive and legalistic. When one reads some parts of the Old Testa-ment the law comes across strongly. But this is only one genre of the Old Testament, one which has been heavily emphasized, especially in Judaism.

We have seen the importance of the law within the context of the his-torical beginnings of a people with the giving of the Ten Commandments, but we looked at it chiefly within an ethical context. However, the religion of Israel wasn't always legalistic. Before the law comes the covenant, and in a sense the laws are a natural result of the obligation by Israel to keep the covenant. And much of that covenant is an act of grace by God – the relationship was a natural one between God and people until the people started to go astray, and then more laws were needed. The understanding of the covenant as 'two-way' with the stress put on Israel's obligations is a development away from a more harmonious ideal.

I would argue that in fact the sheer diversity of the Old Testament is one of its attractions. The very fact that scholars can't agree on what the theology of the Old Testament is because it is so diverse, opens the door to many presentations of God and God's dealings with the world. Many traditions from different times and places converge to make up the texts that are in so many different types and genres. The literature includes laws, proverbs, folk tales, sagas – a whole variety of genres accompanying a whole host of religious perceptions and convictions varying with period, with social group, even with geographical location. Yet there are enough unifying themes and common features for the theology of the Old Testa-ment to be recognized and described. The tensions and inconsistencies lead to a kind of openness in the Old Testament message that is its strength. This meant that the New Testament was able to develop the Old Testament for itself, while Judaism took it in other directions.

## The Relationship of Old and New Testaments

This point is helpful when it comes to looking at the relationship of Old and New Testaments. The Old Testament is the Bible of Jesus and he used that tradition to explore new possibilities and to give new meaning to the 'old'. But the Old Testament is only called *old* in the context of the New Testament[4] and it is only known as that in Christian circles. In Judaism it is the Hebrew Bible, and has found no fulfilment in Christianity. Thus, although we can assert continuity between Old and New Testaments, it is only in relation to the Christian revelation, that states itself to be a continuity of the revelation to the Israelites, that it takes on that meaning. We need to remember that the earliest Christians saw themselves as being within the Jewish family and so simply presumed a relationship to their scriptures. In a sense this is a 'faith' reading of the Old Testament, a view that treats it along with the New Testament as 'Holy Scripture', as it has been read by centuries of Christian tradition. Hauer and Young[5] make an insightful comment on the influence of the Bible on faith in its role as the scripture of both Judaism and Christianity: 'Every minute of every day, the Bible is being read, studied, taught, and used in religious contexts' (p. 365). That is quite a claim for any book!

In Matthew 5:17 Jesus says, 'Do not think that I have come to abolish the law or the prophets; I have come not to abolish but to fulfill.' This was what Jesus believed – he taught his disciples using the very scriptures that were his own religion and which he himself was to progress onto a new level. In verse 21 the same chapter in Matthew continues: 'You have heard that it was said to those of ancient times, "You shall not murder" . . . But I say to you.' Here Jesus is quoting one of the Ten Commandments. Jesus is using the Old Testament as his stepping-stone – this was what people knew, so he expounded it further and sometimes deliberately contradicted it.

This is why the Old Testament is included as scripture for Christians with the New Testament – these texts were authoritative for Jesus and for those who wrote the New Testament.[6] This is why texts are quoted so much within the New Testament, often as 'proof texts' reflecting genuine learned interpretation of the scriptures within the gospels and elsewhere. There are also allusions and echoes that are less obvious than direct citations.[7] The word of God was seen to have been decisively revealed to Abraham, Isaac and Jacob, to Moses and to Israelites and Jews in the history of their nation up to the time of Christ and beyond. For Christians, there was a fundamental turning point, a decisive new step in the God-human relationship. So, while for Jews these scriptures are the only authoritative word from God to man, for Christians they are 'part one' of two covenants of God, the second made through Jesus. As the author of Hebrews puts it: 'Long ago God spoke to our ancestors in many and various ways by the prophets, but in these last days he has spoken to us by a Son' (Hebrews 1:1–2a). There is clearly an attempt here to stress the continuity of old and new and yet it is made quite clear by the writers of the New Testament that in their eyes the new revelation has overtaken the old in significance.

The writers of the New Testament express themselves in the categories and concepts of the Old Testament, not just to stress continuity, but because that was their language. The Old Testament, despite the bloodthirstiness witnessed earlier, contains expressions of a just and loving God who acts faithfully on behalf of the Israelite people. It contains a profound analysis of the nature of righteous and wicked behaviour (both in legal and wisdom terms) and it contains the concept of God's forgiveness of a wayward people. All these theological understandings, while they stand alone in their own right within the context of the Old Testament itself, also find a new resonance in relation to the New.

Many basic theological categories found in the New Testament are taken from the Old. It is arguable that the New Testament could not have come into being (especially theologically) without that background. Titles and phrases from the Old Testament are used to make sense of the significance of Jesus, the language of kingship, the language of sacrifice and so on. Scriptural passages often provided the means by which Jesus' followers could understand and speak about Jesus and his significance. Much theological development had already gone on within the pages of the Old Testament. The Christian concept of God and the way God acts in history and in universal salvation are all worked out in the Old Testament and presupposed in the New. As John Goldingay writes in *Approaches to Old Testament Interpretation*,[8] 'The Old Testament lays the theological foundations for the New and sometimes explicitly looks forward in a hope which the Christian sees confirmed or fulfilled in Christ' (p. 34). This point about hope is important, as by the end of the Old Testament period much emphasis was being placed on future fulfilment of old promises. Expectations of a brighter future, possibly messianic, were around. It was this hope that Christians saw fulfilled in Jesus.

## The Old Testament Canon in Relation to an Emerging New Testament

Christopher Evans writes in *The Cambridge History of the Bible*,[9] 'Christianity is unique among the world religions in being born with a Bible in its cradle' (p. 232). He goes on to say that the effects of this are twofold.

| New Testament timeline | | |
|---|---|---|
| 10 | 14–37 Tiberius | |
| 20 | | 26–36 Pontius Pilate<br>28/29 John the Baptist actively ministering<br>29 Baptism of Jesus |
| 30 | 37–41 Gaius Caligula | 33 Crucifixion of Jesus<br>33 Pentecost<br>34/35 Saul (Paul) |
| 40 | 41–54 Claudius<br>43 Invasion of Britain | 41–44 King Herod Agrippa<br>46–47 Paul's first missionary journey<br>48–51 Paul's second missionary journey<br>48 Jerusalem council |
| 50 | 50 Edict of Claudius<br>54 Nero | 59–93 King Herod Agrippa II<br>54–57 Paul in Ephesus<br>59–62 Paul in prison |
| 60 | 64 Burning of Rome<br>68–69 Galba<br>69–79 Vespasian<br>69 Otho<br>69 Vitellius | Festus 60–62<br>62? Death of James the Apostle<br>64? Martyrdom of Paul and Peter<br>66–70 First Jewish revolt against the Romans |
| 70 | 79–81 Titus | 70 Fall of Jerusalem and destruction of temple |
| 80 | 81–96 Domitian | 81–96 Persecution of the Christians |
| 90 | 96–98 Nerva<br>98–117 Trajan | c. 95 John banished to Patmos |
| 100 | | c. 100 Death of John |
| 110 | 117–138 Hadrian | |
| 130 | | 130 Jersualem rebuilt by Hadrian and renamed Aelia Capitolina<br>132–135 Second Jewish revolt against Romans |

Rabbinic refers to the work of the Jewish rabbis (teachers).

On the one hand they were positive, since already by the time of Jesus there were people engaged in considerable **rabbinic** activity, in research and debate. A wide range of exegesis was on offer, and some interpretations were less orthodox than others. This kind of milieu provided the background for Christian speech and writing. The existing scriptures – the Old Testament – were able to play a large part in Christian thought. On the other hand, the negative effect of already having a Bible was that there was already a fairly firm idea of what the canon of scripture consisted of. The sense of having a canon would have inhibited any thought of producing fresh books, and there is more of a suggestion in the early church of a reluctance to write.

With the exception of the **Pauline letters** the New Testament writings were relatively slow in appearing, and a high proportion of them are anonymous. They have a very different character to Jewish writings in that they are more personal and less literary in style. Evans continues:

> **Pauline letters** are those written by St. Paul. Thirteen letters are attributed to him, seven of which are thought by scholars to be definitely his. Three others are possibly from Paul and are known as Deutero-Pauline. The remainder are thought to be post-Pauline, incorporating authentic Pauline fragments.

> So long as Christianity stood close to Judaism, or was predominantly Jewish, scripture remained the Old Testament, and this situation can be seen persisting in such a document as 1 Clement[10] with its frequent and almost exclusive appeal to the Old Testament text. The elevation of Christian writings to the position of a new canon, like those writings themselves, was primarily the work of **Gentile Christianity**, whose literature also betrays a feeling that the very existence of the Old Testament was now a problem to be solved, and that there was need of some new and specifically Christian authority. (p. 234; my footnote)

> **Gentile Christianity** refers to the move away from Jewish Christians to the inclusion of Gentiles, as begun by Paul.

It should not be forgotten that Jesus' own interpretation of his Bible proceeded from his recognition of the canon of sacred books accepted by the mainstream Judaism of his day. He too would have held the conviction that these writings, rightly understood, were the expression of the mind of God through faithful prophets. In teaching his followers and in debating with his opponents, Jesus constantly engaged in exposition of the received scripture. I would posit against some interpreters that Jesus doesn't oppose the Torah or other parts of the Old Testament *per se*; he merely provides his own understanding, which is often in opposition to the expositions of those around him. This becomes apparent in Jesus' encounters with rabbis in numerous debates, some of which the Evangelists have been careful to retain.

Both Jesus and the New Testament writers give a prominent place to the Old Testament in the formulation of their teachings. Biblical quotations are concentrated on certain portions of the scriptures, as was the rabbinic pattern, especially the Pentateuch, Isaiah and the Psalms; and quotations are used more in some New Testament books than others. In all likelihood

**Figure 5.1**   Scripture written on a scroll. In Jewish synagogues today Torah scrolls are particularly venerated. © Z. Radovan/www.BiblelandPictures.com.

this reflects the gospel writers' selected themes, traditions and interests, and not their limited acquaintance with or regard for the Old Testament.

There are striking similarities in methods of exegesis between the way Jesus and early Christians interpreted scripture and the way the Jews did. This underlines the extent to which the formation of the New Testament is a product of its time. However, the unique contribution of Jesus and the gospel writers to first-century Jewish exposition is their thoroughgoing reinterpretation of the biblical writings to the person, ministry, death and resurrection of Jesus the Messiah. In a sense Jesus and those who proclaimed and wrote the gospel need not have chosen to take the path of wanting to use the Old Testament as their Bible and hence of seeing Jesus as a fulfilment of the messianic hope of the Old. They could have broken with existing scripture, as they eventually did with Judaism, since a new covenant of God was involved that was seen to have overtaken the old in its significance. But the old remained an important part of their understanding, of their identity and of their heritage. The new covenant was not just something completely fresh but a fulfilment that was prophesied by the writers of the Old Testament – hence it retains a relationship with the old.

C. K. Barrett writes in *The Cambridge History of the Bible,*

> It is only the shortest books of the New Testament that do not contain numerous references and allusions to the Old. A very large majority of New Testament books quote the Old Testament explicitly and often in such a way as to make it clear that their authors regarded the Old Testament as an authoritative body of literature which claimed the attention and obedience of Christians. It was used as the basis of theological argument and of ethical instruction. In their reliance upon this sacred literature the Christian writers followed directly the example of their Jewish contemporaries, who made similar use of the same Old Testament and, somewhat less directly, that of many others in the ancient world who also looked for guidance and inspiration to ancient books. (p. 377)

## The Use of the Old Testament in the New Testament

So how did the New Testament writers use the Old Testament? Barrett argues that there are three main categories. 'There is no doubt that the New Testament writers viewed the Old as prophecy, and interpreted it as such; that is, they understood the Old Testament to predict certain events, which had duly taken place in the experience of Jesus or of the Church' (p. 410). So, in Matthew's gospel, for example, we find fulfilment formulas: 'This was to fulfill what had been spoken by the Lord through the prophet' (Matthew 2:15). Some attempts to show the fulfilment in Jesus are more

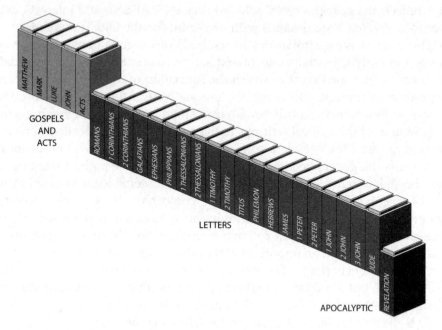

GOSPELS
AND
ACTS

MATTHEW MARK LUKE JOHN ACTS

ROMANS 1 CORINTHIANS 2 CORINTHIANS GALATIANS EPHESIANS PHILIPPIANS 1 THESSALONIANS 2 THESSALONIANS 1 TIMOTHY 2 TIMOTHY TITUS PHILEMON HEBREWS JAMES 1 PETER 2 PETER 1 JOHN 2 JOHN 3 JOHN JUDE

LETTERS

APOCALYPTIC    REVELATION

**Figure 5.2** A line of books, drawn as matchboxes, to represent the New Testament.

convincing than others. For instance, Matthew 2:15 quotes Hosea 11:1: 'Out of Egypt I have called my son.' These words in Hosea refer to Israel coming out of Egypt in the Exodus, and Matthew draws the parallel with Jesus as representative of the new Israel. Matthew 1:22–3 quoting Isaiah 7:14 is a good example of the way the prophecy of Isaiah is directly linked to the events of Jesus' conception and birth. The words of Isaiah are quoted in connection with the virgin birth of Jesus: 'Look, the virgin shall conceive and bear a son, and they shall name him "Emmanuel", which means "God is with us"' (verse 23). However, there is no original reference to a virgin in Isaiah 7:14, although of course the passage has been translated that way. Rather, the reference is to a young woman.[11] This is a clear case of how the New Testament understands the Old in ways which may not have been intended by the original authors. But this is not a problem; they very rightly reinterpreted the text for their own day, a technique evidenced within the Old Testament itself.

A second approach to the Old Testament by New Testament writers, according to Barrett, was to interpret it allegorically: 'that is, they believed that the Old Testament, or parts of it, contained hidden meanings that had been concealed from earlier generations but had now come to light with the Christian revelation' (p. 410). This is reminiscent of the 'hidden things' emphasized in apocalyptic literature in which symbolism abounds and in which there are many levels of interpretation. It is a form of fresh exegesis of old texts – the servant image of Deutero-Isaiah would be a good example, seen to have its fulfilment in the death and resurrection of Jesus. Its application to Jesus would have been hidden to the writers and interpreters of the Old Testament until the Christian revelation opened up its true significance. We also find the writers of the New Testament engaging with Old Testament stories on this level, such as Paul's engagement with the story of Sarah and Hagar in Genesis 21 in allegorical mode in Galations 4:24–6:

> Now this is an allegory: these women are two covenants. One woman, in fact, is Hagar, from Mount Sinai, bearing children for slavery. Now Hagar is Mount Sinai in Arabia and corresponds to the present Jerusalem, for she is in slavery with her children. But the other woman corresponds to the Jerusalem above; she is free and she is our mother.

The inference here from Paul is that the Genesis text now fully revealed means something other than its literal meaning.

A third way was to employ typological interpretations – typology 'seeks correspondences between persons and events not (as allegory does) in meanings hidden in language but actually in the course of history, and looks not to the fulfilment of a prediction, but to the recurrence of a pattern' (Barrett, p. 410). Barrett points out that most New Testament examples in fact combine typology and prophecy:

> The New Testament writers do see recurrence of patterns of divine activity (since the God of the Old Testament is also, in their belief, the God and Father of the Lord Jesus Christ); but the event of Jesus Christ, itself the fulfilment of the Old Testament as a whole (cf. 2 Cor. 1:20), is for them so final and radical that after it no pattern could be simply reproduced. (p. 411)

As it is stated by Paul in 2 Corinthians 1:20, 'For in him [Jesus Christ] every one of God's promises is a "Yes." For this reason it is through him that we say the "Amen," to the glory of God.' Barrett continues:

> Of course it is doubtful whether any New Testament writer ever formulated for himself the question, What is the authority of the Old Testament? So far as they were Jews the question was one that could take care of itself. Of course, the Old Testament had the authority of the voice of God himself. This attitude was adopted in turn by Gentile converts to Christianity. Yet the attitude of Christians to the Old Testament was not the same as that of Jews . . . it was

due above all to the conviction that Jesus himself was the fulfilment of the Old Testament, and thus the living and abiding word of God. Out of a complicated but creative attitude to the Old Testament scriptures a new scripture was born, in testimony to the incarnate Word. (p. 411)

One might add that without the Old Testament there would be no witness to Jesus Christ, no fulfilment to fulfil.

All scripture was essentially seen as a single fabric with different patterns interweaving in and out. That fabric was the mind of God that held it all together. All scripture, while it had a historical perspective, was essentially seen as 'guidance for today' and so overtly **christological** readings were inevitable in Christian circles. So, for example, Paul in Galatians 3:16 paraphrases Genesis 13:15, the promise to Abraham, and interprets Abraham's 'offspring' in relation to one person – Jesus Christ – in whom the promise is fulfilled.

**Christological** means pertaining to Christ.

Titles and phrases from the Old Testament are used to make sense of the significance of Jesus; for example to illuminate such questions as that of the status of Christ. In Mark 12:35–7 Jesus is portrayed as quoting Psalm 110:1 in his debate with the scribes over whether it is appropriate to speak of the Christ as the Son of David. In the psalm, 'my Lord' would have originally referred to the Davidic king, but in the New Testament it is taken to refer to Christ, a messianic interpretation that was probably already around in later Judaism. Furthermore, the language of sacrifice is used to make sense of Jesus' death – all this reveals a very strong sense of continuity with the Old Testament tradition. As Goldingay writes:

The first Christians appropriated the Jewish Bible in the conviction that their faith was one with its faith. This conviction they held to despite, or perhaps because of, their additional belief that Jesus was the messiah. Thus these scriptures substantially shaped their idea of God, of man and of how he related to God, and of the position and calling of the people of God. (p. 16)

As Brevard Childs comments when speaking of the validity of identifying a separate Old Testament theology:[12]

The Old Testament functions within Christian scripture as a witness to Jesus Christ precisely in its pre-Christian form. The task of Old Testament theology is, therefore, not to Christianize the Old Testament by identifying it with the New Testament witness, but to hear its own theological testimony to the God of Israel whom the church confesses also to worship. Although Christians confess that God who revealed himself to Israel is the God and Father of Jesus Christ, it is still necessary to hear Israel's witness in order to understand who the Father of Jesus Christ is. The coming of Jesus does not remove the function of the divine disclosure in the old covenant. (p. 9)

It is clear that the Old and New Testament have had, right from the time of Jesus himself and certainly of the gospel writers, a vital interrelationship. It is important not to caricature that relationship and think in terms of a sharp contrast between the two Testaments. It is patently not true that the whole of the Old Testament is cruel and vindictive, nor that the New Testament is without harsh words. Leviticus 19:18, for example, states 'you shall love your neighbour as yourself' – the very words Jesus so famously echoed (Matthew 19:19; 22:39; Mark 12:31). The New Testament also contains harsh words of judgement, such as in Matthew 25, the parable of the talents, in which the servant who failed to make good use of the money entrusted to him by his master is cast into 'the outer darkness, where there will be weeping and gnashing of teeth'. A few verses later, in a description of the final judgement, the wicked are told 'You that are accursed, depart from me into the eternal fire' (verse 41).

The division often made between law and gospel is also unfounded. There is legal material in the Old Testament, but there is also material (particularly from the time of the Exile) which talks of God's free grace in giving Israel the ability to be faithful to him (Jeremiah 31; Ezekiel 36). In the New Testament Paul may put an emphasis on grace, but the Epistle of James stresses the need for faith to be expressed in good deeds. The tension between demand and grace is therefore vital to both testaments. There are no black and white contrasts which might lead us to deny the place of the Old Testament in the New.

## Jesus as the Fulfilment of Old Testament Relationships

When we turn to the New Testament we find an interest in seeing Jesus as the fulfilment of various types of relationship that have been explored in the Old, reinforcing the point that without the Old Testament the theological outlook of the New Testament would not have developed in the way that it did. So Jesus is seen to fulfil the covenant promise, he is the full expression of the prophetic hope and embodies in his person the creative purpose of God. He fulfils the different kinds of covenant – he gives two commandments to supersede the ten that made up the legal covenant of Moses, he is the new David and Messiah and is often described in kingly terms, and he is likened to Abraham by Paul, as we have seen, in particular in reference to the promises made in his name. His own covenant with the world is like that after the Exile – unconditional, one of grace, the only condition being faith.

One aspect of covenant in the Old Testament is the ratification of it with a covenant meal – in Exodus 24, for example, we have seen that God, Moses, Aaron and the seventy elders sit down together to eat to ratify the covenant. The obvious link with the New Testament here is with the Last Supper, seen as the covenant meal of Jesus and his disciples. This is then symbolically and ritually repeated each time the Eucharist is held and is the way of keeping the relationship alive and reminding us of the promises made. Also connected with covenant is sacrifice – another ratification of the relationship between God and the people in the Old Testament is the presentation of sacrifice, which may well have accompanied covenant elements in festivals. In the New Testament Jesus is the sacrificial lamb who lays down his life once and for all for the sins of the world.

This links up with the hopes and promises made by the prophets. As we have already glimpsed with Isaiah, there are large chunks of the prophets quoted in the New Testament with the purpose of seeing Jesus as the fulfilment of the Old Testament hopes, hence authorizing him as a continuation of the promises made in the past. It is hard to distinguish between quotations being put into Jesus' mouth by the gospel writers and those he might have said himself. It is likely however that he himself made appeal to the Old Testament, which, after all, was his Bible, as a key source of authority, for example when he reinterprets the law – and he was certainly regarded by some as a prophet (Mark 6:15).

It may have been a slower development in New Testament thought, but we have the portrayal of Christ in more cosmic terms starting to emerge in the Pauline letters and in John's gospel. We find such language in Colossians 1:15–20, where Jesus is likened to the firstborn of all creation. This links up with the portrayal of Jesus as the eternal Logos (John 1), which has so many connections with the Old Testament portrayal of the female figure of Wisdom. Just as Wisdom was the means through which God was able to create the world and build a bridge between God and humanity, so Jesus is identified with this creative and life-giving purpose that existed from the beginning. Wisdom, traditionally seen from a human perspective, now gains a cosmic dimension – not only is Wisdom from below, gained by human beings, but it is also from above, from God. So the appropriation of wisdom by humans is to enter fully into human relationships, but also to engage with the creator God. In the same way, Jesus is both a human being and the son of God and he too forges the bridge between the two realms so that, because of the sacrifice he made, Christians can walk across this bridge in their quest for meaning in human relationships and in the search for God.

There is also an important link between the way Jesus was seen in terms of future hope and the Old Testament genre of apocalyptic. This is not a genre that we have dwelt on much. Its main representatives in the Old

Testament are the book of Daniel and part of a prophetic book, Zechariah
9–14. It combines elements of wisdom and prophecy – it is about revelation of knowledge and yet it is also about future events. It usually consists
of highly symbolic visions purporting to reveal knowledge of the end time
to some kind of wise man or seer. In the New Testament it is mainly found
in the book of Revelation, but it is glimpsed in the gospels (e.g. Mark 13;
Matthew 24, Luke 21) and in Paul's letters (especially 1 and 2 Thessalonians, 2 Peter and Jude) when they speak of the end time or of the
significance of Jesus in more cosmic terms.

## Christian Use – or Abuse – of the Old Testament

There is of course a historical dimension to the use of the Old Testament
in history by Christians. There is the famous rejection of the Old Testament
by Marcion in the second century CE. The main ground on which he
opposed the inclusion of the Old Testament was its Jewishness. He asked
the question, 'What relevance could these texts, produced by the ancient
Israelites, possibly have for a church which had broken away from its Jewish

**Figure 5.3** Stone carving from Capernaum thought to depict the Ark of the
Covenant. Photograph: Douglas Hamilton.

moorings?' His agenda was to argue for a total break with the church's roots in Judaism and in the service of that he drew an extreme contrast between law and gospel. He also argued for a different God in the New Testament on the basis of the cruel aspects of the Old Testament. Marcion has had a surprisingly strong influence on the church's attitude to the Old Testament over the centuries, even though he was not really attacking the Old Testament *per se* but as part of a greater agenda against Jews.

Another way in which the Old Testament was interpreted in Christian history is the allegorical interpretation of medieval times. This approach took as its starting point the difficulty that much in the Old Testament was inconsistent with the New, which was seen to be a major problem. Rather than appreciating the Old Testament as it stood, this method sought to find the real meaning of the Old Testament in a christological interpretation. For example, the Song of Songs, which is probably secular love poetry, was interpreted as referring to the relationship between Christ and his bride, the church. The apparently vindictive and cruel parts of a number of the Psalms (e.g. Psalm 63:9–10: 'But those who seek to destroy my life shall go down into the depths of the earth: they shall be given over to the power of the sword, they shall be prey for jackals') were often understood to refer to the sinful tendencies within us – violent language directed against these sinful tendencies rather than against real human enemies. This led to a complete distortion of the meaning of Old Testament texts. As Brevard Childs writes:[13] 'the approach of much medieval theology in shifting the entire semantic range of the Old Testament to a non-literal metaphorical level, in order to retain a reference to Jesus Christ, destroyed the integrity which the Christian canon had assigned to this portion of scripture' (p. 8).

Nevertheless, like Marcion, the findings of these scholars have had an immense influence on the church's approach to the Old Testament and we still find much allegorizing going on today when the Old Testament is preached upon. Of course, allegorical interpretation has its place and can be highly illuminating.

## Modern Approaches to Interpreting the Old Testament

Nowadays such approaches are often seen as a distortion of the Old Testament taken at face value. With the rise of biblical criticism in the late nineteenth century came an interest in the history and theology of the Old Testament in its own right, without New Testament concerns in the picture. Or at least that was the claim made by Christians interested in writing theologies of the Old Testament. It is interesting that Jewish scholars have not generally participated in the writing of biblical theologies.

Perhaps this suggests that Christian presuppositions cannot be helped if one is writing from this perspective – no one is ever bias-free. However, in contrast to medievalists, commentaries are written by Christians on the Old Testament alongside Jews and this is done without an overtly Christian agenda. This is not to say that a Christian agenda is wrong – one simply needs to be aware of one's own agenda and realize that there are other people with other agendas and indeed that no one is agenda-free.

In fact it is important that Christians should read the Old Testament in this way as part of faith. As Brevard Childs writes, 'To suggest that the Christian should read the Old Testament as if he were living before the coming of Christ is an historical anachronism which also fails to take seriously the literature's present function within the Christian Bible for a practising community of faith' (p. 8). Perhaps that is the difference in my agenda here as a scholar of the Old Testament who wishes as far as possible to take it on its own terms, and the agenda of the community of faith whose understanding is led by Christian concerns. I would claim, however, to that Christian community of which I am also a part, that to open and read the Old Testament on its own terms is always an illuminating business, even if one might wish to draw out Christian aspects as a separate concern.

Indeed, we have at least three options in front of us as Christians studying the Old Testament today: ignore it, overemphasize it or affirm it. The first involves an embarrassing silence and a corresponding ignorance about the Old Testament (which is what we have in many churches). The second involves a fundamentalist approach which, while it gives a high degree of authority to the Old Testament, reads the text in a very literal way. Inconsistencies tend to be harmonized and differences played down, while harsh elements of God's activity are taken seriously. This often results in a Christian theology in which the aspect of divine judgement looms large. The third involves Christians using the Old Testament in their own context – whether they be liberation theologians, feminist theologians or just plain people in the pew. This approach seeks relevance for today from the ancient texts, but with a proper respect for its original context.

In my view, Christians should try to develop a more positive evaluation of the nature of the Old Testament. We have seen the kind of authority given to the Old Testament within the Christian tradition. Those who ignore the Old Testament do so with a misunderstanding of its true nature and with a lack of appreciation of their own tradition. Jesus' own teaching presupposed the Old Testament. The authors of the Old Testament, as they spoke about God's activity in the history of their own day, gave to posterity concepts, vocabulary and above all hopes which proved invaluable to the theologians of the early church as they sought to give expression to all that they had experienced in Jesus.

We have noted a positive relationship between the two testaments in Christian circles from earliest times which we should strive to keep alive today. Goldingay aptly writes:

> While God's activity did not begin with Jesus, it came to its fulfilment in him. Thus God's activity in Old Testament times must ultimately be understood Christologically, and one can agree with Luther that all experiences of grace, even those of Old Testament times, are finally to be seen as experiences of Christ . . . Indeed, for a Christian everything of which the Old Testament speaks has to be seen in the light of Christ. But immediately one says that, one has to add again that everything in the New Testament has to be seen in the light of the Old Testament. For the Christian view is that Jesus is the one on whom the faith of Israel ultimately came to focus. But faith can only be Christian if it is built on the faith of the Hebrew scriptures. (p. 37)

## A Liberationist Approach

Focusing on the third way in which Christians can use the Old Testament, I wish to consider some recent interpretative approaches. One way that the theology of the Old Testament has been brought back to central relevance in modern times by theologians is in the use of Old Testament themes and texts, as well as New Testament texts, by liberationists. In their theology ideas of justice and salvation for the downtrodden of society are taken from the Old Testament rather than the New. God is seen to be where God was at the time of the exodus: on the side of the poor and oppressed against those who have enslaved them. This viewpoint is reinforced in the prophetic books in which there are denunciations of injustice and defence of the rights of the poor.

Latin American theologians have applied the example of slavery in Egypt to their own experience of repressive regimes. The Promised Land is not literally another country: it is their own country, so changed as to be unrecognizable. What they are seeking is a Latin America in which free and dignified human life is possible for all, because the exploitative structures of old and corrupt regimes have been entirely eliminated. P. Berryman, in his book *Liberation Theology*,[14] writes:

> Without a doubt, the exodus is the central event in the Hebrew Scriptures, the event that constitutes Israel as a people . . . When the pharaoh . . . pursues them, the waters return, drowning his troops. This act of deliverance is a basic paradigm of God's saving action. In a Latin American reading the focus is on God's concern to liberate the people . . . This is a God who can hear the cry of the oppressed, who comes down, and who leads them to liberation.

'Exodus' is not simply an event but a pattern of deliverance that provides a key for interpreting the Scriptures and for interpreting present experience. (p. 121)

With liberation theology, then, the relevance of the Old Testament to Christians today resounds loud and clear. The teachings of Jesus are also interpreted in liberationist terms.

There is a particular formulation of themes that speak to the poor. Scripture is read as a book of life and is applied to current situations. There is no attempt to seek a bias-free vantage point, but rather the idea is to make one's own bias come as close to that of the scriptures as possible. Thus, for example, Gustavo Gutierrez interprets the exodus as an act of political liberation which inaugurates the construction of a just society. He assumes that his third-world perspective is 'right'. He does not elaborate on what other readings of the exodus are possible or why his perspective is better or more appropriate than others. His basic assumption is that the exodus should be read in this way because it is in this situation that it has its meaning.

Thus the interpretation of the exodus story that sees it as encapsulating the liberation themes of the Bible and as providing a normative guide to the truth that God sides with the poor is decidedly one-sided. In fact, the exodus is probably not to be exclusively appropriated by any one group; rather, its message is for all God's people. Although God's liberation is portrayed in terms of deliverance from the oppression of the Egyptians, in principle it is a greater story about the death of evil and of human exploitation and oppression. It is therefore an under-interpretation of the exodus to look for an oppressor and an oppressed and to understand its liberation merely in relation to social revolution.[15]

## Moses

This talk of the exodus leads us to one of our key figures in this chapter: Moses. Perhaps no book on the Old Testament would be complete without some consideration of him. Moses is the central figure in the exodus, in liberation from slavery and also in the giving of the law, itself often seen as liberating. The story of Moses begins in Exodus 2 and ends with his death in Deuteronomy 34. This is a long span of text and so we will simply pick a few key chapters of Exodus to look at. We are probably all familiar with the story of Moses as a baby, hidden in the bulrushes by his mother and sister because of Egyptian oppression that means that Israelite babies are being slaughtered (Exodus 2). He floats downstream in a reed basket and is picked up by none other than Pharaoh's own daughter, who decides to raise him as her own and unknowingly employs the boy's mother to be his nursemaid. His origins then were most precarious.[16]

This story is followed in chapter 2 by three short episodes in which we see Moses coming to the aid of others. First, he rescues a Hebrew who is being beaten by an Egyptian (vv. 11–12). He kills the Egyptian. This is a slightly difficult text to come to grips with – that the great leader of Israel killed a man is often glossed over. He may have killed a foreigner who was killing his kinsman and thus shown his loyalty to his kinsman, but he is living among Egyptians and has been shown kindness by some of them, so it is not quite the same as killing foreigners in war, for example. He also intervenes in an argument between two Israelites (vv. 13–14) and finally he helps some women who are being maltreated by the men in their place of work (vv. 16–17).

Exodus 3 is also a famous passage in which Moses encounters God in the burning bush and the divine name Yahweh is revealed. God's purpose for his life is made known to him in the proclamation of God's desire to liberate the people from slavery and that he will have a key part in that process (verse 10). This then becomes the mission of Moses and his brother Aaron – the liberation of God's people. They confront Pharaoh in Exodus 5 with God's demand for Israel's release, but Pharaoh does not recognize their God (verse 2) and responds by increasing the hard labour of the Israelites. Moses complains to God bitterly that God has done nothing as yet – this is the impetus for the succeeding plagues.

The plagues are described in chapters 7–10, but nothing seems to move Pharaoh to let the Israelites go. Nine plagues have occurred and the tenth is announced in chapter 11. It is to be the worst of all – the death of every first-born child of every Egyptian family. The Israelites are to be spared by the marking of the doorposts and lintels of their house with the blood of a sacrificed lamb which has been ritually eaten. This is the first Passover – God literally passes over houses where the blood is found. We then read prescriptions in chapters 12 and 13 for the keeping of the Passover, which becomes a great Jewish festival – this is probably added later to this narrative to spell out its significance.

So the Israelites are at last free to leave and the presence of God in cloud and fire leads the people into the desert (Exodus 13:20–1). The Egyptians, however, are close behind – Pharaoh has not given up the fight. The first key event of liberation is the crossing of the Red Sea. The Israelites question the wisdom of leaving even hard labour for seeming death in the wilderness. After all, normally a sea would be quite a stumbling block for escape unless you happened to have a number of boats handy! God speaks to Moses and rebukes the people for their cries. God tells Moses to lift up his staff, stretch it out over the sea and divide it. We perhaps have seen artists' impressions of the parting of the Red Sea, or the film *The Ten Commandments*, with Charlton Heston as Moses, and its impressive special effects for the parting of the Red Sea. The sea rises up on both sides and the sea floor is dry for the Israelites to pass through. Once the Egyptians try to follow, the sea will be parted no more and they will all drown. The pillar of cloud with its guardian angel is still there and makes a barrier between the Israelites and the army behind them.

Interestingly, the language of the flood makes a reappearance with the turning of 'the sea into dry land; and the waters were divided' – there are some resonances of that event here and even of the creation, which later Psalmists and other writers (such as Deutero-Isaiah) were quick to take up. God again shows mighty power over the elements by stirring up a strong east wind[17] in order to effect the parting, so that the waters formed a wall on right and left of the Israelite group. Some Egyptians follow them into the mud[18] with their chariots, and their wheels get bogged down – not long after, Moses stretches out his hand once more and the sea gradually returns to normal, drowning the Egyptians in the process. We have God the warrior here (see Exodus 15:3), acting on behalf of the people and drowning Israel's enemies – there is thus a slightly less palatable side to this 'miracle'. But in general it is recalled from the angle of the liberation of the Israelites. This is the first act of their liberation.

Exodus 15 contains a 'song of Moses', putting into hymnic form the wonder of the people at their deliverance. The theological themes of praise and wonder at God's salvation of his people come through. This may be a later psalm added in at this point in the story (verse 17 mentions the temple in Jerusalem, which had not yet been built). The song has been used by the Christian church for many centuries in the celebration of Easter – new life out of old, praise and wonder at the miracle of God – these are all transferable themes. Here the song is put into the mouth of Moses, for whom God is his 'strength and might . . . his salvation'.

The miracles continue in the wilderness. The end of Exodus 15 describes the transforming of 'bitter' water into drinkable 'sweet' water. Water in a desert is a crucial commodity. God leads the Israelites to an oasis called Elim (Exodus 15:27), where there is water in abundance. Food is the second essential of life after water and in Exodus 16 God feeds the Israelites with manna (or bread) from heaven during the day and with quails at night. We find in this chapter a number of sabbath commandments which are probably later accretions, borne out of the manna story.

The Israelites have a tendency to be rebellious – they do not always trust in God as they should and in the story of water from the rock in Exodus 17 they quarrel with Moses and blame him (and God) for another water shortage. Moses is in the difficult position of mediator – he is the

**Figure 5.4**   Jerusalem from the Mount of Olives. The old city and Temple Mount area can be clearly seen. © Israelimages.com/Hanan Isachar.

one chosen to be the channel for God's miraculous happenings, yet God does not simply act on demand, so Moses gets the blame when immediate divine actions are not forthcoming. It is almost as if the Israelites are greedy for miracles and impatient for more.

In the second half of Exodus 17 we have a rather difficult and little-known text. We find an enemy of Israel called Amalek. Joshua gets the job of fighting him, but Moses is assigned the divine favour of victory on the condition that he lifts up his hands. Moses is only human and so his arms grow tired. It is quite touching that Aaron and Hur hold up Moses' hands for him so that defeat becomes a reality. The difficult part is again the warrior God. We are not told who Amalek was, why he threatened Israel or why he needed to be defeated. The final insult is the wiping out of all remembrance of this man – the ultimate defeat in Hebrew thought.

**Midian** is east of the Gulf of Aquaba. It is the land where Moses stays with Jethro, a priest of Midian, and meets and marries his daughter, Zipporah. It is there that the divine name was revealed to Moses, leading to conjecture as to whether Yahweh was also the Midianite god.

Moses is a married man – he met his wife in **Midian** at the time of the burning bush incident (Exodus 3). She is Zipporah, the daughter of Jethro. In Exodus 18 we meet her again and her father – they come and visit Moses. Jethro seems to worship the same God and rejoices in the great story of deliverance that Moses relates to him. The second half of the chapter shows Moses as leader of the people getting tired by all the demands on his time. Jethro advises him to delegate. We could all learn from this chapter!

The next climax as described in Exodus 19 is the arrival at the holy mountain – Mount Sinai – where God dwells. God calls Moses up on the mountain and makes a promise to him to make Israel his special nation. God states here that 'the whole earth is mine', but this is a call to a special covenant with God for a special nation. This introduces a tension seen throughout the Old Testament between chosen people and the God of the whole world with the chance of universal salvation. This is an important theological theme within the Old Testament, the development of which one could trace. Here, the people are consecrated ritually to be fit to receive God and then there is a theophany from the mountain. There are injunctions upon the people that they may not look on God or approach God – only Moses can do this. This is a statement of God's holiness, otherness and power. Only priests can penetrate into God's holy space. Such a belief continues to this day. We are now on to the giving of the Ten Commandments and the laws concerning everyday and cultic life known as the 'Book of the Covenant' (Exodus 21–3).

We do not return to the narrative until Exodus 24, when the covenant is made between God and the people and we have the various trips up the mountain of God (already discussed in chapter 3 in the context of source criticism). Many of the chapters that follow are prescriptions for the life of Israel in the future, but they are probably back-projections from the time of the settlement when the tabernacle was being set up and the priesthood to serve it. Perhaps the most famous interlude in these chapters is that of the golden calf in Exodus 32, another example of the questioning and easy rebellion of the people. This time they do not only worship another God, but they use an image, something forbidden in the worship of Yahweh. It takes all Moses' strength to try to turn God's anger away from the people – he begs God to reconsider punishing them, he reminds God of the promises to the patriarchs and he succeeds. Moses is indeed a man with God's ear. Moses is so angry when he sees the golden calf that he breaks the tablets of the law. He destroys the calf, grinds it to powder and makes the Israelites drink it in water.

An uneasy part of this chapter is the command to the loyal 'sons of Levi' who will become a branch of the priesthood to 'kill your brother, your friend and your neighbour' (Exodus 32:27b). The result is the slaughter of three thousand Israelites. This is regarded as a blessing and clearly establishes their credentials for priesthood. It sounds a strange and bloody rite of passage to our ears. It is about the imposition of order on the increasing chaos all about, the triumph of obedience to God over disobedience. A

**Figure 5.5**   Moses holding the tablets of stone. This painting by Rembrandt shows him holding up the tablets containing the ten commandments. © Gemaldegalerie, Berlin, Germany/Bridgeman Art Library.

further punishment from God is a plague upon the people, which no doubt removes more of them, although we are not told that here. God has kept his promise to Moses and not destroyed the people, but they have taken a heavy toll for their disobedience. This establishes a pattern that is seen throughout the Old Testament: punishment for sin of the special people themselves. Because they are chosen, they should show more allegiance and loyalty to God, not less.

Exodus 33 sees the troupe leaving Mount Sinai to make their way through the desert once again. God is unwilling to accompany them any further, but again Moses intercedes on the people's behalf. God rescinds the decision and acknowledges that the Israelites are God's special people and gives an additional promise of 'rest' in the wilderness. The focus here is on Moses' relationship with God. We are told in verse 11, 'Thus the Lord used to speak to Moses face to face as one speaks to a friend.' Yet even Moses is not allowed to see God's face, only God's back.

It is at this point that we leave the Exodus narrative. There are further famous stories about Moses, especially his ultimate denial of entry into the Promised Land. This time, although he prays to be allowed to set foot in the Promised Land (Deuteronomy 3:23–5), his prayer is denied: the leader

**Figure 5.6**  The Judaean hills viewed from the foothills of Moab. This was the threshold to the Promised Land beyond which Moses was not allowed to go. © Israelimages.com/Garo Nalbandian.

of the people must share the punishment of the people in being denied this final promise. Moses is allowed to view it (Deuteronomy 3:27), but it is Joshua who will now lead those allowed to receive the promise into their new life in the land. Deuteronomy 34 describes Moses viewing the land from Mount Nebo and dying there. We are told:

> Never since has there arisen a prophet in Israel like Moses, whom the Lord knew face to face. He was unequalled for all the signs and wonders that the Lord sent him to perform in the land of Egypt, against Pharaoh and all his servants and his entire land, and for all the mighty deeds and all the terrifying displays of power that Moses performed in the sight of all Israel. (Deuteronomy 34:10–12)

The figure of Moses dominates the Pentateuch and is regarded by many as the greatest leader and prophet that Israel ever had.

## Cultural Difference

Among the texts we have just examined, it is interesting that some are well known and much loved and that others are relatively obscure and cause us problems. In addition to the warlike nature of God in the hard-won liberation of the Israelites, another problem is cultural difference. Indeed, perhaps the warlike passages illustrate in particularly stark fashion the cultural divide between the world of the Old Testament and today's world. Polygamy as exercised by the patriarchs is another example (itself an inconsistency with other parts of the Old Testament, notably Genesis 3 where monogamy is advocated). Clearly, in the culture of the time it was important to multiply and the best way of doing so was for men to take a number of wives. This practice continues with the kings (e.g. Saul and David). It also continues in today's world, notably in Arab culture. So it is not even a question of the modern world versus the ancient, it is more a matter of cultural difference, depending on where one is standing. This is a postmodern recognition. What is acceptable to me may not be acceptable to you. Some texts have a timeless nature; others are very time-bound and culturally bound. Even the Ten Commandments with their initial aura of timelessness are, as we saw, also quite culture-bound: the final commandment, for example, about 'goods and chattels' – including the wife!

This is a problem in dealing with the Bible because of course we are more likely to prioritize texts that are timeless, especially theologically. Expressions of God's liberation of the people of Israel, of God's love and creative power are bound to have more of a resonance than the slaughter of Amalek and the wiping out of his name, to use but one of many examples. This is not a problem if we simply read the Old Testament as an interesting historical, literary or even theological document. The problem arises when we seek to engage with the morality in the Old Testament and to apply it to our own lives, or when we seek to understand the nature of the God that we know in relation to God's past revelations. What do we do with prescriptions that we find difficult today? We might ignore details of ritual or sacrifice or temple furnishings as irrelevant to our situation, but pronouncements such as those on homosexuality being so wrong as to be punishable by death (e.g. Leviticus 20:13) are difficult for any seeking to find moral guidance in the Old Testament. Of course, we can say that these particular texts come from a time and a place in which homosexuality was not fully understood in medical or spiritual terms. We can eliminate those texts from our lectionary, but then what do we do with other texts – shall we cut out *all* the bloodthirsty bits, *all* the unpleasant stories?

This leads us back to the point with which we started this chapter. Are we right to pick the highlights and ignore the rest of the Old Testament? Isn't it better to wrestle with difficult texts, as Brueggemann advocates? Some texts, however, are so unpalatable as to have led people away from faith, to reject the Bible as having any kind of authority in their lives, and so on. Does reading the Old Testament 'the hard way' necessarily lead to this conclusion?

We can't expect every text to speak to us with equal profundity, but it is also true that different texts speak to different generations. For example, slavery, war and capital punishment can be justified from the Old Testament and also rejected. Perhaps we cannot expect every text to have the same authority for us. Perhaps we need to take, with Childs, a canonical approach and evaluate texts on similar subjects within the Old Testament and possibly also in conjunction with the New and find a collective authority in them. But then aren't we then in danger of going down a purely thematic route, rather as the lectionary does? The problem with this is that many texts contradict one another and so a cumulative approach tends to deaden the distinctive message of each one.

## Pick and Mix

It seems to me that differing viewpoints, different genres, different theologies and different witnesses are so much a feature of the Old Testament that it is possible to steer a path through the difficulties mentioned here. Some stories are simply about a time in which values were different, but often even in a time-bound story some moral or theological message can shine through.

Unpalatable presentations of God can be explained within a cultural context even if they can't be condoned by our current moral sensibilities.

It is perhaps in the 'mix' that is the Old Testament that different groups with different ideologies can find texts that speak to their situation. That this book of books should have spoken in many ways to other situations over the centuries is quite a mind-blowing thought. This perhaps brings us back to the point that interpretation depends largely upon where you are standing at a particular point in time. Yet it is not quite as subjective as that. We can perhaps agree on some more authoritative and important texts for us as a collective, even if not for everyone in the world. Christian writers did that – they selected the texts that spoke to their understanding of who Jesus was and of his significance within the fulfilment of the promises of his religion. We are the inheritors of rich and diverse texts that make up the Old Testament – why should we think we have the right to all the answers, to the final word in interpretation or to iron out all the contradictions?

## A Feminist Perspective

Perhaps more than any other part of the discipline of study of the Old Testament in recent times, the influence of feminist criticism has been the greatest in relation to our interpretation of texts. Little-known texts have come to the fore again, nameless and voiceless women have resurfaced, well-known characters have been reappraised, and even female authorship posited. Beyond that, the recognition of female readers of all kinds and from all cultures, past and present, has made the enterprise a fascinating and diverse one. Feminist criticism has take up the point that some texts are time-bound and others liberating.

The situation of women in the Bible reflects a very different culture to our own, although with closer connections to more tribal arrangements in the world elsewhere today. And yet the texts are not culture-bound in the sense that one situation cannot speak to another. We can all empathize with Sarah's jealousy of Hagar when she was used as a 'surrogate mother' and gave birth easily to a son, while Sarah had been living for years with barrenness. We can all empathize with her disbelief and laughter when she was told in her old age that she was pregnant with a son who was to become Israel's founding father. The time-bound aspects of the text see them as nomads in a tent, in a polygamous situation, with the women as subservient, and yet the timeless aspects are in the stories themselves and in the moral or theological points extracted from them. The story of barrenness to birth, repeated in many other places in the Old Testament, is a story of God overcoming even the most difficult barriers to effect his plans for the people of Israel.

In addition to many texts about women, there is also much feminine imagery in the Bible, a good deal of it negative in that it is used to portray 'sinful Jerusalem' regarded as a woman (especially Ezekiel). There is also, in counterpoint, the very positive picture of Woman Wisdom in Proverbs who guides young men along the rocky road of educational choices and moral dilemmas. There are a few heroic women – two with books named after them, Ruth and Esther; others hidden within the pages of other books such as Miriam in Exodus and Deborah in Judges, and others in the books of Samuel and Kings. Within the patriarchal context of much biblical literature perhaps it is surprising to find strong counter-currents of affirmation of women; stories that show women's courage, strength, faith, ingenuity, talents, dignity and worth. Such stories undermine patriarchal assumptions and temper patriarchal biases.[19]

Other less palatable heroines such as Jael also did what they could for their nation, albeit violently at times. Other women are victims. Phyllis Trible's *Texts of Terror* gathers together texts about the suffering of women and suggests that women today in patriarchal cultures might be able to relate to them. She talks of Hagar, a slave used, abused and rejected; Tamar, the princess raped and discarded; the unnamed woman of Judges 11, the concubine raped, murdered and dismembered and the daughter of Jephthat, a virgin slain and sacrificed. She presents these stories as a neglected history of female victimization. Women are often portrayed as victims and yet some of them nevertheless found ways to declare their personhood.

We have seen that texts should be read from many angles, not just one. We can read a text within its culture or outside it. We can choose to understand the motivation of a person like Jael and not condemn her as much as some of our forebears as interpreters have done. There has been much work in feminist studies to rectify negative portrayals of women, starting with Eve in Genesis 2. Interestingly, it is the New Testament in 1 Timothy 2:13–14 that has contributed to a negative evaluation of Eve. We might compare other New Testament passages, such as 1 Corinthians 14 and 1 Timothy 2 where women are to be silent in church, and Ephesians 5 where women should be submissive to their husbands. Again, a particular context is being addressed and so one should be cautious in universalizing it to refer to women's behaviour in all circumstances! The creation of woman can be interpreted to mean that she is equal to the man (after all, as we saw in chapter 4, in Genesis 1:28 they are created together in the image of God) and in Genesis 3 man and woman are mutually responsible, even though they are united in disobedience.

## Ruth

I have decided in this chapter to allow the indulgence of two key figures – one male and the other female. There have been more men in this book, and maybe that reflects the balance in the Old Testament itself, but we have already encountered some plucky women along the way. Here we shall turn to consider Ruth, the heroine of the book that bears her name. She is an unlikely heroine, in some ways a pawn in the power-plays between her mother-in-law and her husband-to-be, yet there are some surprising 'twists' in her tale.

Ruth is sometimes described as a 'women's tale'. That sounds disparaging at first, but it perhaps tells us something about the domestic nature of the story. Here we are not in the land of battles, kings, warriors and such like; we are in the world of agriculture, small towns, families and interactions between neighbours and relatives. We learn at the beginning of the book of Ruth that a famine caused a couple named Elimelech and Naomi and their two sons to leave Israel for the more plentiful land of **Moab**. At the time the story opens, Elimelech has died, as have his two sons. This leaves Naomi with two daughters-in-law. She decides that she would like to return to her homeland, a place no longer suffering famine. She tells her daughters-in-law to remarry and make new homes for themselves in Moab.

**Moab** is a land east of the Dead Sea, close to Israel, with whom she had contact over a long period – mostly hostile, but not entirely.

It is Ruth who declines, swearing fidelity to Naomi and to her God, Yahweh, preferring to accompany her mother-in-law. Naomi feels embittered by her situation and says, 'Call me no longer Naomi, call me Mara,[20] for the Almighty has dealt bitterly with me' (Ruth 1:20). They duly arrive in Bethlehem and Ruth suggests that she goes gleaning in the field of a rich relative, Boaz. She sees that two women alone need the support of men, particularly in a culture in which widows were fairly lowly members of society. Boaz accepts Ruth into his workforce and in fact shows her special favour, saying that he has heard about her loyalty to her mother-in-law. Interestingly, Naomi and Boaz never meet, but Ruth is caught between the two of them. However, she is not without initiative of her own and certainly shows much loyalty and steadfastness which is praised in the text. It is Naomi's suggestion that Ruth go down to the threshing floor in the quest for 'security'.

In perhaps the best-known part of the book of Ruth, Ruth lies on the threshing floor at Boaz's feet and he sleeps the first part of the night not knowing that she is there. He wakes with a start at midnight and finds her there.

**Figure 5.7** William Blake's drawing of Naomi entreating Ruth and Orpah. © Victoria and Albert Museum, London/Bridgeman Art Library.

This puts him in a compromising position in the morning, even if nothing happened (and scholars debate whether in fact anything of a sexual nature did happen, which may hang on the interpretation of 'uncovering his feet'). This leads on to Boaz's desire to marry Ruth. He sees her actions not as trickery but as an act of loyalty to her kin because she has not gone after young men but has dedicated herself to him, presumably an older man. He even allows her to remain the rest of the night at his feet!

There is a need to clear the path to marriage by the removal of the rights of another 'kinsman' of the family who has first call on Ruth. That stumbling block is removed by Boaz's purchase of Naomi's (formerly Elimelech's) field in which Ruth is included as a part of the acquisition, after giving the other kinsman first call on the property. Boaz and Ruth are then able to be married. One might have thought that was the end of the story – a rather tender romance in the end – but there are two more important points. First, Ruth bears a child. This is then an heir for Boaz and herself, but the text makes it clear that it is also an heir for the line of Elimelech. In fact, Naomi is given the baby to nurse and Ruth doesn't even get to name her own child; that is done instead by the women of Bethlehem.

Then the final twist in the tale comes and it is ostensibly the driest part of the whole story – the genealogy. This turns out to be crucial because we learn that Ruth is none other than the great-grandmother of King David himself! This is perhaps most surprising because Ruth is a foreigner – she is a Moabitess. The Israelites and the Moabites were often at war, so what is a Moabitess doing as ancestress to Israel's most important king? Of course, she converts to the Israelite faith, as we are told early on, and yet one wonders if she was ever fully accepted. Perhaps the writers of the story are saying that foreigners should be accepted into Israel and that **exclusivism** is wrong.

**Exclusivism** is the rejection of foreigners by a group or nation.

The book of Ruth is a short but rich text that can be read on different levels. It speaks volumes about the relationship between two women who are not even blood relatives and the theme of loyalty comes out strongly. It is also about foreignness, estrangement and famine, and ultimate reconciliation and fullness. It is about extending the male line (and the line of King David at that). God takes a back seat in this tale, yet God condones the good behaviour of Ruth and is invoked in the prayers of characters such as Naomi. This reinforces the point that texts are rich and should not be read from just one angle.

Feminist scholarship has opened up appreciation of the book of Ruth, but it is not all positive. Some have seen her as a pawn in the games of others, some have seen her as an 'anti-heroine' manipulated by the patriarchy of the time. It is nevertheless remarkable that there is a whole book to her name and that this simple tale with its powerful themes goes on to speak to us in many meaningful ways today.

## Feminist Scholarly Approaches

The Old Testament can be used in its diversity by many different groups in many situations today, just as it has always been used. Feminist interpretation of the Old Testament, as we have seen, offers an alternative assessment of the biblical evidence as seen through the eyes and experience of women. I should add quickly that reading and interpreting texts as a woman is not necessarily a practice only to be done by biological females. Increasing numbers of men are appreciating the approach and seeing it as having wider value in biblical hermeneutics, for in many ways it has established the whole principle of reader-response criticism. However, feminist interpretation sprang from the point that men had dominated mainstream interpretation for a long time.

It is the opinion of many feminist theologians that hostile attitudes towards women and their low status in many societies have their roots in the history of biblical interpretation, so that what is needed is a reinterpretation of the text in the light of a feminist hermeneutic. While the Old Testament does often reflect the primitive and tribal society in which it began, it provides many examples of women occupying positions of considerable power and influence. Furthermore, the qualities of Yahweh in the Old Testament are not described in exclusively male terms – in Isaiah 49:14–15, for example, God is described as caring for Israel like a mother. We also have the feminine personification of Wisdom in the book of Proverbs – a female attribute of God, described as having been alongside the creator during the creative act.

An interesting question has been raised by feminist theologians about the legitimacy of the canon of scripture that defines our Old Testament. We saw in chapter 1 what a slippery concept this is. What is the status of the canon, they ask? Elizabeth Schlüssler Fiorenza in *Searching the Scriptures*[21] explores extra-biblical material, much of it contemporary with the New Testament, material which was not admitted into the canon but much of which contains imagery and stories that speak to women in particular. She asks, 'Was the canon shaped by men for men, perpetuating a status quo of patriarchy? How therefore can these scriptures speak to us today? Are they the only writings with authority?'

We have already encountered the canonical approach to scripture of Brevard Childs in which he saw the time of the formation of the canon as decisive.[22] He argued that it is what is in the canon of scripture now that defines the word, that has been read through the generations and to which people have related over the centuries. This is decisive for scripture in a way that it is not for other writings, in that they have not exercised the same kinds of influence. One's stance towards scripture and towards the canon of scripture very much affects one's relationship to it. Some extreme feminist scholars have broken away from Christianity, unable to accept the Bible as the authoritative word of God. Others continue to live with its anomalies, to face the difficulties and meet the tensions and contradictions head-on. We need to ask what kind of authority the Bible has for us in our own lives and how we are to expound its insights afresh to an ever-changing society.

## The Old Testament as a Rich Resource

The Old Testament can be used to find support for ethical positions we might want to adopt. Themes such as the perversion of justice and the denial of rights to the weak and the poor resound throughout the Old Testament prophets. There is agreement in the Old Testament that such actions should be condemned. The duty of the strong to support and to protect the weak is stressed. Above all, appeal is made to God's grace in redeeming the people of Israel as the ground for gracious treatment of others. It is important to find the dominant social and moral imperatives of the Old Testament and to work them through with reference to our own moral sensitivities today. As Goldingay writes,

> Christian theology needs to be open to Old Testament insights on the nature of God, on the world and on everyday human life as God's gifts, on the continuing theological significance of Israel, on what it also means for the church to be the people of God, and on how the individual believer relates to God. (p. 35)

We can turn to the Old Testament for thoughts on war, on social justice, on economic justice, on issues of life and death, wealth and poverty – the list is endless. The sheer diversity of the Old Testament makes that possible.

It seems that not only every generation but every race, creed and colour, interest group and faith community can explore different facets of the texts that make up the Old Testament. They can explore those texts for guidance in matters of faith, ethics and worldview, or for a deeper understanding of the lives and deeds of patriarchs, matriarchs, prophets, kings and wise men. Opening the Old Testament is not something that can be done once and from one angle – you might open it from yours and with your own reasons for wishing to explore further, and I might with mine.

What I enjoy about the Old Testament is its literary diversity – there is always some part of the Old Testament that one comes across afresh, for the very first time, even though, in my case, I have been working with it for more than twenty years. Its different genres reveal the complexity of life and the many angles that can be applied to life. It speaks to us with many different voices and in turn we hear it with a similar diversity of voices depending on who we are and where we are in our journey of faith.

As Davidson puts it: 'There is a rich and varied country here waiting to be explored, a country whose secrets only reveal themselves to those who traverse it with an open mind and a healthy dose of curiosity.'[23] He likens our interaction with the Old Testament to a journey, with ups and downs, challenges and experiences, which will widen your horizons, question your prejudices and enrich your heart and mind. This is a challenge not just to dip into the Old Testament, but to go on and study it in more depth. We might complain with the author of Ecclesiastes that 'of the making of books there is no end, and much study is a weariness of the flesh' (Ecclesiastes 12:12), but I hope that is not your feeling at the end of this quest to learn more about this diverse and fascinating set of books.

# Notes

1   K. J. Dell, 'Hospitality in the Old Testament', *Guidelines* Vol. 20/3, ed. J. Duff and K. J. Dell, Oxford: Bible Reading Fellowship, 2004, pp. 100–6.

2   P. Trible, *Texts of Terror: Literary-Feminist Readings of Biblical Narratives*, Overtures to Biblical Theology 13, Philadelphia: Fortress Press, 1984.

3   W. Brueggemann, *The Bible and Postmodern Imagination: Texts Under Negotiation*, London: SCM Press, 1993.

4   In fact the New Testament itself refers to what we call the Old Testament as 'the Scriptures' (Matthew 21:42) or 'the law and the prophets' (Matthew 5:17) or 'the law of Moses, the prophets and the psalms' (Luke 24:44). The term 'Old Testament' is a later one than New Testament times.

5   C. E. Hauer and W. A. Young, *An Introduction to the Bible: A Journey Into Three Worlds*, 5th edn, Upper Saddle River, NJ: Prentice-Hall, 2001. This is an excellent and very thorough introduction to the whole of the Bible with good coverage of the historical context as well as the literary genres found in both testaments.

6   It is likely that the writers of the New Testament knew the 'Scriptures' in Greek in the Septuagint form.

7   Scholars cannot fully agree on the precise dimensions of such allusions and echoes, so it depends which scholars you read as to what impression you get of the extent of such thematic links between the Old and New Testaments. It might also reveal that it is hard to reconstruct exactly reading practices of the first century CE. See R. Hays, *Echoes of Scriptures in the Letters of Paul*, New Haven: Yale University Press, 1989.

8   J. Goldingay, *Approaches to Old Testament Interpretation*, Leicester: Apollos, 1990.

9   C. Evans in *The Cambridge History of the Bible*, Vol. 1, ed. P. R. Ackroyd and C. F. Evans, Cambridge: Cambridge University Press, 1975, pp. 232–84.

10  1 Clement is a first-century CE extra-canonical book. 'Extra-canonical' refers to any book that was rejected from the canon of scripture but which still exists. R. P. C. Hanson, 'Biblical Exegesis in the Early Church', *The Cambridge History of the Bible*, pp 412–53, writes on 1 Clement: 'The author of 1 Clement, in the tradition of that hellenistic Judaism which drew much of its inspiration from Stoicism, ranges over the Old Testament to find examples of good and bad conduct applicable to the church of his day, and finds a prediction of the contemporary form of Christian ministry, not in the old Jewish priesthood, but in a passage of Isaiah (60:17; 1 Clement 42:5), and he sees a prediction of the blood of the Lord in Rahab's scarlet thread (13:7f.)' (p. 414).

11  Hebrew word, *almah*.

12  B. Childs, *Old Testament Theology in a Canonical Context*, London: SCM Press, 1985.

13  Childs, *Old Testament Theology in a Canonical Context*.

14  P. Berryman, *Liberation Theology: Essential Facts About the Revolutionary Movement in Latin America and Beyond*, London: Taurus, 1987.

15  Cf. Guttierrez's views on Job, whom he sees as the champion of the poor who are suffering at the hands of a cruel regime. His book is entitled *On Job: God-talk and the Suffering of the Innocent*, Maryknoll, NY: Orbis Books, 1987.

16  This seems to have been a popular story in the ancient Near East and beyond (e.g. Sargon, Cyrus, Romulus and Remus).

17  This has echoes of the spirit or wind (Hebrew, *ruah*) of God brooding over the waters in Genesis 1.

18  One suggestion by scholars is of a Reed Sea rather than the Red Sea, a marshy, muddy area that could nevertheless be crossed, rather than a sea in a conventional sense. This, of course, plays down the miraculous element in the story and attempts a more rational explanation for the events described.

19  See T. Dennis, *Sarah Laughed: Women's Stories in the Old Testament*, London: SPCK, 1994.

20  Mara means 'bitter', the same word used in the passage in Exodus 15 about the bitter water.

21  E. Schüssler Fiorenza, *Searching the Scriptures*, Vols 1 and 2, London: SCM Press, 1994.

22  B. Childs, *Old Testament Theology in a Canonical Context*, London: SCM Press, 1985.

23  R. Davidson, *A Beginner's Guide to the Old Testament*, Edinburgh: Saint Andrew Press, 1995, p. 147.

# Further Reading

## Introductory Textbooks

P. Alexander and D. Alexander (eds), *The Lion Handbook to the Bible*, Oxford: Lion, 1999.

B. W. Anderson, *The Living World of the Old Testament*, 4th edn, London: Longman, 1991.

J. Barton and J. Bowden, *The Original Story: God, Israel and the World*, London: Darton, Longman and Todd, 2004.

L. Boadt, *Reading the Old Testament*, New York: Paulist Press, 1989.

J. Bowker, *The Complete Bible Handbook: An Illustrated Companion*, London: Dorling Kindersley, 1998.

R. Davidson, *A Beginner's Guide to the Old Testament*, Edinburgh: St Andrew's Press, 1992.

C. E. Hauer and W. A. Young, *An Introduction to the Bible: A Journey into Three Worlds*, 5th edn, Upper Saddle River, NJ: Prentice-Hall, 2001.

G. McConville, *Teach Yourself the Old Testament*, London: Hodder and Stoughton, 1996.

J. Rogerson and P. Davies, *The Old Testament World*, Cambridge: Cambridge University Press, 1989.

J. Stott, *Understanding the Bible*, London: Scripture Union, 1984.

## Biblical Studies Overviews

J. Barton, *The Biblical World*, 2 vols, London: Routledge, 2002.

L. G. Perdue (ed.), *The Blackwell Companion to the Hebrew Bible*, Oxford: Blackwell, 2001.

J. W. Rogerson and J. M. Lieu, *The Oxford Handbook of Biblical Studies*, Oxford: Oxford University Press, 2006.

## Method in Biblical Study

J. Barton, *Reading the Old Testament: Method in Biblical Study*, London: Darton, Longman and Todd, 2nd edition, 1996.

J. Barton, *What is the Bible?* London: SPCK, 1991.

E. Charpentier, *How to Read the Old Testament*, London: SCM Press, 1982.

*The Postmodern Bible*, New Haven, CT: Yale University Press, 1995.

## History of Israel

P. R. Ackroyd, *Israel under Babylon and Persia*, London: Oxford University Press, 1970.

G. W. Anderson, *The History and Religion of Israel*, London: Oxford University Press, 1974.

J. Bright, *A History of Israel*, 3rd edn, London: SCM Press, 1980.

J. Drane, *The Old Testament Story*, Tring: Lion, 1983.

J. Drane, *Old Testament Faith*, Tring: Lion, 1986.

E. W. Heaton, *The Hebrew Kingdoms*, London: Oxford University Press, 1968.

M. Noth, *The History of Israel*, London: A. & C. Black, 1958.

## Bible Dictionaries

G. Buttrick (ed.), *Interpreter's Dictionary of the Bible*, 5 vols, New York: Abingdon Press, 1962.

R. Coggins and J. Houlden (eds), *A Dictionary of Biblical Interpretation*, London: SCM Press, 1990.

D. N. Freedman (ed.), *Anchor Bible Dictionary*, 6 vols, New York: Doubleday, 1992.

D. N. Freedman (ed.), *Eerdmans Dictionary of the Bible*, Grand Rapids, MI: Eerdmans, 2000.

B. Metzger and M. Coogan, *The Oxford Companion to the Bible*, New York: Oxford University Press, 1993.

L. Ryken, J. C. Wilhoit and T. Longman III (eds), *Dictionary of Biblical Imagery*, Leicester: Intervarsity Press, 1998.

K. van der Toorn, Bob Becking and Pieter W. van der Horst (eds), *Dictionary of Deities and Demons in the Bible*, Leiden: E. J. Brill, 1995.

## One-Volume Commentaries

J. Barton and J. Muddiman, *The Oxford Bible Commentary*, Oxford: Oxford University Press, 2001.

M. Black and H. H. Rowley (eds), *Peake's Commentary on the Bible*, London: Thomas Nelson, 1963.

C. M. Laymon (ed.), *The Interpreter's One Volume Commentary on the Bible*, London: Collins, 1972.

J. L. Mays (ed.) *Harper's Bible Commentary*, San Francisco, Harper San Francisco, 2000.

C. A. Newsome & C. H. Ringe, *The Women's Bible Commentary*, London: SPCK, 1992.

J. W. Rogerson and J. D. G. Dunn (eds), *Eerdmans Commentary on the Bible*, Grand Rapids, MI: Eerdmans, 2003.

*The New Jerusalem Bible*, London: Darton, Longman and Todd, 1966.

## Introductions to the Old Testament

W. Brueggemann, *An Introduction to the Old Testament*, Louisville, KY: Westminster John Knox Press, 2003.

B. S. Childs, *Introduction to the Old Testament as Scripture*, London: SCM Press, 1979.

O. Eissfeldt, *The Old Testament: An Introduction*, Oxford: Blackwell, 1965.

G. Fohrer, *Introduction to the Old Testament*, London: SPCK, 1976.

O. Kaiser, *Old Testament Introduction*, Oxford: Blackwell, 1975.

J. A. Soggin, *Introduction to the Old Testament*, London: SCM Press, 1989.

## Atlases

Y. Aharoni, *The Land of the Bible: A Historical Geography*, London: Burns and Oates, 1979.

J. J. Bimson, J. P. Kane, J. H. Paterson and D. J. Wiseman, *New Bible Atlas*, Leicester: Intervarsity Press, 1985 (reprinted 2005).

L. H. Grollenburg, *Atlas of the Bible*, London: Nelson, 1956.

H. G. May (ed.), *Oxford Bible Atlas*, 3rd edn. ed. J. Day, Oxford: Oxford University Press, 1987.

J. Pritchard with M. White, *Harper Collins Concise Atlas of the Bible*, London: Times Books, 1991; New York: Harper Collins, 1997 (reprinted 2005).

## Archaeology

K. M. Kenyon, *Archaeology in the Holy Land*, 4th edn, London: Methuen, 1985.

A. Millard, *Discoveries from Bible Times*, Oxford: Lion, 1997.

P. R. S. Moorey, *Excavations in Palestine*, Guildford: Lutterworth, 1986.

J. Murphy O'Connor, *The Holy Land*, Oxford: Oxford University Press, 1992.

D. Winton Thomas (ed.), *Archaeology and Old Testament Study*, Oxford: Clarendon Press, 1967.

## Collections of Ancient Texts

W. Beyerlin, *Near Eastern Religious Texts Relating to the Old Testament*, London: SCM Press, 1978.

J. M. Charlesworth, *The Old Testament Pseudepigrapha*, London: Darton, Longman and Todd, 1983.

W. W. Hallo and K. Lawson Younger Jr, *The Context of Scripture*, Leiden: E. J. Brill, 2000.

J. B. Pritchard, *Ancient Near Eastern Texts*, Princeton, NJ: Princeton University Press, 1950.

D. W. Thomas (ed.), *Documents from Old Testament Times*, New York: Harper and Row, 1961.

## Surveys of Old Testament Study

G. W. Anderson (ed.), *Tradition and Interpretation*, Oxford: Clarendon Press, 1979.

R. E. Clements, *A Century of Old Testament Study*, Cambridge: Lutterworth Press, 1976.

A. D. H. Mayes (ed.), *Text in Context*, Oxford: Oxford University Press, 2000.

H. H. Rowley (ed.), *The Old Testament and Modern Study*, Oxford: Clarendon Press, 1951.

A. Yarbro Collins (ed.), *Feminist Perspectives on Biblical Scholarship*, Chico, CA: Scholars Press, 1985.

## Old Testament Theologies

W. Brueggemann, *Theology of the Old Testament: Testimony, Dispute, Advocacy*, Minneapolis, MN: Fortress Press, 1997.

W. Eichrodt, *Theology of the Old Testament*, Vols 1 and 2, London: SCM Press, 1961–7.

G. von Rad, *Old Testament Theology*, Vols 1 and 2, Edinburgh: Oliver and Boyd, 1962–5.

## History of Interpretation

J. W. Rogerson (ed.), *The Oxford Illustrated History of the Bible*, Oxford: Oxford University Press, 2001.

# Index